The Labors of
Sir Francis Drake

The Labors of

Sir Francis Drake

Erma Armstrong

ISBN: 978-0-9860856-4-2

Tanglewood Hill Press
PMB 203
170 W. Ellendale, Suite 103
Dallas, Oregon 97338
tnglwdhp@q.com

"Not far without this harbor did lye certain Islands, we called them the islands of Saint James, having on them plentiful and great store of seals and birds with one of which we fell July 24, whereon we found such provision as might competently serve our turn for a while." — Francis Fletcher

Note to the Reader

The writer—myself—in forming an opinion about Sir Francis Drake, has felt compelled to understand the historical setting of his time as I have come to understand it. Just as "the research for what you're writing is your whole life"—according to Oregon poet William Stafford— the research for Sir Francis Drake must take into account the evolution of a culture vastly different from ours. Hence my propensity to analyze and expound upon that culture and its history. This may be a problem, therefore, for the reader who wishes to follow only my main thesis: his labors which have come to such neglect.

Friends and potential readers have advised that certain chapters had best be relegated to an appendix, since historical trivia leading up to the bloody Tudor dynasty might be beyond a reader's interest in these our busy lives. Likewise, effects of Drake's neglect and subsequent history after his time might be beyond the interest of my readers.

I am especially grateful to Pam Porter of Portland and Phillip Costaggini of Corvallis, Oregon who have given me much significant feedback, the latter suggesting that certain chapters might best be presented as appendices for those with extended interests. Since I am unable to accomplish this, I will suggest to the reader that you peruse and skip such Chapters, e. g., 2, 3, 4, 5 and again 12, 13, and 15.

My great wish to publish the work regardless has two other incentives: 1) the desire to make it available to readers, and 2) recent notice in certain journals that there is a sudden interest in the possibility of Drake's sojourn in Nehelem Bay. I want to contribute what I have learned to that interest.

—Erma Armstrong

CONTENTS

x

INTRODUCTION

A book is born, we must assume, with a writer's sudden insight into some transcendental truth or reality that has not come forward or has been unaccountably neglected. This may be true of a fictional writer searching for a new dimension in human relations or of a researcher who amasses facts of history without being stimulated to react until some element stirs his emotions.

The site of Drake's landing on the North American continent had never interested me until I read Samuel Bawlf's 2003 account of his sojourn as far as Alaska in 1579 and his claim for an English colony by establishing a "point of position" survey at 45 degrees above the Spanish claims in California. It was to have been a challenge at that time to Pope Alexander VI's bull of 1493 dividing the whole New World between Spain

Tillamook County Pioneer Museum

and Portugal which had led to surreptitious trade with their colonies and plunder of their gold and silver.

It was the following passage from Bawlf's study, *The Secret Voyage of Sir Francis Drake 1577-1580*, describing the above, that captured my emotions and sympathy for Drake's expectations upon his return. I became aware that a great error had occurred and was being forever neglected:

"He had undertaken and performed the most important voyage in the history of his nation, and in consideration of his ***labors*** [Italics mine], he must have thought, he surely would be given command of the great enterprise he envisioned being founded on his discoveries."

"Point of Position" relics from Neahkahnie Mountain

Records of his discoveries, however, were lost to history because Elizabeth I confiscated all his maps and journals upon his return in her fear of inciting a war with Spain and revealing the route of his return to the Portuguese.

Knowledge of his achievement would perhaps have drawn the attention of the entire European world at that time. Elizabeth's denial of her part in the planning of it and a confiscation of his records meant that the meaning of his ***labors*** would take a nose-dive, not to be noticed through 48 years, from 1580 to 1628, when his story was finally told in the publication of the journals of his chaplain Francis Fletcher, entitled *The World Encompassed by Sir Francis Drake*. By that time his story was of no concern to anyone any longer; England was fighting her own Barbary pirates, and Drake would be remembered only for his own role in that enterprise.

What had happened and why began to concern me. Surely an historian as qualified as Bawlf could arouse the academic world to such an injustice, so contrived and hidden in the sands of time. So great an error deserved attention and analysis.

Fast forward four hundred years from 1579, and we have the artifacts Drake left behind at "point of position" and the discovery of these archaeological treasures by M. Wayne Jensen, Jr. and Donald M. Viles, residents of the Nehalem area. Failing to arouse any academics or federal agencies to investigate the meaning of these discoveries, they engaged a young engineering student at Oregon State University, Phillip A. Costaggini, through his advisor, Robert J. Schultz A.S.C.E., to conduct an analysis of the relics and their meaning in the positions in which they were found. Phillip had studied analysis of historical surveys at Columbia University and in 1982 completed his unpublished thesis, *Survey of Artifacts at Neahkahnie Mountain Oregon*.

Costaggini's maps were produced in Bawlf's study and his entire thesis appears in Garry D. Gitzen's 2008 book, *Francis Drake in Nehalem Bay 1579: Setting the Historical Record Straight*, a book I found in 2011 in the bookstore of the Tillamook County Museum while inquiring about

"Point of Position" relics from Neahkahnie Mountain

the five relics from Drake's survey in the basement floor there. The book and the relics soon captured my full attention. I found Gitzen's book a real treasure in unfolding the story of Drake's encounter with the Indians of Nahalem Bay and his sojourn there.

Jensen and Viles' discoveries along with Costaggini's study of 1982 have been virtually ignored by historians for 32 years—a comparison akin to the neglect of Drake's labors up to 1628, when Fletcher's volume was finally published—and, as in that time, the Bawlf and Gitzen books are also threatened to be swept under the rug. Where, according to the National Historic Preservation Act of 1966, amended 1992, was our Secretary of the Interior and State Historic Preservation Officer who should have investigated the site at Neahkahnie Mountain, acquired the relics and Costaggini's analysis, and deemed them eligibile to be designated as a National Historic Landmark? Attempts were made, as will be recalled in the final chapters of my book, and then ignored. Such artifacts should have had federal protection and the public should have access to them.

With the realization that nothing further is being done, I therefore have conducted a study of my own and am but the third person to seek permission to reproduce Costaggini's charts. In my research I have also drawn heavily on the work of the aforesaid Bawlf and Gitzen, being the only two to protest this dire neglect of history. Bawlf's academic position in British Columbia and Gitzen's access to the Jensen Collection left to him by his predecessors have enabled them to use sources unavailable to me.

I have had, however, a 25-volume set of *Historians' History of the World,* hereafter referred to as HHW, published in 1904, 1907 by the Enclyclopedia Brittanica, a rare collection left to me by my family, which gives me a unique look at 17th, 18th, and 19th century historians and their consensus at that time. Since acquiring interest in this topic I have added to my sources through purchases and the local library's inter-library loan facilities. As an amateur I endeavor to take a fresh look at the events which have led to this neglect of history.

In addition to my intent to write in support of Drake's labors at Nehalem Bay, I wish to attempt to understand an English society under the control of absolute monarchs who used the most sadistic and masochistic means to control their subjects. Elizabeth I, following in the footsteps of her father Henry VIII—who manipulated his subjects, and wives, in cruel and bloody ways—performed her strategies by manipulating the men in her life: her "favourites" [British spelling], which did not include a "commoner" such as Francis Drake. To me, the intrigues within the Tudor court, in addition to the strife between countries, play an important part in understanding his neglected role in history. They are the essential factors to explain how and why his "labors" were lost.

In addition, forbearance is requested for comparing Drake's labors with those of the ancients, where those of certain heroes were denied by their gods and kings; and, lastly, for citing the discovery of the ruins at Troy as a wakeup call to currrent archaeologists.

It is hoped also that this small treatise will expand the historical groundwork of Garry Gitzen and Samuel Bawlf and assist in drawing attention to it among history buffs around the world.

— Chapter 1—

Drake's Legacy

A Labor Lost

The loss of Sir Francis Drake's claim of territory for England, documented in stone at Nehalem Bay on the northwest coast of America in 1579, was regrettable and unnecessary for England and the world. Under the cloud of Pope Alexander VI's line across the Atlantic the year after Columbus's famous voyage in 1492, dividing all new discoveries between Spain and Portugal, England was barred from the New World. Drake's claim was to have been a dramatic first step in the direction of reclaiming a New World in the grip of the Catholic Church for the progress of mankind, after a century during which all who would not submit to that yoke were considered predators and subject to attack.

If Queen Elizabeth I had had the courage to acknowledge Drake's magnificent achievement of 1579, her triumph over the Spanish Armada a decade later would have had some meaning. In so many ways the daughter of Henry VIII was indecisive, using her power over the greatest sea captain the world has ever known to discredit him and placate her enemy. Unfortunately, that was not just a momentary decision. It affected the whole relationship of the European world at that time and for a long time to come.

Although the first Tudor king, Henry VII, had promoted John Cabot and his son Sebastian in their Northwest voyage of discovery in 1497, its purpose was to establish fishing rights and was carefully watched by the Spanish. By 1509, however, Sebastian Cabot was in the employ of Spain who claimed the entire continent of South America and eventually the American continent up to the 38th parallel on the California coast. It would be over 200 years before Spain got around to extending her territory. What an opportunity lost to recognize England's prior claim.

A hero, proving himself capable of maritime achievements above those of any other mortal at that particular time, Drake was denied the honor of his greatest labor, which was like a thorn festering in his side he could never complain about nor acknowledge. He was the first man to live among the North American natives, where he was regarded as a demigod, worshipped, adored, and still in their memory after two hundred years. Yet he was betrayed, stripped of the honor of his greatest deed and in time thought to be a mere self-seeking privateer.

After confiscating his records, Elizabeth kept him waiting for over three months at his harbor in Plymouth, communicating through agents whether she would receive him or throw him in the Tower to show her disapproval of his pirating to the Spanish throne. The share of the immense treasure he had robbed in their colonies finally got to her conscience and she summoned him, knighting him for his circumnavigation, but carefully concealing the true nature of his voyage.

She took care publicly not to honor him. There was no celebration for Drake. There was little said of his voyage, except a coin featuring his ship, the *Golden Hinde,* in order to acknowledge his circumnavigation. During the next eight years she used him for further privateering and raids to curb Spain's buildup of the armada, while she surreptitiously supported the Netherlands in their war with Spain. Meanwhile Philip II of Spain, in his way also carrying out a surreptitious activity, continued to promote the ascendancy of Catholic Mary Queen of Scots to replace Elizabeth on the throne of England.

In this introductory chapter, before we tell the tale of Drake's life and efforts, we would present the following episode as evidence of the lack of honor shown to him and his achievements. It is a moment in time seven years after his notable journey, which had netted him only a knighthood and the commemorative coin to acknowledge his circumnavigation.

It was a moment in time after the decision to behead Mary for her treachery and threat to the throne and its accomplishment. London was in a mood of great rejoicing. There was no need any longer to dread a papist successor to Elizabeth. "The bells of the city's hundred steeples. . . proclaimed the stern exultation of the citizens that the voice of the parliament had at last been listened to."[1]

Elizabeth had seized this opportunity to stir patriotic feelings of the people in a funeral parade to honor Sir Philip Sidney, diplomat, courtier, and poet of her court, who had been slain in battle in the Netherlands, one we will later examine. But it was the opportunity she wanted to honor her "favourite" of the courts, Sir Robert Leicester, earl of Dudley, whom she had sent to command that battle, which, incidentally, had been a failure. In spite of the show of the train-bands marching three abreast in all their finery, it was Sir Francis Drake whom the people cheered.

"In the pomp of that funeral of Sidney there was something more than empty pageantry." The people had known of the unacknowledged treasure and that their great general had been the first sea captain to circle the globe, Magellan having died in the Philippines before his ship made it home. The crowds gazed upon Drake and cheered him. It was their opportunity to see the great mariner who had circumnavigated the world and had carried terror of the English flag through all the Spanish settlements.[2]

It was a moment to savor in England: "After Mary's death the attack on England would have to be conducted in open day. It would be no advantage to Philip and the pope that Elizabeth should be murdered if her place was to be taken, not by Mary, but by Mary's Protestant son, James of Scotland."[3]

In addition to the distrust and hostility between Spain and England due to England's support of Holland against Spanish monarchial claims, there were ensuing battles wherein England monitored Spain's buildup of the armada. Drake's strike on Cadiz was one of these, which we will eventually describe in more detail. Though England claimed the victory, there was enormous loss of life on her side.

Sir Philip Sidney
(1551-1586)

It is evident from the record that Drake did tend to disobey Elizabeth's instructions in that war. He was instructed to limit his presence to observing Spain's preparations for war and their gathering of naval vessels, and, especially, monitoring the safety of her then current "favourite," the earl of Essex. Instead Drake burned and ravaged Cadiz, allowed Essex dangerous participation which included, it turns out, humanitarian gestures to curb Drake's ferocity. Upon their return, she made a point of denying Drake any appropriate honor for his triumph. This is an event we will relive in detail as we recount the events following his journey.

One has to recognize the personal vendettas going on between various of Elizabeth's favorites and how they affected the decisions she made for the good of her country. These were all made in what we would consider an absolute monarchy in England during that century. Parliament had no power, except to grant money for the wars she decided upon in conjunction with her ministers. She alone had the power to initiate war.

We mention here certain major events and tendencies of that century, expecting to analyze them further in the course of this study, especially the ways that they affected Drake's relationship to his queen. We would, however, in Chapter 2, first make an extensive overview of the centuries before these events in order to trace the evolution of power through the ancient Greek, Roman and medieval world before the Tudor monarchy. We hope to show a relationship also of Drake to heroes of the ancient world and to recall how other "black holes of history" have obscured their glory and the ways that Christianity was used to maintain that power.

When the Tudors came to power with Henry VII in 1515 after a struggle between the houses of York and Lancaster—the Wars of the Roses—all previous power of the nobility was essentially canceled. The new monarch staged immediate battles to suppress it. Royal hereditary power still remained in Scotland, but proprietary power among the nobility could be granted by the king only, as it had originally been since the time of William the Conquerer in 1066, except briefly after the Magna Carta in 1215. A greater treatment of the Plantagenet kings, the rise of the Tudors, their wars and Spanish connections will be dealt with in Chapter 3.

In a brief summary here of Chapter 4, we mention that when the young Henry VIII assumed control of that power in 1509, it led to a century of external harmony, to a fair degree. But there was much internal strife due to religious upheavals as a result of his defying the pope in order to divorce his Catholic wife, which became the focus of his reign.

This internal strife had its effects upon the people individually, in the form of the prosecution of heretics on one side or the other. During the reign of Henry VIII and his invalid son Edward VI, who briefly succeeded him, at least 200 persons were tortured, burned or otherwise lost their lives by failing to adhere to the newly emerging Church of England. His Catholic daughter Mary, who succeeded Edward, outdid her father by murdering some 300 who would not revert to Catholicism; and then Elizabeth, who followed, devised ways of punishing those who would not revert back to Protestant worship. This overview, we hope, provides an outline up to the time of Drake, which we will expand upon in the next several chapters.

Historians' Estimates

In the foregoing we have recounted the status of Drake with his contemporaries. We would consider now the summaries of historians in two later eras, and, finally, those negative assessments of present historians, save those mentioned in the Introduction, Gitzen and Bawlf, who are endeavoring to redeem his reputation and achievements.

First, it is important to understand the extent to which the legacy of Sir Francis Drake was denied throughout the 17th, 18th, and 19th centuries. When Drake returned from his labors he was cast aside and his legacy lost, which might have been for all eternity. As with the tragic hero Heracles when he returned from his labors—a reversal of triumph and tragedy as told in Euripides' version—Hera drove him mad because of Zeus' betrayal with a mortal woman. In anguish he slew his wife and children and then spent a lifetime of expiation and service to his fellowmen. Drake suffered no such extreme, but Elizabeth's failure to credit him caused him to continue to lose favor, and there are many in history who have judged him in that light.

Being a mere mortal he was perhaps lucky he didn't eventually suffer a beheading, as did so many in the Tudor age, who, once useful, were judged expendable, including another brilliant sea captain, Sir Walter Raleigh, in the reign of Elizabeth's successor, James I. Whereas Spain had burned heretics at the stake by the hundreds and exiled all her unbaptized Jews and Moors, England, through the Tudors, destroyed many of her most useful supporters to the crown because of their failure to carry out the more extreme strategies of their sovereigns. In this Elizabeth was but following in the footsteps of her father, the great Henry VIII, who suffered no man, nor woman, to come between him and his heart's desire. His story of blood lust and that of his daughter, "Bloody" Mary Tudor, set the stage for Elizabeth's reign.

We review another evidence of Drake's destroyed legacy during the intervening centuries. George Bancroft gives this egregious summary of his character and attainments, while elsewhere eulogizing the attainments of the explorers Sir Humphrey Gilbert, Martin Frobisher, Sir Walter Raleigh and others:

"Embarking on a voyage in quest of fortune (1577 to 1580), Francis Drake acquired immense treasures as a freebooter in the Spanish harbours on the Pacific, and, having laden his ship with spoils, gained for himself enduring glory by circumnavigating the globe. But before following in the path which the ship of Magellan had thus far alone dared to pursue, Drake determined to explore the northwestern coast of America, in the hope of discovering the strait which connects the oceans. With this view, he crossed the equator, sailed beyond the peninsula of California, and followed the continent to the latitude of the southern borders of New Hampshire. Here the cold seemed intolerable to men who had just left the tropics. Despairing of success, he retired to a harbour in a milder latitude, within the limits of Mexico; and, having repaired his ship, and named the country New Albion, he sailed for England, through the seas of Asia.

"The lustre of the name of Drake is borrowed from his success. In itself, this part of his career was but a splendid piracy against a nation with which his sovereign and his country professed to be at peace. The exploits of Drake except in so far as they nourished love for maritime affairs, were injurious to commerce; the minds of the sailors were debauched by a passion for sudden acquisition; and to receive regular wages seemed base and unmanly, when, at the easy peril of life, there was hope of boundless plunder." [4]

This summary seems an unwarranted curse upon his memory emanating from the history's neglect of his original plan. One has to believe that Elizabeth and her advisors set him up to accomplish a mission for the good of England and then failed to acknowledge their complicity at his expense. One thing led to another, and his being in disgrace, or at least unacknowledged in the accomplishment of their plan, his other attainments in their name were passed on to others. Notice Bancroft's further disclaimer:

" Thus was the southern part of the Oregon territory first visited by Englishmen, yet not till after a voyage of the Spanish from Acapulco, commanded by Cabrillo, Portuguese, had traced the American continent to within two and a half degrees of the mouth of Columbia river (1542), while, thirteen yeas after the voyage of Drake, Juan de Fuca, a mariner from the Isles of Greece, then in the employ of the viceroy of Mexico, sailed into the bay which is now known as the Gulf of Georgia (1593), and, having for twenty days steered through its intricate windings and numerous islands, returned with a belief that the entrance to the long-desired passage into the Atlantic had been found. " [5]

In the above we see a legacy denied and unavailable since the initial labor was unacknowledged. First of all, Cabrillo's voyage in 1542 resulted in no claim of territory for Spain. He didn't even land his ship. Most damaging to history, however, is the fact that details of Drake's records in Elizabeth's control, or from those he had managed to retain, emerged through those trusted not to reveal their source.

The Queen's admonition was that the records, as well as her complicity in the original plans, were not to be revealed "upon pain of death." It must be assumed therefore that the maps of the straits of Anian, as the projected northwest passage was initially termed, and the descriptions of the islands in the Puget Sound were appropriated by Juan de Fuca through secret diplomatic channels for his own ownership. This is one of the recent assertions in the twentieth century by Bawlf, which will be expanded in our final chapters. Once denied and disinherited from the original purpose of his journey, it was easy for others to gain access to his maps through inside channels and to claim what he had discovered. By 1593 Drake was much in Elizabeth's disfavor, and he had no access to setting the record straight without fear for his life.

In a broader view of the legacy of Drake we find that by the end of the Tudor era and the two failures of Raleigh to establish a colony in Virginia, hope was engendered that England might be able to compete with Spain in colonization in the New World. This was especially true after the defeat of the Spanish Armada and the fact that Spain, in spite of the wealth of her earlier colonies, had suffered a severe decline and eliminated her intellectual base by expelling the Jews, the Moors, and her more progressive minds through the Inquisition. In addition, there were emerging in England those who were prepared to found a different type of colony not subject to the class divisions engendered in Spanish possessions. In the 17th, 18th, and 19th centuries historians were positive about the progress of the British Empire (which would then include Scotland and Ireland), her great sea power, and her overthrow of the absolute monarchy in the 17th century.

Therefore historians such as Bancroft in the 19th century could express this optimism and minimize the errors of the 15th, 16th and 17th centuries as necessary forerunners of their emerging power. It is disheartening to read their summaries of the career of Francis Drake as that of a pirate of the most self-serving sort, useful to England only in her naval warfare. The "privateering," in which France had led the way in the preceding centuries was no longer an official government-approved warfare, but a disgrace for individuals thus engaged for their own profit.

Drake was eventually given a bit of credit as a forerunner who assisted in breaking down Spain's territorial claims, however. As two 19th century historians have claimed:

"The expeditions of Drake and his fellows were little better than buccaneering forays. Yet their work was of the first importance. It was something to have asserted the right of England to colonize. England had been brought face to face with Spain on many and various occasions, and had invariably proved the stronger on the sea. Finally, when James [I] proceeded to follow in the footsteps of his predecessor [Elizabeth I], the way had been prepared for him and the difficulties smoothed away. What had shortly before seemed impossible became an accomplished fact. " [6]

In the ensuing chapters about the career of Francis Drake you will read more statements by some of the more notable historians of the 19th century in regard to Drake. The burden for piracy was all on his shoulders, as though international law had existed at that time and he was guilty of disobeying it.

We have presented in brief the distortions of his achievement in the immediate aftermath of his journey and in the summaries of historians of the 16th 17th, and 18th centuries. Now we would examine some current estimates.

Current Estimates

Even more deplorable than the disclaimers of earlier centuries in regard to Drake's legacy have been the assessments of more recent 20th, and even 21st century historians, who no longer have so great a cause to eulogize the success of the once mighty British Empire. Now, it may even be surmised, England might have had villains who had led to her decline.

A flagrant example of the above is in a 1998 book by Harry Kelsey called *Sir Francis Drake: The Queen's Pirate* which recalls episode upon episode throughout Drake's life which confounds his actions and motives and puts him in a bad light. It ends with these statements:

"The Drake myth started when his victims complained to the Spanish king that they could not be expected to defend themselves all alone in the New World. To make their point, they described Drake as a man of terrifying stature, an enemy of their king and their church. As their dozens of reports reached the Spanish court, the name of Francis Drake came to represent the English enemy, and stories of his exploits circulated through the diplomatic circles of Europe. . .

"Response was different in England, whose chroniclers originally viewed Drake as one of a group of adventurous seamen, but not necessarily a national hero. Some years after Drake's death, in response to comments at home and abroad, his nephew began trying to refurbish his reputation by publishing a sympathetic version of Drake's exploits. Revised and amplified, this work became the basis for a new type of patriotic book with

Drake no longer a pirate but a hero, defending God and queen against a threatening Spain.

"That sort of biography no doubt served a national purpose, but history ought to say what the man was really like. Francis Drake was a rogue, an able seaman, and a pirate. Drake was a commoner who made himself rich and in the process became a friend of the queen, who tried to turn him into a gentleman. This is the Drake who emerges from the historical record, an interesting fellow but not the Francis Drake of patriotic myth." [7]

The above summary of Drake is not, fortunately, true of all books and papers which have been published in the past century, especially those writers collected and published in the Hukluyt Handbook of 1974. In this collection are many proofs of the extent of his northern journey and his assistance in producing maps to verify it. But there are still those who continue to put down efforts to recognize these proofs and revise their estimates of Drake's achievements.

In the preface for Gitzen's book, a natural science professor from the Oregon Institute of Technology in Klamath Falls has this to say, which to me is typical of academics when they encounter the work of laymen:

"What is it about these amateur historians, each brazenly challenging the Ph.D.s and learned experts who have made their scholarly pronouncements on what happened, when and where? Should we even bother to read their accounts, much less take them seriously? What do they know or what have they learned that the professionals have missed?"

The man—oops, academic—redeems himself, however, and states what we all should endorse: "I recommend the volume you hold in your hand, for your consideration. . . then come to the Oregon coast, visit the Tillamook Museum, and poke around the Nehalem Bay region. Do the ghosts of Drake's men whisper in the wind? Enjoy!" [8]

In other current books, incredibly, even Drake's circumnavigation—the only achievement Elizabeth would give him credit for—is not mentioned. One account, by Angus Konstam, calls a subsequent voyage of plunder in the Caribbean his "Greatest Voyage" without mentioning his achievements of 1577-1580. No mention is made of this greater voyage of discovery, in which the greater plunder, the circumnavigation, the first claim for England at the 45th parallel of North America for England, and, God forbid, the first peaceful encounter and description of the natives took place. [9]

In our present account of Drake we hope to let it all hang out, while explaining why he did what he did, how he accomplished being the greatest sea captain England ever had—because he learned how to captain a mixed set of men on his ships, gentlemen with sailors, in a way that

England was just learning to manage. Never could he have accomplished this, except that he saw a difference between defensive and offensive behavior when nations were at war, and he knew how to survive.

A Legacy Revealed

As indicated earlier, certain documents existing in isolated places finally came together and told a different story about Francis Drake than had been current during the preceding three centuries. These include attention to Fletcher's *The World Encompassed* and numerous research papers emanating from the Hakluyt Society which gathered them, including certain discoveries in Mexican archives.

SIR FRANCIS DRAKE
(1540–1596)

Gitzen and his predecessors showed that there had to be another element in the story of Francis Drake. He had done more than careen his boat in Spanish territory before his arduous return by way of the Moluccas. As Elizabeth in her better moments had authorized him to do, he had sought the Northwest Passage—the Straits of Anian—all the way to the present southern coast of Alaska, made his first claim for Nova Albion at Vancouver Island, and, finding no suitable port and the Indians hostile, made his way past "a mighty river"—the Columbia—to a point on the coast of the present state of Oregon at a place now called Nehalem Bay at the 45th parallel.

His greatest achievement, at Nehalem Bay, was to carry out a plan to survey and thus claim the chosen Nova Albion in accordance with the then established scientific procedure, of which Elizabeth had assisted, by introducing him to those experts in England who could instruct him in the process. This was like a key, a permission,—like Jason's to seek and find the Golden Fleece—and her permission, if not her blessing, was essential for the task upon which she had sent him.

It is well to introduce a statement from Garry Gitzen's book which points to the logic of Drake's claim, something that seems to have escaped that of historians through the ages: "Was Drake trying to circle the globe while financing his trip at the expense of the Spanish treasuries? It is unlikely that such venture would have been permitted, much less financed, by Elizabeth for the sole purpose of irritating so formidable a foe." [10]

After his work with M. Wayne Jensen, Jr. and Donald M. Viles— who amassed the incredibly inscribed relics from the Neahkahnie Mountain above the bay, initially wrote about their possible origin, and engaged the surveyor, Phillip A. Costaggini to analyze their scientific intent— Gitzen ultimately cited four major 16th century sources which, when analyzed, confirm Drake's landing site and activities in Nehalem Bay:

1) *The World Encompassed,* a journal kept by Reverend Francis Fletcher

2) The Jodocus Hondius Broadside Map circa 1593-1595

3) The Nicola van Sype Map

4) The John Drake Depositions to the Spanish Inquisition of 1584 and 1587

The latter two proofs were discovered by Zelia Nuttall in 1908 in Mexican archives, among other 20th century contemporary geological and anthropological documents, [11]

In addition to the above significant discoveries and their ramifica-

Nehalem Bay and Neahkahnie Mountain

tions, Gitzen added another proof he discovered, which is also described by Helen Wallis in the Hakluyt Handbook, the Edward Wright's World Chart of 1599 which he put forward in an article of 2012, published in 2014, which placed Drake exactly at the 45th parallel. [12]

We will here give a brief explanation of the above in order to claim their significance as proofs of Drake's neglected legacy. We cannot here, however, go into the history of how they came about. That important background will be covered in Chapter 14 as we review the distortions which occurred after Drake's journey.

The Fletcher journal had been abridged and adjusted to meet the requirements of the court of Elizabeth, and, failing that, had finally been published with the many omissions and changes it had undergone. It was finally published by Drake's nephew, also named Francis Drake, in 1628. Gitzen has used its passages extensively to describe the events of Drake's voyage and, especially, his sojourn at Nehalem which identify the particular features of the climate, geographical surroundings, native culture, but not the survey which was called his "point of position."

In one of the edited accounts of Drake's journey, *Anonymous Narrative,* which had crept into public domain before Fletcher's journal, there

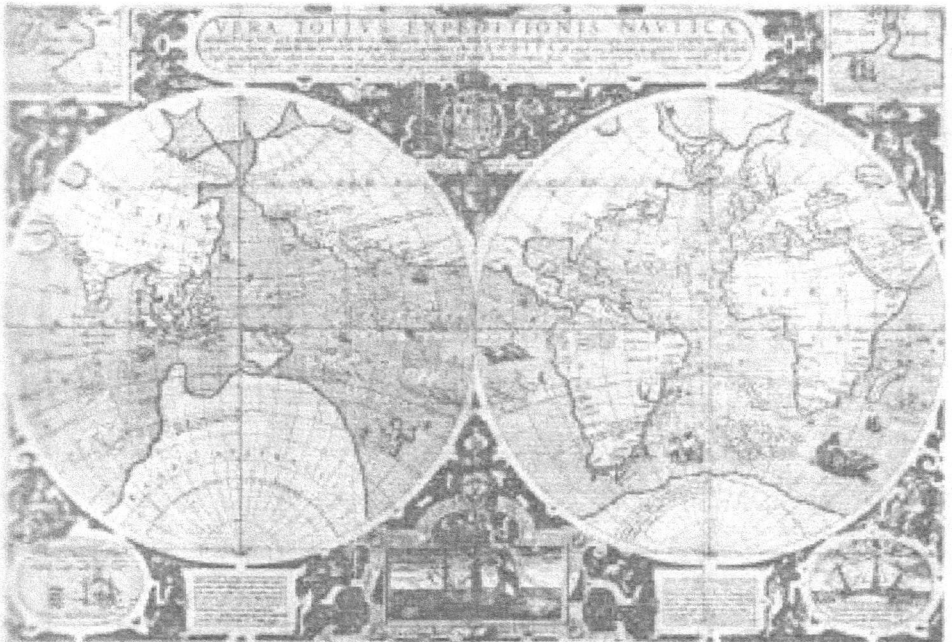

The Hondius Broadside Map

are broad gaps in the calendar, especially during the time he would have been seeking the Straits of Anian. Even references to the activity of the survey during the five weeks at Nehalem Bay are missing, which would have been forbidden knowledge at the time others were editing and compiling it. As indicated in our Introduction, however, its publication date, 1628, was after two generations had passed and any real interest in his aims had expired.

The Hondius Broadside Map of 1593-95, shown here, is the most remarkable evidence of Nehalem Bay that could possibly be given. Here in the left hand upper corner appears the outline Drake gave to Hondius of the Nehalem Bay as it was when he proclaimed it Portus Nove Albionis, or Nova Albion, as it is best known. Its contours, its convergence with the recorded events of Fletcher's journal, and its undisturbed elements of the present day make it alone the only evidence needed. When compared with the contours of the present bay, one need only superimpose upon its outline the changes of entry caused by the tsunami of 1700.

The Nicola van Sype Map, not here included, shows the demarcation line of Drake's claim across the North American continent to the 48th parallel in the east. The Library of Congress states, "One of the greatest cartographic treasures of the Elizabethan era is a map bearing the legend [translated]: 'A map seen and corrected by the aforesaid Sir Drake.'" This

Drake's "bay of fires" in the upper left corner of the Hondius map

marked the territory which England ought to have claimed and which even the Spanish honored when they resumed their exploration in 1774, carefully avoiding the latitudes between 38 and 48 degrees north in recognition of Drake's claim. "Also," as Gitzen writes, "why would Drake, with leaking treasure-laden ship, ever want to sail no closer to Spanish territory than need be, when he believed the Spanish could be searching for him?" [13]

The John Drake depositions of 1584 and 1587 to the Spanish Inquisition are also remarkable discoveries. This cousin of Drake, who was with him on his voyage, was subsequently captured by the Spanish when he sailed with William Fenton in 1582 and subjected to the Inquisition. He revealed in the depositions that Drake had sailed as far as the 48th parallel, a fact denied by the Elizabethans. Incredibly, it was in 1908 that a researcher of Mexican archaeology at the Mexican National Archives, Zelia Nuttall, discovered both the van Sype map and the depositions of John Drake, confirming Drake's sojourn at the 45th parallel.

The discovery of these great evidences have been ignored by historians who instead induce their students to concoct fake brass plates to establish a Drake's Bay in California and will not be convinced otherwise. As Gitzen remarks in regard to this information, "Would this not have been a precious discovery to keep from the Spanish?" Why indeed? [14]

Very interesting quotes cited by Gitzen include Fletcher's statements about the location for the careening, that "the Spanish had never been there" and that Spanish discoveries were "many degrees Southward of this place." [15]

He also stated that those who "survey and measure. . . have been thus bestowed [of] their studies and endeavors," which was as much as could be preserved of his writing to suggest the scientific nature of Drake's claim. In his journals was also recorded his firm belief that "God has provided this planet for all men's trading and colonization," a reference to the affirmed purpose of their journey. [16]

In our chapters about Drake's troubled voyage and command we will again visit Gitzen's analysis of Fletcher's journal, as well as Bawlf's, which Drake took from him upon arrival back in England, for what it tells us about his journey and for what it deliberately skips in what must have been many rewritings.

First, however, our story requires a trip through the ages in order to understand the absolute monarchy of Tudor times which denied him his legacy.

Chapter 2

A Historical View

Black Holes of History

It may seem presumptuous to take issue with the neglect of Drake's arduous labors at a time when individuals had little importance except as they served church and state. My point, however, is to report that occurrence and to assist in recovering evidence of that neglect. This may again be a "black hole" such as has occurred at other times in the history of the world. In regard to Francis Drake, we need to recognize the "black hole" of history that allowed ecclesiastics to claim the whole New World for Spain and to bow to any attempt to challenge that claim..

In this chapter we deal especially with the role of historians and how they interpret history in such a way as to stand the test of time. One "black hole of history" lasted over fifteen hundred years, from the time Diodorus summarized a history of the known world up to the Christian era until the late eighteenth century when historians Gibbon, Hume, and others began an objective account. We also give credit a century and a half before to Sir Walter Raleigh, who began a modern account of the ancient world while in prison. These are, of course, the histories which have survived, and the point is that authentic histories do survive the test of time, while those which glorify the gods and kings are always in controversy and tend not to be passed on.

In our earliest extant histories the reciting of the deeds, real or alleged, of a king, Ramses or David, or of a god, Osiris, Ishtar or Yahveh was the principal content, and the reader was expected to do homage to the glorified monarch, human or divine. Their deeds have been assessed through stone tablets, monuments, mythologies and the oral histories passed down through the ages which found their way at length into the written history of particular groups of people. The histories were meant to be a guide to conduct and allegiance to the present ruling authorities.

We would here introduce a rough division of histories: the mythological, the heroic, and the classic. This can be only from a personal understanding, admitting that elements of each overlap the others. The mythological, which would include the origins of all religions, are those which are used solely to justify the powers that be. In that they defeat their purpose, however, which ought to be to present universal precepts for the betterment of mankind. It is seldom, however, that their purpose is not also to divide mankind into sets of believers and non-believers.

Where then, ought we to receive guidance? From numerous resources and an open mind, but, finally, if we are to form an opinion, it should come from within oneself. As the Oregon poet William Stafford expressed it: "the research for what you're writing is your whole life." To the writer this means judging historical events, especially those in controversy, with one's own experience. Likewise, if one is searching for answers and summaries from a wide range of history, one must also endeavor to capture the predominant feeling of an age, with its many contradictions.

In this writer's summary, history might be divided first into that age which glorifies the gods and whomever would claim to represent them in a society; next the age of heroes, who claim direct authority from the gods or powers that be but act to defend the people; and finally, those who claim and defend the rights of individuals to determine their lot and promote the rights of others.

Within this pattern and division, however, there are bound to be many "black holes" in history, when those representing the gods or are claiming the power they represent would be defended in writings which would not pass the test of time. Herein we would analyze briefly the so-called Mycenaean Age 1600-1200-- B.C. which encompasses the Trojan War of 1250 B.C. which we would assign to mythology, but where we see also elements of all three.

It is important to recognize that in that war, so important to the standing of the Greeks in defending the abduction of Helen but which lasted over a decade, began the breakdown of a clear division between east and west which festered through the centuries, led eventually to the

Persian Wars under Xerxes, and delayed the development of classical Greece.

During the archaeological Bronze Age 3500-1125 B.C. the so-called Mycenaean culture spread throughout the Mediterranean area 1600-1200 B.C., and there emerged also the so-called "Heroic Age", best identified in Homer's *Iliad* and *Odyssey*, which sought to glorify heroes, neither gods nor kings, but the representatives of the people. The *Iliad* dwells on the achievements of Achilles, Ajax, and Hector rather than of Menelaus or Priam, the opposing kings. Thus individuals of lesser rank have a hearing. It is understood that the gods, however, had exceptional power over these individuals in their actions. [1]

The power of the gods, indeed, gave these heroes an excuse, actually, for their own natural impulses. We learn that Helen, according to one interpretation, was actually extolled for her exploits with Paris which started the Trojan War, even by her husband, since it was Aphrodite who motivated her. [2]

Apollo

Another claim has it that she actually had nothing to do with that war, fought over a phantom, as in Euripides' *Helen* (412 B.C.), and never eloped with Paris. This playwright also wrote a play on the hero Hercules which in some ways parallels our view of Drake's labors lost. It was written when Euripides was in his sixties in the mid-410's B.C. By that point the Peloponnesian War was in its second decade and the Athenian state seemed to be characterized by moral inconsistency, in a state where he was motivated to present Heracles—the demigod son of Zeus who epitomized Hellenic heroism and whose Labors made the world safe for civilization— to become unrecognizable to his family, friends, and himself. He is driven mad by the vengeful goddess Hera, perennially enraged at the hero as the product of a liaison between her husband Zeus and the wife of a king called Amphitryon, who, in a frenzy, murders his wife and sons.

The shocking aspect of Euripides' play is that he reversed the order, the murders followed the Labors, in fact, they came just as *Herakles*,

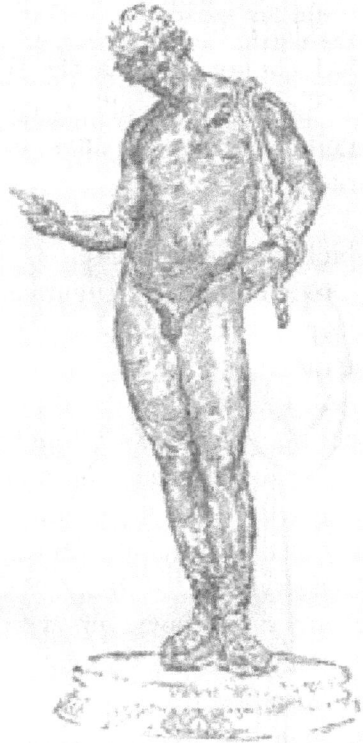

as Euripides called him, returns from the last of his exploits. It is as though Herekles is being punished for his splendid Labors on behalf of mankind. "Brought low by the arbitrary whim of the jealous Hera, the hero is pointlessly transformed into a villain, the Labors are emptied of any ethical significance, and greatness is rewarded with . . . a world empty of moral structure." [3]

The Trojan War, which occurred 1250 B.C. in the generations which followed the exploits of Hercules and lasted more than a decade, is thought to have inaugurated the many wars and controversies which occurred between east and west, being totally different cultures, and had the inevitable result of the defeat of the Greeks in the Persian Wars of 490-479 B.C. The Greeks had overextended themselves, and after the battle at Thermopylae were overrun by the Persians.

Having been put in their place, however, the Greeks began to focus on their city-states, to somewhat curb distant wars and to develop one of the most remarkable cultures that have existed on the planet. Called the "Classical Age," 478-336 B.C., focused in Athens, there began an era of reformers and lawgivers which progressed into what is considered a democracy.

Mount Olympus had been the shrine where mortal men might call upon the gods for power to conquer other cities, tribes, and nations. It is interesting that this did not work as a

The pass at Thermopylae

cohesive power over the entities conquered. In order to accomplish that, each man in a nation conquered would have to become either a slave to bring back home, or a free man to call upon his own chosen gods for power and authority. Otherwise he must be kept under constant surveillance.

Democracy was said to exist in Greece in the age of Pericles, but its participants formed but a small part of the population, since it did not include slaves or resident foreigners. As they defined it, it was said to begin when the barrier had been thrown down whereby all political rights that had been the inheritance of certain families, excluding those lacking sufficient property, was by law then available to those capable of acquiring the latter. Democracy thus achieved by the ancients, however, was overthrown at the end of the Peloponnesian War by the 400 tyrants, a move back toward despotism. [4]

This shift from the heroic to the judgment of a populous is consistent with a shift of historical focus from the egoistic to an altruistic standpoint, as indeed Herakles in Euripides's version is made to expiate his sins by a lifetime of service to the people which did nothing to restore his name. This shift therefore describes the not unworthy focus of the great historians Thucydides, Xenophon, Herodotus, and Polybius, who endeavored to glorify, not the individual, but the people. Thus the historian marks the progress of civilization in the Greek and early Roman periods.

Herodotus

In these histories these writers were involved for thirty to forty years, a life's work, involving travel to all known civilizations and an endeavor to portray mankind in its most typical and best light. These were followed among the Romans by Tacitus, Livy, Caesar, and finally, Diodorus, a Greek of Sicilian origin who codified the ancient world in the most definitive manner. These, as previously stated, were not to be equaled nor replaced until Gibbon and Hume in the late eighteenth century, followed by Macaulay and Bancroft in England and Schlozzer and Muller in Germany. Here we have a school of secular historians with broad vision and high views not dominated by a single idea wherein "events are mean-

ingless unless we can know something of the human motives that led to their enactment."[5]

In regard to Diodorus, he is considered at the epitome of the ancients in the scope and grasp of their world which sufficed until modern times. It should be emphasized, however, that he looked out upon the world with the eyes of the first century B.C., not with the eyes of the 20th century A.D. "The accepted faith of nineteenth century Europe would have seemed to Diodorus as absurd and fabulous and as mythical as any tale which he has to tell us can seem to the 20th century critic."[6]

The Age of Pericles became a model to retrieve in the Renaissance after what became a veritable "black hole" in history. In that brief enlightenment in ancient Greece there came about a glorious age, with its open antithesis of political parties, universal liberty of speech, and manifold individual energy which we have described. An assessment of that age is given by Beaty and Johnson:

"This relatively brief respite was brought to a close by the armies of Philip of Macedon and his son, Alexander the Great, in the latter part of the fourth century B.C. Though the Greeks produced much of value in later years, particularly in science and philosophy, the great period of Greek civilization was ended in this long and costly struggle. . . . But while it lasted, the Greeks perfected a civilization whose achievements still stand as objects of admiration and inspiration for the Western world"[7]

Grote, another renowned historian of the nineteenth century has written that after the Persian war no Grecian state except Athens could have sufficed to organize such a system. The very circumstances of her own democracy, with its open antithesis of political parties, universal liberty of speech, and manifold individual energy sufficed to provide cohesion and to release the energies of its members. But they were unable to repel the overruling march of "the man of Macedon" a half a century later.

"When we reflect how infinitely superior was the Hellenic mind to that of all surrounding nations and races, how completely its creative agency was stifled as soon as it came under the Macedonian dictation, and how much more it might have achieved; if it had enjoyed another century or another half century of freedom, under the stimulating headship of the most progressive and most intellectual of all its separate communities— we shall look with double regret on the ruin of the Athenian empire, as accelerating, without remedy, the ruin of Greek independence, political action, and mental grandeur."[8]

The Roman Mind

Rome possessed a capacity for expansion and an ever-increasing extension of civil rights. The Roman mind offered the strongest contrast to the churlish spirit of the Greek cities, according to Dr. Edward Meyer in an essay written especially for the *Historians' History of the World*.

"In the latter, purity of descent and the exclusion of all foreigners from civil rights was an axiom of political life, to which radical democracies, like Athens, clung even more tenaciously than the rest, and the consequence was that every success abroad led to the subjugation of the vanquished under the yoke of the ruling city.

"Rome, on the contrary, for all her conquests, made no subjects in Italy. . . Conquered communities were usually admitted to the Roman political confederacy on equal terms, and allowed to retain local autonomy under Roman supervision. She extended the franchise and the right of voting in the Roman popular assemblies, being withheld only from countries of alien languages.

"When Rome had vanquished a foe she took possession of a portion of public lands and established citizens there to cultivate the soil; the rest of the citizens retained complete liberty and political autonomy." [9]

We might consider this admirable, except as it resulted in the progress of civilization. Greece held on to her inner core, the rights and progress of a select group and produced a golden age of philosophers, artists and historians. Rome excelled in the law, the extension of rights to her territory in the direction of all who would otherwise oppress her, and the extension of civil rights to all her conquests. In this manner, however, she did not protect her core but allowed factions to rip it apart. Members of the First Triumvirate, much as our political parties today, were at war with each other and would divide the nation rather than to unify it, thereby rendering it incapable of creating a homogeneous state.

Symbolic of this tendency is the famous "crossing of the Rubicon" where in 49 B.C. Caesar led his army, defying the Roman senate and commencing a civil war which would divide Gaul from Italy. Thus, the dissenting factions at home, and by reducing all neighboring states to helplessness and impotence, she deprived them of the power of exercising the proper functions of a state. They found themselves constrained to appeal to Roman arbitration in every question. It would have been better if she had embarked on a systematic conquest. As Dr. Meyers continues:

"Finally, let us point out the effects of the policy of Rome on the development of civilization. Rome and Italy more and more assimilated the culture of Greece, and the latter, in its Latin garb, assimilated more and more ways to exercise dominion over the entire West. . . In the East, however, a retrograde movement sets in. . . and the connection of the Greek cities of the East with the mother country was severed from that time forward." [10]

In medieval times, after the Romans had failed to manage their vast conquests and had turned to religion to exact control, any analysis that passed muster among them used that religion to frighten men into submission. Religion became the method of attacking their conscience, and hagiography largely took the place of secular history.

The more recent eighteenth, nineteenth, and twentieth century periods have been a time of searching out obscure or forgotten records, finding old letters and state papers, searching forgotten and neglected archives, and applying a critical analysis to the conflicting statements of alleged authorities previously accessible. Unfortunately for Sir Francis Drake, records of his principal achievements were destroyed and it has remained to contemporary researchers to put together threads which still remain in order to try to reconstruct his true legacy. In our chapter on the aftermath of his voyage we will consider the ways that it was lost in Tudor times, and in our final reprise we will amass and again explain those threads of evidence which attest to his principal labor which might have changed history had it been properly recognized.

Caesar Crossing the Rubicon

Of the ensuing historians who attempted to rescue world history from the ecclesiastics the work began prominently with the Englishman Edward Gibbon, who undertook a thousand years of European history in his *History of the Decline and Fall of the Roman Empire*. His great work was followed by that of Bartold Georg Niebuhr, a German born in Denmark, who rescued a few centuries of Roman history in three volumes (1811-1832) which "may be said to have inaugurated modern scientific historical method. In it he related individual events to the political and social institutions of ancient Rome." [11]

A MONK OF THE MIDDLE AGES

In order to understand the man Drake, the subject of this story, his character and motivation for his labors, and the moment of his epiphany, we must recognize that his world was not our world. It was a world alien to us now, not at all attuned to our concepts of liberty, equality, and freedom of action. The setting might be explained in brief before we can understand the absolute power of the Tudors over the individual.

Our understanding envisions the progress of democracy and freedom of conscience arising as a phoenix from the slavery of the mind from organized religion which had reached unquestioned acceptance. It requires going into the mind, empathizing with the soul unexposed to its own power. This transfer must be done before one can understand Sir Francis Drake, or Walter Raleigh, or Columbus, even. They had no recourse, legal or moral even, to challenge the judgments made against them.

The setting was Tudor England, and its absolute authority was determined in the Star Chamber, established by Henry VII, where the royals conferred with their chosen councillors, including those bishops and cardinals approved by the pope, before they themselves chose the best course of action. Another tragedy is that so many of the councillors themselves eventually faced exile or execution for any mistakes in their actions or

opinions in disagreement with the royal sovereign or, simply, any failure
to carry out his or her will.

In partial explanation as to how this came about, through Christianity, the tribes of Israelites, existing in the Middle East and Egypt through
the same millennium the Greeks experimented with democracy, had a
direct relationship to their god, the same one god for all their people, who
also had the power to inflict both good and evil upon them. This was eventually codified into their Bible, which set forth the main elements of their
history, some mythical, and the commandments and rituals for daily living
which occupied their existence and solidified their cohesion. Their god had
an enviable power over them, which would capture their minds and build
upon their individual strengths, far above the ordinary. Wherever they
were they were recognized for their extraordinary abilities and focus, but
they were also used, abused, ostracized and persecuted throughout history, They were conquered by the Romans and their temple was destroyed
in the first century A.D. Their strength they attributed to their god, who
himself they greatly feared, even to look upon his face. [12]

The Rise of Christianity

The Romans, who gradually achieved ascendancy over the entire
Mediterranean and most European tribes, scarcely noticed that
obscure tribe of monotheists, the Hebrew race, nor could they assume such loss of power in a direct relationship to God. Yet they required
a means of control over conquered peoples which would appeal to their
spiritual allegiance. What was needed was an intermediary, a personal
god to monitor human failures if necessary. The Romans eventually found
that monitor in Christianity, for it was Jesus Christ, a supposed savior
of mankind, who would intervene for man's salvation with his Father in
Heaven. If a man needed to be reminded, there was that spiritual god, ever
present, the Holy Ghost, to arouse his conscience and urge him to confess
his transgressions. [13]

This new religion, which after the crucifixion St. Paul preached
throughout the Roman world, was the perfect tool for the Romans in con-
trolling their growing empire: they would eventually establish a clergy to
monitor the behavior—the civil and moral obedience—of all their conquered subjects, a power parallel and answerable to their own authority.

Those Dark Ages—when the minds of men of all stations of life came to be monitored by the ruling factions through the clergy of the Catholic church—saw also a reversal of that hierarchy at times, because the power of the church was universal whereas the nations and principalities, after the gradual disintegration of the early Roman Empire brought on wars between them. In fact, there was never much cohesion between tribes and nations, for they were isolated in their localities, each a lord with his knights and serfs. It was an age of chivalry, brought into convergence gradually by the crusades against the waves of Arabs, Moors, and Saracens who had established their own religion under Mohammed in the seventh century A.D. Without the Catholic church, there might not have been any cohesion at all.

The disintegration of the Roman Empire brought on wars between the many composite factions which fed upon rivalry and chivalry. The wars were initially for territory and enslavement, but gradually they became wars of succession as their rulers intermarried. As we approach the Renaissance those wars became more and more for religious hegemony, when the powers of the church began to be challenged and men emerged who would speak out for a more direct, personal relationship with God, as in the Protestant movement. A challenge to the clergy, however, also led to a challenge to the absolute rule of kings, who would be gods themselves if necessary.

As a consequence of absolute rule, strife between those of the nobility which supported their powers and those who didn't was inevitable. Therefore occurred the civil wars in England to bring to heel those factions who differed. We view the complications of understanding the mindset of those under the absolute authority of kings, as in the Tudor time of Francis Drake, as important to consider. The recourse we would have to freedom of speech and conscience did not exist. Neither had they in any sense access to courts who would address their grievances of mind and spirit were they put forward. They existed only to handle civil strife and petty crime and as an avenue to inform the people of the will of the throne. Parliament was called only to support the crown in the wars of their sovereign.

In this study we will consider the rise of the Tudors after the Hundred Years' War and its culmination in the Wars of the Roses, which brought them to power. We will see briefly significant events in English history which touched upon questions of human freedom, only to lapse back into total submission. Inevitably we see the role of religion as the fall back position to effect that.

Perhaps it should be explained that we see the arrival of the Renaissance in England considerably after that in Italy and elsewhere in Europe. That delay allows us to deal with the rise of the Tudors and all their corruption of the human spirit before considering the influences which finally gave rise to such humanists in England as Sir Thomas More, Erasmus, and finally to Spenser and Shakespeare.

— Chapter 3 —

The Rise of Tudor England

The Plantagenets

W e might begin with the conquest of William of Normandy in
1066, while not the first king of England, he totally reorganized
the property and ownership of the entire country, bringing over
and bestowing titles upon French nobility he wished to honor. This organization he published in a Domesday Book which established from that time
forward the nobility of England and regulated to each its possessions.

During the rule of the kings of Normandy in England, from 1066 to
1154 only French and Latin were spoken by the court and clergy. William
was followed by William II, who brought over Eleanor of Aquitaine with
the elegance of the French courts; and, with Pope Urban II, launched the
First Crusade, recapturing Jerusalem at a terrible cost.

Then Henry I and Stephen came to the throne, during which the
Second Crusade ends in failure and a schism develops between east and
west factions of the Catholic church.

The Plantagenet kings, from 1154 to 1399, included Henry II and
Richard I, known for the qualified success of the Third Crusade, followed
by John the Gaunt, associated with the Fourth Crusade in which the sack
of Constantinople by Western forces took place and when the Magna Carta
charter confirmed the liberties of the English church and set out the feudal
duties in the monarchy. There followed, in a long line, Henry II, Edwards
I, II, III, and Richard II.

The Lancasters ruled from 1399 to 1461: Henry IV, V (of Agincourt), Henry VI; then the Yorks, from 1461 to 1485: Edward IV, V and Richard III, all of whom we still consider as members of the Plantagenet line, since they were all interrelated, vying for control during the Hundred Years' War with France—which may be confusing since rule overlapped—and ending with the Wars of the Roses between the houses of Lancaster and York within the Plantagenet line. It is well to include a quote here from Knight, an early historian:

> "With Richard, the last of the Plantagenets, expired the political system under which England had been governed by that house for more that three centuries." [1]

The story of Richard III we will include as leading into the first of the Tudors, being concerned with the ways that the sovereigns disregarded royal succession and their lack of diligence in allowing parliamentary participation. Having usurped the crown from Edward V in a hypocritical farce and holding in the Tower of London Edward's heirs, Richard proceeded to Westminster and took possession of his pretended inheritance, with the Lord Howard, afterwards duke of Norfolk, on his right hand, and the duke of Suffolk on his left.

The story is told, also by Knight, in his words:

"As far as we can discover, however, the accession of the duke of Gloucester to the crown was not an unsanctioned usurpation, resting only on the resolute will of one man, surrounded by a few unscrupulous partisans, and having the command of a strong military force. . . The heir of the last king, to whom the nobles of the land had twice sworn fealty, was, with his brother, in mysterious confinement, which, according to the natural destiny of deposed princes, would probably end in secret murder, and yet, in less than a fortnight after Richard had seated himself on the marble bench of Westminster Hall, thirty-five of the peers of England and seventy of her knights—names among the highest in the land—did homage to his coronation. . . . Prostration before the despot of the hour was so absolute as to throw a colour of legality over all his proceedings. . . and when Buckingham, Norfolk, Suffolk, and Northumberland—the highest of the nobles—were ranged on the side of Richard, the heads of lesser lords of the soil did not trouble their consciences with the prob-

RICHARD III

able fate of the children of their late master.[2]

The true heir to the throne and his brother were indeed murdered, but Richard III is said to have taken measures thereafter that seemed to promise a reign of peace and security. The people of town and country were utterly weary of these feudal struggles, and had sunk into the worst state of public feeling, into that of indifference. Following the lead of the duke of Norfolk and others, parliament was ready enough to confirm his title, by passing an act for the settlement of the crown upon him and his issue hence forward, thus paving the way for the establishment of the Tudor dynasty, Richard being under both. [3]

Of the measures taken for peace and security, Richard enacted fifteen statues regulating the law of the land "protecting the liberty of the subject; and putting down abuses in the administration of justice which had sat since the time of Edward I [4]

Another improvement noted by Knight was that

"For the first time these laws to be obeyed by the English people are enacted in the English tongue. But, beyond this, they are the first laws of the land which were ever printed. . . . fifteen years after Gutenberg. . . . [The statutes] also enacted a claim for the dissemination of knowledge, a tribute to the merchants and artificers of knowledge. . . But the spirit of the feudal ages was still a living presence. As the commercial classes were pressing forth to the honours which wealth commanded, and the gates of knowledge opened wider, the claims of blood came to be regarded even more than when the only social distinction was that of lord and vassal." [5]

Another factor had had a decided effect upon the feudal society in the previous century, the Black Death of 1345 during the reign of Edward III, which had taken a third of the population, causing the remaining serfs to demand higher recompense for their labors and a move toward independence in other occupations in the cities. With the statutory importance, however, of every man's status and occupation, the claims of blood became ever more confining, hence the importance of guilds and apprenticeships.

Throughout the Wars of the Roses the claimants to the throne disappeared so fast, that on the death of Edward V and the usurpation of the throne by Richard III, there appeared a Welch gentleman by the name of Henry Tudor, being descended also from John the Gaunt, who could put forth a claim for the throne of Lancaster and was prepared to challenge Richard. He took refuge first in Brittany and then in France. Taking advantage of the unpopularity of Richard, he landed with a small force in Wales, inspiring enthusiasm for his claim and enabling him to raise a small army in his support. Then, with the help of a few English adventurers and supporters, they won a battle at Bosworth Field against a king for whom the mass of his English subjects were ashamed to fight. These are the summations of two historians, Trevelyan and Ramsey:

> Here, indeed, was one of fortune's freaks: on a bare Leicestershire upland, a few thousand men in close conflict foot to foot, while a few thousand more stood aside to watch the issue, sufficed to set upon the thrown of England in the person of Henry VII the greatest of all her royal lines, that should guide her through a century of change down new and larger streams of destiny, undreamed of by any man who plied bow and bill that day in the old-world quarrel of York and Lancaster. [6]

> Thus the Red Rose of Henry VII had avenged the White Rose of Edward IV and his sons. Ultimate victory had fallen to the house of Lancaster, and the war of succession was at an end.— [7]

We won't expect that founding a royal line would take care of all problems of succession, however. The next year, 1486, Henry married Elizabeth of York, and continued the policy of diverting the power of his nobles, further weakening the hold of parliament on his actions and canceling out their action against royal prerogative established in 1215 in the Magna Carta, and leading to a century in which Elizabeth I could personally manipulate wars and intrigues. His actions, however, brought in an era of internal peace—if you can leave out the religious persecution of individuals and skirmishes to control factions which supported usurpers to his throne.

It was a peace, described thus by the Spanish ambassador De Puebla at that time: "The English crown was now more secure than it had been for five centuries." Henry's despotic machinations did however establish a royal control over the people that in time would make it possible for the Reformation to take place, i. e., unilateral and royal dictum to switch from one faith to another and the power to control the decorum of the people which made the Renaissance possible. By the time of Elizabeth—and Spenser and Shakespeare—the people were docile to the rule of law and the expectation that right and retribution would quickly follow any controversy. [8]

We note again, a fact close to the book's main subject, that in 1497 Henry sent the Cabots on a voyage to America, closely watched by the Spanish and the world. Indeed, Cabot was the first European explorer to reach the American continent. Here again, the pope's ruling prevented any explorer from making a claim. It is this grievous problem that held back progress of the English nation in that area of the world for over a century. It was understood that colonization was forbidden, and this included the initial voyages into the areas around Newfoundland. The establishment of fisheries by the English and French kept to that rule.

Neglected in this study are details of the many wars and skirmishes between England and her near neighbor to the north, Scotland, as well as those with Ireland and Wales. Pertinent to our understanding of the British succession, however, is the understanding that at this time James IV was ruler of Scotland and that in 1496 he married Margaret, the eldest daughter of Henry VII, then but twelve years of age. Such was the procedure at the time, the joining of alliances through marriage in order to avoid wars and to insure that sufficient heirs to the throne might emerge. Naturally, neither did the custom prevent wars nor prevent problems of succession.

Henry died on April 21, 1509 of gout. Others say of tuberculosis. He left three children: Henry VIII; Margaret, married to James, king of Scotland; and Mary, afterward the wife of Louis XII, king of France.

Not all historians are generous to Henry's memory. Langard also confirmed that the first Tudor king Henry VII assumed his throne through murder and intrigue, the vengeance of which continued to haunt him throughout his twenty-four year reign. His ability to divert the power of his nobles, thereby weakening the hold of parliament on his actions, canceling out their action against royal prerogative established in 1215 in the Magna Carta, would lead to a century in which Elizabeth I could personally manipulate wars and intrigues.

It is important to establish here, however, that Henry VII, while not encouraging transoceanic adventure in the face of predominant Spanish power, made possible the future liberation of his country's energies by the only means possible—the foundation of a Royal Navy.

With this overview of the Tudor Age under Henry VII, we proceed to that of Henry VIII whose reign brought him into controversy

Henry VII
(1456-1509)

with the Catholic church. We give here a brief overview of his controversy with the church, intending to go into particulars of his reign in the
next chapter. When his marriage to Catherine of Aragon proved to be in
the way of his desire to marry Anne Boleyn, Henry VIII challenged its
legitimacy. If the reader wishes to understand its complexity, the pope had
already granted a papal dispensation for his marriage to Catherine. He
was already the nephew by marriage to Charles V, Holy Roman emperor,
who was also Catherine's uncle. The pope would have had to reverse that
dispensation in order to grant his wish to annul that marriage. One of the
early mentors of Henry's youth, John Fisher, bishop of Rochester, lost his
head for protesting that "(n)ot even popes could set aside, nullify the stated
will of God," that is, the Bible.

Leviticus provides that in the case of "childlessness" a man must
marry his brother's widow. Deuteronomy makes a correction, that it referred only to lack of "sons" that obligates such a marriage. Henry claimed
that, in any case, the Jews had abandoned such a requirement; therefore,
he had no such obligation and the marriage was invalid.

Catherine's and the church's argument was that since the marriage
with Arthur, Henry's older brother, was never consummated—which Henry would challenge—the marriage was indeed valid. [9]

Another irony is apparent, that in the same year of Catherine's
marriage with Henry, his older sister Margaret, widow of King James IV
of Scotland and mother of the young James V, secured an annulment of
her second marriage in order to enter upon a third, and Henry boiled over
in indignation.

This was an immense complication for Wolsey, cardinal and Henry's chief minister, who regarded Pope Clement VII as "a sort of orien-
tal potentate on a high golden throne." Wolsey hoped to establish peace
across Europe between Charles V and France for control of North Italy.
Clement was allied with France, and Charles' victory in 1525 at Pavia and
sack of Rome left the pope humiliated. Henry's request was minor, and
Wolsey did not want a resumption of war. This difficulty would finally
cause Henry's great rift with the Catholic church in order to effect the marriage with Anne, who would be the second of his six wives. [10]

The question of Henry's bid for annulment of his marriage to
Catherine went on for some years, gaining some possibility of the pope's
agreement when he was at one point prisoner of Charles V. A special court,
therefore, was set up in England under the pope's counsel. That counsel of
two would be of Wolsey himself and his long-time friend Cardinal Lo-

renzo Compeggio of Rome. Before Compeggio, of frail condition, could arrive in England, Henry sought opinions of John Fisher, Thomas More, and Erasmus of Netherlands in hopes of swaying public opinion, but to no avail. Needless to say, Fisher and More were eventually on Henry's death list.

When the special court finally met, actually bearing the hoped for opinion of the pope, the arguments compounded the issue resulting in outbursts from Henry. First he extolled the virtues of his queen Catherine to try to win favor, and then in his sudden anger vowed that **"there was no head so fine that he would not make it fly."** [bold by author] In the final vote, which was put to the nobles, only three signed his petition to nullify the marriage: Anne's uncle, the Duke of Norfolk; Thomas Boleyn, her father, now Viscount Rochford; and her brother George, a junior courtier.

The outset, as we know, was finally a complete break with Rome, the details of which will be given in greater detail in the next chapter. What we mean to say is that Henry's outbursts over rational issues would soon become uncontrollable. His early defense of certain church positions would become a complete rejection, and his method would be to designate himself as supreme ruler of the church of England. He would gradually organize his church around elements from the Protestant movements in Germany, France, and Scotland.

The Spanish Connection

We backtrack, however, to an earlier period when the first Tudor king, Henry VII, after his breakthrough in the Battle of Bosworth in 1485, was able to arrange the betrothal of his little son Arthur to a daughter of the royal house of Spain. That connection had been a triumph for Henry, Spain being much the greater nation in population and influence because of the union of Aragon with Castile and its strict adherence to the powerful Catholic church.

This union had come about through the marriage of Ferdinand II of Aragon and Isabella of Castile in 1469, bringing together in power the two greater provinces on the peninsula. At the time of their marriage Ferdinand became also the ruler of Sicily as well as Aragon, and in due course he began to compete with France for the dominance of Italy.

Not to forget nor pass over the principal events of their reign—the overthrow of the Moors, who had overrun the peninsula in various waves for six hundred years; the promotion of Columbus' voyage of discovery; the tragic expulsion of the Jews, Moslems, and the destruction of their own people through the Inquisition—these events will be covered again in our chapter on the rise of Spain preliminary to Drake's great voyage into their colonial territory.

    The marriage of Henry's son Arthur with Catherine of Aragon was a public event, proof that "the Tudors had arrived." However, he was still a boy, and soon died of a "sweating sickness" and Catherine, also ill, became a virgin widow at sixteen. Henry was devastated at the loss of this powerful connection to a potential ally, and he also wanted to retain the half of Catherine's dowry. There were some bad years for Catherine, Henry not wanting her to return home and contriving himself for a papal dispensation for her to marry the young prince Henry VIII. By the time this was granted, in 1504 and with the death Queen Isabella, her income from Spain was to cease. It was Ferdinand this time who favored the marriage, to counter improved relations between England and France.

    At Henry's death, finally, in 1509, the connection was quickly reestablished with the marriage of his successor, Henry VIII, who now desired to marry Catherine, his elder brother's widow. Henry was 18 and Catherine, 23. There was great ceremony and much rejoicing, especially due to the continued alliance between Spain and England. [11]

    It was a good marriage for a long time. Wars and controversies continued, England and Spain vs. France which resulted in the Treaty of Westminster and the seizing of Navarre by Spain to add to their kingdom. Catherine played her part in granting clemency at one point to four hundred foreign pillaging rioters in London and in her letters of encouragement to her husband as he led his forces in battle.

    When Ferdinand died in 1516, all of Aragon, Castile, Naples, Sicily, plus New Spain (as the new colonies in Caribbean were called) passed to young Charles I, the son of Catherine's apparently insane older sister

Juana and the grandson of Maximilian of the Hapsburg empire, who then became Charles V, Holy Roman Emperor.

As we make connections of England with Spain we learn that Catherine's daughter Mary, her sole remaining child with Henry after many miscarriages, was at one time betrothed to Emperor Charles. Charles withdrew, however, from the engagement when Mary was 10, and he, at 25, then married his first cousin of Portugal.

This was a big shock to Henry and he plotted another scheme to substitute for the desired alliance: he elevated his six-year-old bastard son, Henry Fitzroy, of mistress Mary Boleyn, Anne's sister, to positions of nobility and spoke of making him king of Ireland and perhaps his successor. This infuriated Catherine, of course, and with their marriage dead, and also the dream of an alliance with Spain and the Hapsburgs dead with it, the end of the stage was set for many troubles to follow. [12]

In Henry's extended bid for an annulment of his marriage to Catherine, its blockage, and the failure of aligning himself to powerful countries through marriage, it might be asserted that his character appeared to lose control. Absolute monarchy had arrived, and the character of Henry no longer awaited approval of his people and his ministers. Many heads would fall.

As stated previously, the Black Death in the fourteenth century had begun the first loosening of the bonds of serfdom due to the demise of a third of the population, and episodes of the plague continued at intervals into the fifteenth and sixteenth as well as drought and crop failure. The dearth of peasants to run the properties of the nobility resulted in a gradual change from the production of grains and produce on their lands to converting them to "enclosures" which would accommodate the raising of sheep and the harvesting of wool for trade abroad. By the time of Henry VIII there were but fifty or so Lords in the kingdom, who at that time were finding it difficult to meet his demands for taxes due to the many wars.

As Henry's controversy with the church proceeded, he became aware that there were other reasons why he should challenge it and the

papacy. The crown owned so much land that as a rule it was expected to pay the costs of the government, except in times of war when it would then call a parliament to pay their share of "benevolences." With hostility developing even with his own people over the break with Rome, he conceived a new plan.

The church, in contrast to the crown, owned even more that a third of all the acreage of England, belonging to cathedrals, parish churches, colleges and hospitals, and monasteries. These altogether provided not only the broad spectrum of religious life to the people but also meals and shelter for those in need, stores of food against famine, lodging for travelers, care for the sick, a network of schools, and two universities. Henry, in his need of support for wars to challenge the papal authority, became aware of the conspicuous sums that were taken in offerings from the people which maintained the church hierarchy in princely splendor. [13]

The numerous wars, the depopulation of cities due to disease, the population replacement from the country where labor was needed, and his conspicuous spending—in addition to his apparent unpopularity—was creating a crisis for Henry. It cannot be supposed that his attack on the church was due only to their stand on his desired annulment. It was becoming obvious to Henry that the wealth of the church must be a solution to his problems.

First he would ask the monasteries for an "amicable grant" of their properties to the good of the crown. There was no protest of the clergy, but the people blamed Wolsey, who, in fact, was the pope's man in England. Henry nagged Leo X to appoint Wolsey cardinal and then took into service Thomas Cromwell, a self-made lawyer, to assist in closing some monasteries, diverting their income and managing them for the crown and his own benefit. [14]

The pope protested that the usurpation of church property was becoming a violation of the "praemunire statute." Wolsey had turned over Hampton Court to the crown years before, and now Whitehall, which had belonged to Archbishop of York, was to become the new home for Henry and Anne Boleyn.

To the pope's protests, however, there was no reply, only a continuation of Wolsey's help in closing the monasteries. They were learning how to tap a seemingly endless reservoir of wealth. By not defending himself against ridiculous charges, the pope had shown the king how potent a weapon the "praemunire statutes" could be. [15]

Not to tax the reader's understanding, what this tactic amounted to was the astonishing assertion that the church had no power at all except to forgive sins. The Catholic Europe of the 1520s was sustained less by raw power than by consensus on how and for what purposes society should be organized.

This was somewhat a breakthrough, for over the centuries, no one had succeeded in overturning the authority of the church. Without pursuing more details, Henry was burdening Wolsey with the wrath of the Roman church, and after his fall, nobles directed their hatred toward the system that had produced him. This was a veritable victory for Henry over the papacy's hold over his marriage. The people were ready for change.

In Germany Martin Luther was expressing discontent with the powers of the church. By 1529 such ideas were bursting into print via the newly developed printing press; and Tyndale claimed that the king had as much authority as the Bible. He said, "He that judgeth the king judgeth God," quoting the kings of the Old Testament. Said Henry, "This is a book for me and for all kings to read."

Here we sense a victory of Henry over the church. With this kind of support who but the basest of men would undermine his supporters in his war against the church. We have suggested Wolsey's end, which was as a man totally stripped of his wealth and position and dying in failure. We would also cite Sir Thomas More, raised to the chancellorship, who had once stood at the king's side with exceptional political flattery, saying in all conscience, "Genuine and legitimate powers come to the prince not from above but from below, from the community that is governed," and, "Society functions when princes act in harmony with the will of the people," straight from the Magna Carta and Parliament. Yet in the end his words, hedging on the church's authority, would lead to his imprisonment and beheading. It would have been better if More had never assumed the chancellorship. [16]

Were we to follow the gradual decline of the Catholic church in England, we might start with 1530 when there were 9,000 parish churches, 21 dioceses, each headed by a bishop or an archbishop. There were two provinces: York with three sees and Canterbury, with eighteen. There were 10,000 monks and 1600 nuns in 600 monasteries and 200 houses of mendicant friars responsible for the education of the populace. At that time Erasmus had said, "England is the great hope for the future of European scholarship."

As the influence of the Inquisition in Spain and threats against Henry proceeding from Rome took effect, heresy was feared, not only for the church hierarchy but for the structure of society as a whole. As pressure from Rome increased Wolsey had taken a relaxed stance about searching out, never mind punishing, possible cases of heresy. Yet the ordinary people were strongly attached to their church. They really believed what the church taught. Therefore Henry took careful measures not to change the manner and order of worship while gradually changing the liturgy and beliefs of the emerging Church of England. In his attachment and sale of the monasteries to the nobles to replenish his economic resources, he was also careful not to arouse the people.

Changes emerging in the Church of England also met with approval because of attitudes toward deviant behavior. Unlike public deportment in Spain which might arouse interrogation on church principles, in England, a deeply Catholic culture also, unacceptable behavior was not condemned, nor hated. This is evident in Chaucer's description of the common folk in *Canterbury Tales*. The only essentials were perhaps belief in and adherence to the seven sacraments. These Henry would preserve. [17]

Chapter 4

Henry VIII, Character and Legacy

Early Years

We have taken a brief journey into the Middle Ages in the previous two chapters through nineteenth century historians, including Gibbon, Knight, Ramsey, Campbell and Lingard. Continuing on we include Trevelyan in the nineteenth and G. J. Meyer in the twentieth, each doing their part to restore reason from the "black holes" of history. We have also noted briefly Chaucer's role in his portrayal of the common people in the fourteenth.

We pass by, however, St. Thomas Aquinas of the thirteenth, whose *Summa Theologica* had the most influence on Christian thought, and Dante, whose *Divine Comedy* gave the most vivid picture of life at that time in our endeavor to pursue the more dispassionate assessments of the status of mankind under the rule of sovereigns who used religion to subdue the minds of men. Reporting the ways that they have done this is unavoidable, but our wish is to expose this perfidy and not accept the many factors of injustice that were unquestioned at the time they occurred.

With the death of Henry VII there succeeded to the throne in 1509 his younger brother, crowned Henry VIII. Soon to follow was his marriage to Catherine of Aragon, since his older brother Arthur, who was to have enjoyed the lady and the realm, had prematurely died. Archbishop Warham, the chancellor; Bishop Foxe, lord privy seal; and Howard, earl of Surrey, lord treasurer, were the king's chief ministers. The young king was eighteen years old, and it must be said that he didn't exactly rule: he turned over most affairs of state to the newly appointed Cardinal Wolsey, who gradually in effect ruled England while Henry hunted every morning, engaged in sports of all sorts, and kept open activities each evening in his court of a most extravagant manner. It was also said that in Henry's court there was a better store of learned men than in any university. According to Trevelyan:

"These early friends of his implanted in his mind a dislike of monks, of image worship, of relic worship, and a respect for the study of the Bible—all perfectly compatible with doctrinal orthodoxy on the Eucharist, as his subjects were to find out in the days to come when this handsome young athlete and all things noble had been turned by thirty years of power and worship into a monstrous egoism moving remorselessly over the bodies of old friends and new foes toward a clearly conceived middle policy in religion, with the Royal substituted for the Papal power." [1]

It will not be necessary in this study to go into all of the wars and intrigues which continually disrupted life for the people of England and made them docile to royal authority. Two early wars in his reign, however, might be reviewed for additional information pertinent to the development of our story. .

In the battle of Flodden Field, Sept. 9, 1513 against Scotland, James I did fall, along with 9,000 of his men, the prime of their nobility, gentry, and even clergy. The English army under the earl of Surrey also suffered great losses and did not pursue the enemy into Scotland, leaving the victory uncertain for the future. Henry himself was not present, and having joined the Italian Holy League against Louis XII in 1511, was simultaneously involved in war with France. It was Queen Catherine who announced the victory to her husband in a very spirited and English letter, calling him "my Henry."

Soon after he returned from France, he awarded Surrey by restoring to him the title of duke of Norfolk, which had been forfeited by his father, who fell in the battle of Bosworth Field (1485) after being on the wrong side. In this, the battle of Flodden Field, instead of invading Scotland, he disbanded the rest of his army as the Scots prepared manfully for the defense of their county. The queen of Scots, at the same time, wrote an affectionate letter to her brother Henry, requesting his forbearance for a widowed sister and an infant orphan. Henry, not incapable of generous sentiments and recalling the unprofitable nature of Scottish wars, agreed to a peace. [2]

The year 1514 saw a peace with France and the marriage of Mary, sister of Henry VIII, to Louis of France, who died, however, shortly thereafter. 1515 is the year that Wolsey was made an arch-bishop, and the pope then made him a cardi-nal and chancellor. Francis I was the successor in France, and a confeder-acy was formed be-tween England and France. 1516 was then the year of the birth of princess Mary of England, who would be the only surviving child of Henry and Catherine.

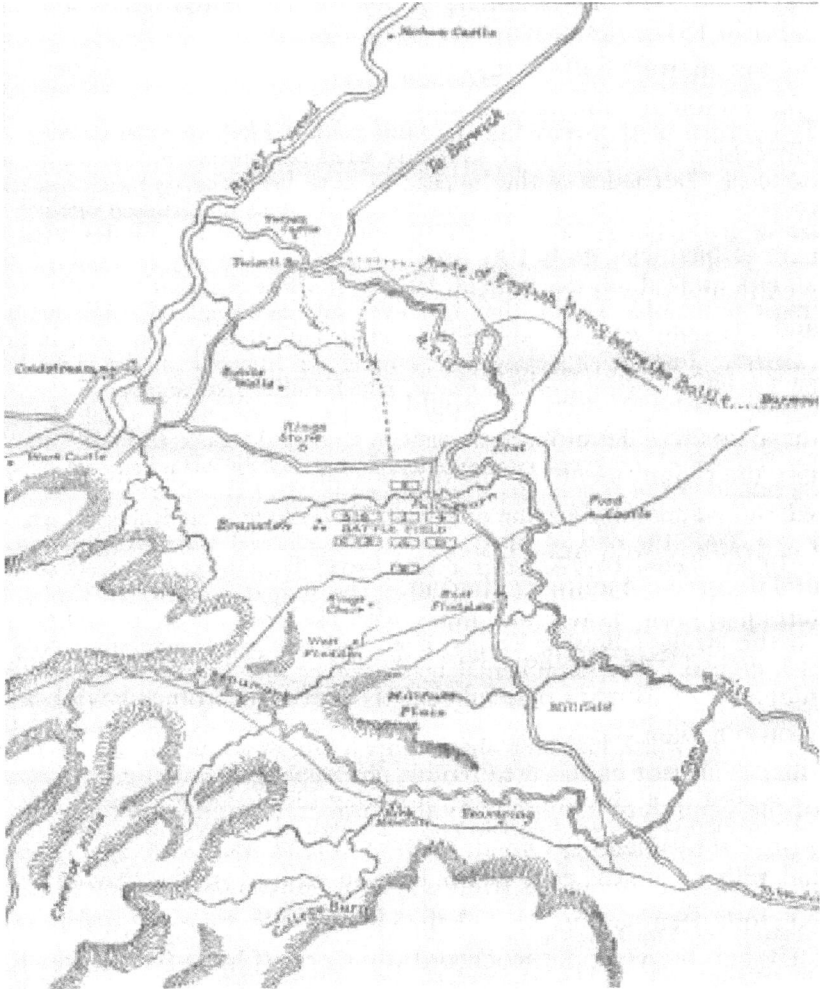

Map of Flodden Field

1518 was the year of a treaty with Spain, but it preceded by a year the death of Ferdinand, whose successor was his grandson Charles who ruled also a larger part of Europe. It is said that the spirit of Renaissance was reaching England slowly, having first emerged in Italy, assisted no doubt by the invention of the printing press.

With scholars in the ascendancy it was likely that Sir Thomas More's *Utopia,* a satire on English government, received much attention.

He was elected to be privy councillor in 1518. Henry was having his quarrels with Luther by
1521, wrote a book against him,
and received the title from the
pope of "Defender of the Faith",
all this while Wolsey was taking
care of business, gathering great
wealth and power for himself,
and even building the Hampton
Court as a gift for the king.

No way, however, could
these positive developments satisfy the requirements of the king
when he suddenly conceived
the desire to wed Anne Boleyn
and divorce the aging Catherine,
who had borne him a daughter,

CARDINAL WOLSEY
(1471-1530)

not a son. By 1530 the divorce would be pending on the grounds of the
illegality of Henry's marriage to his deceased brother's wife, as in the previous chapter.

Demoting his great friend Wolsey, Henry made himself the head
of the Church of England. By this time a divorce from the church of
Rome was indeed assumed. With the break with Wolsey and the church,
he elevated some of his friends whom he was later to betray: the duke of
Norfolk became president of the cabinet; the duke of Suffolk, earl mar-
shal; and the viscount Rochford was created earl of Wilshire. To appoint
a successor to Wolsey in the chancery was an object of great importance.
The office was at length given to Sir Thomas More, treasurer of the household and chancillor of the duchy of Lancaster. [3]

In 1530 Henry's efforts to bring credence to the throne and to
support his objections to the papistry soon caused him to raise Thomas
Cromwell to Cardinal. In 1531 he increasingly endorsed Lutheranism, and
in 1533 was able to bring about his marriage to Anne Boleyn and a complete break with the Catholic church. Regarding the lot of Catherine, men
had the prudence to be silent. But women expressed their disapproval "till
Henry, to check their boldness by the punishment of their leaders, committed to the Tower the wife of the viscount Rochford and the sister-in-law of
the Duke of Norfolk" [4]

There followed, in 1535 an execution of monks in a Catholic Charterhouse, who, defending Catherine, in their unworldly realm, were unable to adjust to the king's becoming head of their church. Fourteen of them were condemned to the flames, and twelve were sent to other towns, there to be burned for example's sake and for the vivid manifestation of the king's orthodoxy. [5]

There followed an Act of Supremacy—of Henry's authority over the church of England— and the execution of John Fisher, bishop of Rochester, for his adherence to the Catholic faith. Fisher at the burning pier opened his Bible and read, "This is life eternal, to know Thee, the only true God, and Jesus Christ, whom Thou hast sent." All had been required to affirm the legitimacy of the king's marriage. Fisher was the only one to sign a declaration that the king's marriage was unlawful. Sir Thomas More escaped, but said, "What is postponed, is not abandoned."

DOORWAY IN CHARTERHOUSE

That same year Thomas Cromwell was made vicar-general with powers over the archbishop of Canterbury. The difficulties of deciding who might exert the powers, even of a reformed church, became great. Two of Cromwell's creatures, Leigh and Ap Rice, came up with a letter of instruction to the clerics that all powers of the church should be suspended for an indefinite period. If any of the prelates claimed authority by divine right, they must produce proofs or petition the king for restoration of their powers. Thus, it was achieved that they must acknowledge the crown as the real fountain of their spiritual jurisdiction.

Step by step the property and authority of the monasteries was usurped. First they were dissolved, then one hundred had their rights restored, subject to giving or selling their larger portion to the king. Soon, however in 1539 "an act for the dissolution of the monasteries" was put forward which encouraged the clerics that of their "free will" they might assign all of their possessions to the king. [6]

First Wives of Henry

Through the Act of Supremacy, Henry was then able to declare his marriage to Catherine unsanctioned by the church of England. Catherine, however, refused to give up the title of "queen" and Mary, her daughter, that of "princess." On that account she was banished from the court in 1536. Having established his supreme authority, Henry was then able to divorce her and marry Anne Boleyn. Anne deserves an introduction. As daughter of Sir Thomas Boleyn, one of the king's most trusted diplomats, Anne had been assigned first to the Brussels court of Margaret of Austria, and then to the court of the queen of France, whose friend she became. She was especially vivacious, educated, and talented in the manners of court life, which set her apart in the courts of Henry when threat of war between France and England caused her return home in 1521. She was twenty-one, a singer, a dancer, an instrumentalist, and by the standards of English court life, a paragon of fashion and taste. In addition she was the granddaughter and niece of two dukes of Norfolk, which alone placed her in the position of an advantageous marriage. Wolsey foiled one of these, for reasons unknown, and it was soon obvious that she had the king's attention. [7]

Anne had the sense to know that her situation with the king was precarious, especially since the king had already sired a son by Mary's older sister, whom he had taken as a mistress. Although Mary had been pensioned off and her father elevated to Viscount Rochford—perhaps because of the affair—this was not going to happen to her!

Her marriage to Henry concluded, however, Anne gave birth to a daughter, princess Elizabeth, a short while after her marriage to Henry and then to a son who was stillborn. But the king was already paying attention to another lass of the courts, Jane Seymour. Unfortunately for

ANNE BOLEYN

Anne, her levity of manner acquired in the French court was no match for Jane Seymour's superior elegance of person and gentle and playful disposition. Anne's finding them together was said to have brought on the son's early birth. Harsh words were exchanged.

Soon, in order to solve his problem of what to do about Anne, Henry was receptive to rumors that Anne had been indiscreet before her marriage to him in the household of her grandmother, duchess of Norfolk. She had thereby also alienated the regard and acquired the enmity of her uncle Norfolk, the second duke of Norfolk, who had probably encouraged Henry's attention to Anne. [8]

When reports injurious to Anne's honor reached the ear of Henry, the first disclosures had come from a female in her service, who, being detected in an unlawful amour, sought to excuse herself by the example of her mistress. This Lady Rochford was also involved as a witness (who later perished for her involvement in the amours of Henry's fifth wife, Catherine Howard).

Eager to rid himself of a woman whom he no longer loved, Henry referred these reports to the council, and a committee was formed to inquire into the charges against the queen, which reported that sufficient proof had been discovered to convict her of incontinence, not only with Brereton, Norris, and Weston, of the privy chamber, and Smeton, the king's musician, but even with her own brother, Lord Rochford.

When thus accused, Smeton, who was a commoner and subject to the rack, after various intimidations, made a full confession of guilt, and Norris soon followed. Rochford, Weston, and Norris had stood high in the kings favor, the first two playing with him for large sums at shovel-board, dice and other games. Smeton, of mean origin but also high in his favor, was hanged and quartered. The others all received a sentence of death by decapitation. Anne's guilt is not known since licentious desire is a question that probably never can be determined. Her uncle Norfolk shook his head and said, "Tut, tut," and abandoned her to the decisions of the court. That behaviors in the court were licentious cannot be denied, as they were to threaten not only Anne, and later Catherine Howard, another granddaughter of the Duchess of Norfolk, but also, it is claimed, threatened the virtue of Jane's daughter, Elizabeth, as we shall also note.

Anne's conviction was tedious, a matter of her denying that a promise of marriage had ever existed with Brereton, which might have saved her life. By the time she was executed, Jane Seymour was already pregnant, and she bore a son on the 12th of October 1437. Their great rejoicing was short-lived, for her death, which soon followed, left the king again alone.[9]

When Henry married Jane Seymour, he had Mary and Elizabeth declared illegitimate, still hoping for a male heir. He also had hoped to name Henry Fitzroy, the illegitimate son of his former mistress, Mary Boleyn, his successor, but in 1534, he died. Mary soon sought a reconciliation with her father, and she and her sister Elizabeth were received back in his graces. In that day bastards by law might be treated as princesses, in fact, be married, to the king's profit, into the families of some of the continental sovereigns.

Wives Four, Five, and Six

In his eagerness to fill this gap in his personal life, Henry called upon Thomas Cromwell to supply him with an advantageous connection with a German princess. Soon he had finalized a marriage with Anne of Cleves, who came over, entered his court and bedchamber, and displeased him immensely with her homeliness and lack of talents pleasing to the court.

A divorce of Anne of Cleves was then con-

Henry VIII
(1491-1547)

cluded, and Cromwell was arrested by the duke of Norfolk at the council table, posing the question: "Had not Cromwell imprudently pressed upon Henry this marriage to a Protestant queen?" Soon, however, the duke would likewise be arrested. Cromwell was attainted for treason and heresy by an act of parliament, and on the 29th of June this servant of twelve years was executed. This 'heretic' was a clergyman. [10]

In 1540 Henry married Catherine Howard, fairest of the young maids of nobility at his court, who was actually a cousin to Anne Boleyn. This was a short marriage, ending as had Anne Boleyn's, in accusations of adultery before her marriage to Henry. Would this not lead to trouble for Norfolk? "Had not Norfolk as resolutely urged upon his master, who now hated heretics more than papists, to consider the charms of his niece, Catherine Howard, who would support him in resisting the 'rashness and licentiousness' that had come upon the land?"[11]

It was only a year after their marriage, in 1541, that Henry was informed through another female under the duchess of Norfolk's roof, now married to Essex, of the profligacy of Catherine before her marriage. She named Derham, a page to the duchess, as Catherine's paramour. She claimed that Essex had told Lascelles, her brother, that Derham had been in the habit of coming into the apartment allotted to females, bringing wine, fruit, and entertainment and behaving with great freedom and rudeness. She said that "on a thousand nights" Derham had come to Catherine's bed chamber. [12]

In her interrogations Catherine admitted that Derham had offered some violence to her person, but, not as Cranmer had urged her to claim, there had been no pre-contact of a marriage, which might have saved her. She was to plead that "all that Derham did unto her, was of his importune forcement and in a manner *Costume of the Sixteenth Century* violent, rather than of her consent and

will." [13]

As stated also by the Catholic historian, Lingard, "There is no inherent improbability in her statement. We shall later find Elizabeth proved by witnesses to have endured similar treatment from Lord Seymour often in the presence of his wife." [14]

There followed the imprisonment and execution of Catherine after the Star Chamber, the king's own court of jurisdiction, had determined that if there was no pre-contract, which would be incompatible with adultery, the court must proceed against her with that charge. Also to be charged was Culpepper, maternal relative and the king's secretary who had been aware of the alleged adultery. Durham was hanged and quartered; Culpepper was beheaded. Lady Rochford, the informer, was allowed to accompany Catherine to the block; however, she was charged as aider and abettor and was later beheaded also.

This was the same Lady Rochford whose testimony against her husband had led to his execution with his own sister, Anne Boleyn. All those convicted of concealment were condemned even though no legal proceedings whatsoever were taken against them.

On the scaffold Catherine avoided all mention of the alleged adultery and gave no protest. She had been enjoined by authority that she might not seem to impeach "the king's justice."

BLOODY GATE IN THE TOWER

Among those thus convicted were Lord William Howard, earl of Surrey; the duchess of Norfolk herself, along with her daughter the countess of Bridgewater. All other inferiors were condemned to forfeiture and perpetual imprisonment. We will learn the fate of other members of the Norfolk nobility presently. [15]

"To make concealment of vice a capital offence was worthy of such a reign," says the historian Mackintosh. As a result, "[there were] no more youthful candidates for the honour of Henry's hand after this enactment. Henry, under this new law of treason, chose the hand of a discreet widow, Catherine Parr, twice married, in July 1543. There would be no more accusations of premarital infidelity. " [16]

For these affairs of the heart Henry had sought further justification by changes in religious worship. He embraced a new version of Tyndale's English Bible in 1539 which coincided with his second usurpation of the surviving monasteries, and his removal of their idols, jewels, and treasury.

He then drew up Ten Articles aimed at defining the new worship and a distinct advance toward Lutheranism, which was in fact an effort to explain rather than reject the creed of the medieval church. This was interpreted perhaps as a signal for the duke of Norfolk, who had been a zealous Catholic and seems to have hoped for a reconciliation with the church, and he was suddenly recalled from France.

There followed then in 1544, further liturgical changes in the Church of England, including the *Book of Common Prayer,* which resulted in challenges to Norfolk's position in Henry's court. In time, both the duke of Norfolk and the earl of Surrey, father and son, were committed to the Tower, as was Lord Seymour—all favored members of Henry's court.

In this limited study it will be hard to pursue the role of each of those arrested. The achievements of Lord Henry Howard, Catherine's uncle who was executed in 1547, should be acknowledged, however, of whom Mackintosh says,

"Henry Howard, earl of Surrey, is so justly renowned for his poetical genius, which had been surpassed by none but Chaucer; by his happy imitations of the Italian masters; by a version of the *Aeneid* of which the execution is wonderful, and the very undertaking betokens the consciousness of lofty superiority; by the place in which we are accustomed to behold him, at the head of the uninterrupted series of English poets; that we find it difficult to regard him in the inferior points of view, of a gallant knight, a skillful captain, and an active statesman." [17]

The writer of this study of Drake's claim traces her ancestry to the aforementioned "Ap Rice," or Rhys ap Griffith, whose second wife was Lady Bridgewater, who was the aunt of Catherine Howard, fourth wife of Henry VIII, hence the focus on this particular family, though there was no blood connection to the Howards. None-the-less, in Henry's reign of terror, the first duke of Norfolk was, as previously stated, at Richard III's right during his inauguration. The first duke was killed, being on the wrong side in the battle of Bosworth, the second duke being restored by Henry, and now this third duke was subject to execution for trifling acts of treason and for being on the wrong side of Henry's religious revisions. These men were among the most valiant in England's history, sacrificed for the personal whims of a despot, and this Lady Bridgewater was one of those sent to the Tower as a result of Catherine's supposed adulteries.

Family historians, i. e., genealogists, name Ap Rice's son, Sir William (Royce) Rice, born previous to his marriage to Lady Bridgewater, as next in line, followed by William Royce (Rice) who was granted a coat of arms in 1535, then Thomas Rice, b. 1558, born in 1568. The author inserts here, for your possible interest, the lineage of her great-grandmother, Fanny Parks.

Continuing our story, the duke of Norfolk was scheduled for execution on the very morning that Henry VIII died, January 13, 1547, and a respite was sent to the Tower. Therefore, his head was spared.

A comparison may be made between the achievements of Lord Henry Howard, who was tried and executed in 1547 whose works are still revered today, and those of Sir Walter Raleigh and Sir Francis Drake, both of whom were distinguished explorers, colonizers or potential colonizers, and principal sea captains against the Spanish Armada. Their stories, yet to be completed here, include their other achievements: Raleigh, having written the first history of the known world of note since Diodorus during his long imprisonment, and Drake, having documented the first English claim and encounter with the native Americans on the west coast of America, a story lost to the world due to the intrigues of the Tudor court.

That Raleigh was beheaded by James I, following Elizabeth's reign, in 1618, as a gesture of compliance with Spanish claims, defies the imagination, as does her poor treatment of Drake in compliance with the ill will and jealousies of her favorites at court as well as in obedience to Spanish claims. In our chapters on Spain and the Inquisition and on the Martyrs we will further catalogue the incredible mistreatment of Columbus, another comparison to Drake which merits our attention. Some of our greatest talents, our greatest contributors to world history, have received shabby treatment.

5th Generation	6th Generation	7th Generation
Fanny Parks Ancestors	60. Elijah Parks b. abt 1742 p.b. Guilford, N.H., CN m. 14 Jan 1772 d. 1790 p.d. Bethlehem, Linch, CN	120. Nathanel Parks b. 20 May 1712 d. 1790 p.d. CN 121. Abigail Clark b. 1715 d. 26 Nov 1794
30. William Parks b. 21 May 1787 p.b. Lebanon, N.L., CN m. 2 Apr 1807 d. 12 Feb 1856 p.d. Louisiana, Pke MO	61. Anna Beaumont b. 15 Sept 1749 p.b. Lebanon, N.L., CN d. 23 Mar 1830 p.d. Livonia, Livingston, NY	122. William Beaumont b. 1725 d. abt 1812 123. Sarah Everett b. abt 1729
4th Gen. 15. Fanny Parks 2) b. 25 Oct 1821 p.b. Livonia, Livins, NY	62. Benjamin Hyde b. 1 Mar 1756 p.b. Norwich, N.L., CN	124. Walter Hyde b. 1737

8th Generation	9th Generation	10th Generation
Fanny Parks Ancestors, cont.	496. Samuel Hyde chr. 1665 N.L. County, CN d. 1742	992. Samuel Hyde b. 1637 d. Jul 1677 993. Jane Lee chr. 12 Sep 1640
248. Daniel Hyde b. 1694 of Windham, Windham, CN d. 1770	497. Elizabeth Calkins b. 1674 Norwich, CN	994. John Calkins b. between 1634-8 d. 8 Jan 1702 995. Sarah Royce (Rice) b. 1634 d. 1 May 1711
249. Abigail Wattles chr. 1702 of Stonington, N.L., CN	498. William Wattles or Waddell* b. 1672 of Lebanon and New London, CN d. 1737	996. John Wattell b. abt 1641 d. 1676 King Philip's War 997. Mary Gould b. 23 Oct 1651

11th Generation	12th Generation	13th Generation
Fanny Parks Ancestors, continued		
1990. Robert Royce 1991. Mary Sims	3980. Thomas Royce (Rice) b. 1564	7960. William Royce (Rice) b. 1521 of Boerner, Buckinghamshire, Eng. Granted Coat of Arms 1555
1994. Francis Gould 1996. Gregory Belcher 1997. Katharine Buckley 1998. Roger Billings 1999. Hannah Savage 2004. John White 2005. Mary Levett 2012. John Dennison 2013. Phebe Lay 2016. James Olmstead 2017. Joyce Cornish	3992. Thomas Belcher 3993. Deborah Hunt 3996. Roger Billings 4024. Capt. George Denmson 4025. Ann Borodel 4032. James Olmstead b. abt 1551 Thaxted, Essex, Eng. d. 2 Dec 1593	7984. Gregory Belcher 7985. Joan 7986. Samuel Hunt 7987. Rebecca 7992. Richard Billings b. 1560 7993. Elizabeth Strong 8050. John Borodel 8064. James Olmstead 8065. Alice Hawkins or Sorrell

14th Generation	15th Generation	16th Generation

Fanny Parks Ancestors,
cont.

14th Generation	15th Generation	16th Generation
	William Danforth	Thomas Dernefextd
15632. Paul Danforth	Isabell	
15633. Katheryne		
15636. William Sudbury		
15668. William Selden	William Selden	
15669. Marian	Alice	
15672. Francis Bushnell		
15673. Rebecca Holmes		
15684. Thomas Gilbert		
15688. Richard Trott or Treat	William Treat	John Trott or Treat
15689. Joanna	b. abt 1480	
b. abt 1512		
15692. Nicholas Gaylord		
15693. Johanna		
15736. Robert Foote	Edward Whetman	
15738. John Brooke		Ralph Kelland
15739. Elizabeth Whetman	Bridget Kelland	
15872. Robert Hyde	Harriet Hyde	
15873. Margaret (Catherine)	Mary Margaret Warren	
Dranfeld		
15874. William Claverly		*Line extends to sixth
15875. Elizabeth Sneyd		century: 20 generations of
15896. Rev. William Browne	John Browne	kings and nobles of South
15897. Magdalene Elsick		Wales.
15898. Richard Patching	Thomas Patching	Thomas ap Griffith*
15899. Margery	Margaret	Elizabeth Griffith
15920. Sir Rhys ap Griffith	Griffith ap Rhys	Rhys ap Thomas
15921. Lady Bridgewater, aunt	Katherine St. Johns	Merch Henry
of Lady Catherine Howard, 4th	Sir Thomas Howard	John Howard**
wife of Henry VIII	Agnes Tilney	b. 1310
15984. Roger Billings	William Billings	Alice DeBoys
15985. Catherine	Joan	Robert Howard
15986. Ebenezer Strong		Margaret De Scales
16128. James Olmstead	James Olmstead	John Howard
16129. Beatrice	Beatrice	Alice Tendring
16144. Thomas Lummys	Laurent Lummys	Sir Robert Howard
16150. William Marler	Thomas Marler	Margaret De Mowbray
16151. Margaret Perye	Margaret White	John Howard
16256. Richard White	Thomas White	Katherine DeMoleyn
16257. Ellen or Helen Kirton	Agnes Richards	
16260. William Allgar	Robert Allgar	**Line extends to Edward I,
16261. Mary	Margaret	King of England, and through
		his 2nd wife Margaret to King
		Philip III of France

Family Genealogy Chart - See 5920 Sir Rhys Ap Griffith

Chapter 5

The Successors of Henry VIII

The Reigns of Edward and Mary

In the previous centuries in Spain and Italy the Inquisition had been in full sway, and orthodoxy had been very clear from early Roman times. But here we have a church that is rapidly changing, at the whim of a despot motivated by his own personal lusts and the control of his own line of power, in some ways more evil because of its unpredictability. It had become obvious that no spiritual advisor, war hero, dissenting cleric, wife, child or personal friend was exempt in Henry VIII's reign from the fire or chopping block. This heritage was not to cease simply because of his death. His legacy was to leave a scattered line of succession that would become even more evil in its extent, if we are to count the lives burnt at the stake, hung, or beheaded.

We have mentioned only in passing Henry's involvement in interminable foreign wars. His success here was not good either. In these he tried to become the third great power, but he lacked both the strength and the skill to have much effect. In the process of trying, he also impoverished the country and alienated his supporters. There had begun a great duel which lasted from 1520 to about 1570 between France and the Hapsburg empire, with England most often on the side of France, and it wasn't over yet.

Before we proceed to Henry's successors, it might be well to quote from a few additional prominent historians of the 19th century in regard to his character. T Knightley said that "Thorough selfishness formed the basis of Henry's character," and that "We may therefore allow Henry to have been a bad man, and yet regard the Reformation, of which he was an instrument, as a benefit to mankind." Peter Heylin said, "He spared no man in his anger, no woman in his lust." [1]

David Hume pointed out, however, that,

"notwithstanding his cruelty, his extortion, his violence, his arbitrary administration, this prince not only acquired the regard of his subjects, but never was the object of their hatred. . . And it may be said with truth, that the English in that age were so thoroughly subdued, that, like Eastern slaves, they were inclined to admire those acts of violence and tyranny which were exercised over themselves, and at their own expense." [2]

In regard to the latter statement, one can wonder how the people could gather and watch the terrible acts of burning and beheading, how Henry's councillors could condone the martyrdom of their own members and the whole entourage of members of the households of his two wives, including nobles who had served him mightily in wars and in the conduct

HENRY VI
(1517-1553)

of his courts, and not raise a finger in protest to defend one another. This was an age hard for us to imagine. It was, therefore, an age when Francis Drake could serve and be discounted among the heroes of the time.

On to the successors of Henry VIII. First in line, but of a different temperament from his father, was Henry's son Edward VI, born in 1537 of Jane Seymour, who came to the throne at the age of nine. He was an invalid, precocious, earnest and severe and much under the influence of Archbishop Cranmer, who nevertheless proceeded in Henry's progress of the Reformation, pulling images down and punishing nonconformists. Some of his actions included prayers in English for the people; at the same time he composed an English litany for the priests and a primer for private prayer, the foundation of which became the *Book of Common Prayer.* [3]

During the period of Edward's minority, known as the Protectorate, there came about a closure and appropriation of common fields, the previously mentioned "enclosures", wherein profits derived from wool and products of growing manufacturers did not reach the people. Yet the people, the learned as well as the illiterate, were profoundly ignorant of this truth, that the increase of

QUEEN MARY
(1516–1558 a.d.)

produce must be finally beneficial to all classes. They were also slow to realize that the effect of precious metals from America, which had enhanced in general the money price of commodities, had not caused a proportional rise in the wages of labor. Therefore the protector, Edward Seymore, duke of Somerset, issued a proclamation against such enclosures. His progress toward Reformation within the church in 1551 also caused the princess Mary to be forbidden the use of the mass. [4]

It was Catherine's Catholic daughter Mary who came to the throne at Edward's death in 1553, a great calamity for the people of England, who were suddenly persecuted for the Protestant faith Henry had established in order to annul his marriages. Her legacy was to burn, as we have mentioned, some 300 at the stake, whereas the Protestants burned or beheaded only 200 non-conforming Catholics altogether before and after that time. We have noted, however, that the latter were more famous for executing their friends and trusted ministers.

There was no doubt that Mary intended to restore Catholicism and to use the methods of the Inquisition to do so. Her marriage to Philip II, son of Charles V of Spain, in 1555 was her first move to establish that intention. That marriage made England a vassal of the Spanish monarch for three years and imposed the conviction that "all thought of a foreign policy anywhere opposed to Spain must be set aside, together with all hope of trade with America—which Philip strictly denied to his island subjects— and all dreams of colonization or sea power. Samuel E. Morison describes the events which followed:

"Next, the capture of Calais by the French in a war with England to please Spain and fought very ill, added to the heavy weight of Mary's unpopularity—however [that capture] was a blessing in disguise to an island whose future did not lie on the continent of Europe.

"Mary's reign was a period of despondency and persecution for England, a fact she became aware of. Her marriage to Philip was of no comfort to her, nor to him. Finally, aware also of her image in eyes of her people, 'childless, hated, slighted, [and] fearful Elizabeth would ruin her work for God, [she] turned away to die.'" [1558]

Men then turned passionately to a young woman, princess Elizabeth, to save them, and to bring them on to harmony and prosperity. [5]

Elizabeth's Court

It is stated by the historian E. A. Freeman that

"the complete character of the English date from the days of the Tudors, and mainly from the reign of Elizabeth. One main cause of this is that the language of the sixteenth century is the earliest form of English which an ordinary reader can understand without an effort. And, as it was with language, so it was with everything else which goes to make up the national life. . . We feel that the men of Elizabeth's day, her statesmen, her warriors, her poets, and her divines, are men who come near to ourselves [the British] in a way which the men of earlier times cannot do." [6]

Elizabeth received the tidings of her good fortune at Hatfield Castle where she had been residing for several years in the mild custody of Sir Thomas Pope, but under the watchful eye of a guard. Elizabeth immediately restored Sir William Cecil to the post of secretary of state which he had occupied under Edward, but from which he had been removed by Mary. He was forthwith sworn a privy councillor, with his friends and followers, Parry, Rogers, and Cave. The same day the earl of Bedford, returning from a visit to Protestant exiles in Zurich, took his seat at the board. Though many were retained of Mary's councillors, the majority of the queen's confidential servants at Hatfield took their post, including

Nicholas Bacon and Sir Francis Walsingham. "But, next to God," as the historian Raumer said, "Cecil was the main support of Elizabeth." [7]

Elizabeth was born September 7, 1533, had lost her mother in the third year of her age, and had been wholly neglected by the timid servants of her passionate father. Later, after his anger against Anne her mother had been somewhat allayed, he paid more attention to her education. She spoke French and Italian as well as English, and Latin with fluency—having studied the classics in great detail— and also Greek, moderately well. Her hand writing was elegant, also in Greek and Roman characters, and she was skillful in music. It was said she had a most ardent love of true religion, and of the best kind of literature.[7]

The years of youth which Mary Tudor, Catherine's daughter, had spent in pleasure, Elizabeth spent in solitude and silence. Many times she imagined the terror of the executioner's axe over her head on which her friends and fellow-believers were cruelly sacrificed during the reign of Mary. She had the good fortune, however, of having a serious, learned education, which prepared her well for her future role.

To her credit and the counsel of Cecil, she took great care in restoring the Protestant religion so as not to again cause great distress to the people as had occurred during the reign of Mary.

First we need to understand her personal setting where all her decisions took place.

ELISABETH
(1533-1603)

In this chapter we will describe that setting, its routines, and the ways it was possible for her to promote or discount individuals within her realm and the reasons for it. While providing a larger picture, we will eventually focus on what was going on in her court at precisely those times when she chose to withdraw from her original authorization for Drake to make a claim for England on the west coast of America. We will be surprised at the deviousness of her behavior and the extent she would go to discount others in the court in order to have her "favourites" at her side.

Some of the following descriptions of court settings are recounted in a recent book by Tracy Borman, *Elizabeth's Women,* Random House 2009. She has had access to innumerable state papers and archives through her capacity in England as Joint Chief Curator of Historic Royal Palaces. These will be supplemented by other descriptions of Elizabeth's heroes and their behavior recorded in principal histories of the nineteenth century. In the next chapter we will then return to her descriptions of court intrigues.

"The queen's chief residence was Whitehall Palace in the heart of London, a vast maze of buildings that sprawled over twenty-three acres. . . Another of Elizabeth's London palaces was Greenwich, the place of her birth. Built on the banks of the Thames, it was conveniently accessed by barge. . .

"Upriver, west of the capital, lay Richmond Palace, built by the Queen's grandfather, Henry VII. Viewed from the river, it was a fairytale palace of domed towers and turrets behind a high curtain wall, set within some of the most beautiful gardens in England . . . Further upriver was Hampton Court, the most splendid and magnificent royal palace of any that may be found in England, or indeed, in any other kingdom, according to one visitor. . . T(t)he Queen found it uncomfortable and unhealthy, and after falling down gravely ill there in 1562, she rarely visited.

"By contrast, Elizabeth was extremely fond of Windsor Castle, where she tended to spend the summer months. Although the castle dated back to the time of William the Conquerer, it boasted a host of modern luxuries. The castle's Great Park was where she could indulge in her love of hunting. She later acquired Nonsuch in Surrey, a fantasy palace built by her father in the style of the great chateaux of the Loire.

"If the Elizabethan court was a carefully stage-managed production, then the Queen herself was the director. . . [At her courts she managed] lavish entertainments, intrigues and flirtations. [She demanded, however,] absolute fidelity, both emotional and political from her male courtiers and would brook no rival for their affections. . . [It was] a highly volatile atmosphere in which men vied with each other for favor and advancement." [8]

Borman's account proceeds to compare Elizabeth's court with those which preceded it:

"In contrast to the hundreds of male councillors, ambassadors, noblemen, and place seekers who flocked to her court, there were only thirty or so women there at any

one
time.
. . a
marked
de-
crease.
. . [as
there
were]
upward
of a hun-
dred in
her half
sister's

WINDSOR CASTLE IN THE TIME OF EDWARD VI

and her father's courts. . . If they were not of her personal household they were not welcome. . .

"In selecting women who would serve her as queen, Elizabeth was motivated by the desire to honor her late mother. . . [There is therefore] regular mention of the Careys, Knollys, Howards, and various other Boleyn relatives. . . [The] number of ladies and gentlewomen of the privy chamber and bedchamber decreased from 20 to 11, [with] just six maids of honor." [9]

Not being content to control outward access to her person and council, she exerted measures to manage the lives of everyone assigned to the management of her inner rooms. As Borman continues, we learn:

"The structure of her household was also carefully controlled. . . [The] layout of rooms . . . followed a similar pattern in all of the royal palaces. Beyond the taller, great hall, and great chamber was the Queen's suite of rooms, and the further a courtier was able to progress into them the more important he was deemed to be. First there was the presence chamber, to which most courtiers flocked in the hope of gaining an audience with the Queen. . . The presence chamber was filled by noblemen and other supplicants, who would regularly spend many hours waiting for Elizabeth to emerge from her more private rooms beyond—often entirely in vain.

"Beyond this, there was the privy chamber, a day room for the sovereign where she tended to take her meals. Only the most exalted members of the court were admitted, such as Privy Councillors, ambassadors, or close favorites. . . [There was] still a more exclusive sanctum, and this was the Queen's bedchamber, served by a small number of her most trusted and high-ranking ladies.

"The bedchamber, privy chamber, and presence chamber would each be staffed by a select group of women who were assigned positions of various status" [10]

Although the queen's women were instructed to be oblivious of the intrigues of the court, they were always present and available to the queen for conversation or appeal. A story is told of one Lady Mary Sidney, sister of Robert Dudley, whom she instructed to give private assurances to two ambassadors of Spain of her interest in pursuing their marriage proposals, only to be caught short with her later denial of the same. The episode was enough to discourage Lady Mary from getting involved with anything but her routine duties at court. [11]

It is said by the historian Knight, however, that the first ten years of Elizabeth's reign were regarded as her halcyon days. It must have seemed so, as the transition from the fiery Catholicism of Mary Tudor to the temperate Protestantism of her sister Elizabeth was accomplished without bloodshed. [12]

Having thus provided the setting for Elizabeth's intrigues, we turn to earlier historians for character descriptions of her favorites and the extent to which Elizabeth would go in order to accept their inadequacies and betrayals.

Her Favorites

We have mentioned Drake's initial contacts with Elizabeth after his famous voyage which led to a dispersion of his treasure and a reluctant knighting as acknowledgment that he had made it around the world.

But then he went off the charts, as he tried to maintain contacts with Richard Hakluyt and others who were allowed to record select episodes of his journey. But he had no power in her inner circle. If he disappeared from the scene it was because Elizabeth no longer gave him an audience. Thereafter he might be enticed to conduct further raids to augment her treasuries or conduct surveillance on the Spanish maritime buildup, but these were under the auspices of other favorites in her court, e. g., Howard, Essex and Leicester. These she would empower; Drake was not to be honored for the commander that he was. Philip II of Spain she would not want to challenge for his total claim on the New World, considering their long history of his being in the Tudor court as her sister Mary's husband and even, at one point, her suitor. She saw no other way to resolve the problem of always being the third party in the wars between France and Spain.

We might observe her actions in dealing with her privy counsel, emulating her father in his role as king, leaving them often without answers until she might make her decisions. As far as Drake is concerned, however, we must understand what was going on in her mind which led to such manipulations. Why did she hesitate and then send some of her least competent figures to dangerous waters with orders that put them at a disadvantage? We do not yet know what was going on in the mind of the woman who was obsessed with her own physical appeal to certain men. She also felt compelled to exact revenge upon the younger, hence physically more attractive, women of her privy chamber.

While others have written extensively of this, it might be well to consider just those years when she had sent Drake on his dangerous journey (1577-1580) and in the decade following, when she could have made a statement to the world that she did not accept Philip's hegemony in the New World. It is as though she still considered him a potential ally should the balance of powers shift among nations. This being at least highly speculative, we can at least investigate what was going on in those years that distracted her from such worthy ambition.

We have summarized the structure of her rule and inner circles, which included a group of younger women who were obliged to attend her and to abide by an act of 1536 which made it treason for any of them to marry or form any sort of alliance with the opposite sex. This would seem a contradiction since their role was to provide her with companionship and attract courtiers of all sorts to her courts. As long as Elizabeth herself could compete, or imagine herself as competing in the realm of physical attractiveness, she could browbeat and punish them without arousing bitterness and revolt among them.

This became a problem, however, as time went on, and her discipline suffered more and more rebellion. She always had the upper hand, of course, and the result was that, while punishing these women she was unable at the same time to punish her "favourites" in court who carried on affairs and secret marriages under her nose. She needed them too badly, as they continued to boost her ego, and she would then reinstate them at court while continuing to punish those who were led astray. Nor could she afford to disenfranchise those nobles of the opposite sex whom she called upon to help finance her wars. It is obvious, also, how easy it was for her favorites to marry secretly and without adequate witnesses and thus, in their passing affairs, to ruin the status of young women of like heritage.

Chief among her favorites, from shortly after her ascension to the throne until his death in 1588 was Robert Dudley, Earl of Leicester, whom she adored as no other and a man as vile and unprincipled as can be imagined. "But Elizabeth seemed to ascend the throne," according to the historian Motley, "only to bestow gifts upon her favourite. Baronies and earldoms, stars and garters, manors and monopolies, castles and forests, church livings and college chancellorships, advowsons and sinecures, en-voluments and dignities . . . were conferred upon him in breathless succes-sion." [13]

Elizabeth came to notice him soon after her ascension and was unaware of his marriage to Ann Robard. Before she would learn of this, however, Ann was poisoned. Over a period of time he would contract sub-sequent marriages and mockmarriages with Douglas Sheffield and Lettice of Essex, which though well-known, escaped her notice. "The list of his murders and near-murders was almost endless. But in his position as the queen's favourite, these crimes were ignored." [14]

Details of the above are as follows: after poisoning, as it is thought, his first wife, Robert Dudley, earl of Leicester, her designated favorite, became enamored of Douglas Howard, youngest sister of Charles How-ard, then married to John Sheffield who was occupied in the conflicts in Ireland. After Sheffield's death Leicester secretly married her, but then took to bed Lettice Knollys, one of Elizabeth's maids in waiting. He then offered Douglas L100 to deny all knowledge of their compact if she would also surrender her young son to his custody.

In the end she did agree, and the other secret marriage took place in the spring of 1578 to Lettice Knollys, dowager countess of Essex. Later we will learn of Drake's former employment in Ireland to assist Essex before his death, also rumored to be by poison. Marriage with Lettie, as she was called, seemed to agree with Leicester, and after she bore a son in 1581 he dared to leave the court and live with her, even effecting a formal wedding at his palace just before the queen's visit there. Incredibly, it still took a year for Elizabeth to find out. She was, of course, furious,

Eventually, as might be expected, Elizabeth could not bear to lose his proximity at her court. She forgave him on the premise that he would pretend his marriage had never happened and that Lettuce would be forev-er banned from the privy chambers. Her son, on whom Leicester counted much as his heir, died at a young age; and it was Leicester's adopted son Robert who rose to prominence in Elizabeth's court as the next earl of Essex. [15]

— Chapter 6 —

Later Years of Elizabeth's Reign

Mary Queen of Scots

Y ou will recall the battle of Bosworth wherein King James V of
Scotland fell in battle a week before his daughter Mary was born.
That Mary, Queen of Scots, had grown to womanhood, married
the French dauphin Francis II who shortly died, and had returned to Scotland, married Lord Darnley, and was somehow a bystander in the murder
of her husband. She was thereafter carried away, forcibly, by her lover,
Boswell, decides to marry him after all, but is unable to convince her lords
of counsel that she is worthy of the throne. It is a long story, but being
run out of her country and leaving an infant son, she sought the succor of
Elizabeth and was being kept safe in a castle under her protection. She is,
however, the granddaughter of Henry's sister Margaret, a Catholic, and
would gladly have declared Elizabeth illegitimate and usurped the throne.
In a nutshell, her story is the cause of much grief in English history, as you
will see.

First, however, we will try to deal adequately with the wars Elizabeth was compelled to engage in, mostly surreptitiously, to maintain a
balance of power with Spain. Her efforts through the years, e. g. expenses
incurred assisting the Huguenots in France, depleted her treasury, and she
was obliged to call Parliament in 1565 and enact an Oath of Supremacy to
command allegiance. A plague in La Havre was also carried into London
at this time during which 20,000 died.

In 1568 she was secretly supplying the French Protestants against the Spanish though technically at peace with Philip II, son of Charles V emperor of Austria and at that time regent of Spain. In public she took care to proclaim her respect for the Spanish ruler and her dislike for all rebellions. She and Cecil were determined to have no open war. She once plundered Philip's ships on their way to supply his men in the Low Countries, saying their cargo belonged to certain Italian bankers and money-lenders, exporting upon speculation. Charles even pursued marriage with Elizabeth as a way of committing England to their cause. But she, in no way tempted, simply replied that her subjects would never tolerate a Catholic prince.[1]

It was soon after that cousin Mary, Queen of Scots, became a problem for Elizabeth. A closeness due to kinship was never meant to be. Mary was always a threat to the queen's throne.

In an age when it was a common practice for individuals to enter into plots against the government for the sole purpose of betraying them and reaping rewards, a scheme developed in 1569 involving too many characters for any hope of secrecy. There was talk of the then duke of Norfolk marrying the Scottish queen to assist her in usurping the throne. Elizabeth confronted him about this, and he replied that "he meant never to marry with such a person where he could not be sure of his pillow," in reference to the beheading at the block of Boswell who had replaced Mary's murdered husband.

Elizabeth was satisfied; yet a day or two afterward, the duke conferred with Murray, regent to the infant Scottish king, and others that if Mary could be restored he would marry her. The Scottish regent assured him that "such a nobleman as himself, courteous, wealthy, and a Protestant, could not fail of restoring tranquility to Scotland, maintaining peace and a perfect understanding between the two countries." [2]

Norfolk did not commit himself to the plot until he was propelled by the insidious Leicester—the especial favorite in Elizabeth' cabinet—in a scheme to throw Cecil into the Tower and to change the minister's system to one that would promote his own interests. Letters were exchanged between Norfolk and Mary, but the earl of Sussex saw ruin for his friend Norfolk. The Scottish regent also approved, but actually plotted Mary's continued imprisonment.

Suddenly Leicester fell ill, very, very ill. And if you can believe this, Elizabeth flew to his bedside where he revealed the plot and was forgiven, but the duke of Norfolk received a reprimand. Elizabeth could not conceal her anger against Norfolk, however, and Leicester began to treat him rudely. The regent Murray further informed her of the plot, saying that he would not have agreed except to preserve his own life. The duke was committed to the Tower. The bishop of Ross in vain pleaded his privilege as the agent and ambassador of a crowned head but was also committed to prison, along with those others involved. The duke was eventually executed in 1572.[3]

Needless to say, the year 1569 also saw efforts of Cecil to draw England into a war with Spain over indications that Philip II had adopted Mary's cause. That same year the French government made a fresh seizure of English merchandise at Rouen, Calais, and Dieppe, since France was also involved in this type of privateering. English privateers retaliated and promised to end this kind of warfare. Inflamed at privateering, some of the queen's troops went over to the Huguenots and "issued a proclamation against privateers and all such as made war without her license upon the French king." Her conduct, giving extra powers to the Protestant French, gave encouragement to the Catholics in England and excited an interest in all the papistical countries of the Continent in favor of the captive Mary. Suspicions increased among Catholics in England that "Elizabeth cared little for the dogmas of either church." [4]

She was altogether free from intolerance as to speculative opinions in religion, unless they were to weaken the royal prerogative. Her intolerance was all of a political kind, and she persecuted, not because men believe in the real presence of Christ in the sacrament, but rather she believed that no Catholic could possibly be a loyal subject. In the months of October, immediately after the duke of Norfolk's arrest, the counties of York, Durham and Northumberland betrayed symptoms of open insurrection.

The earls of Northumberland and Westmoreland, Ratcliff and Dacre, the latter whose wife was Norfolk's sister, converged at the castle of Branspeth with a plan to liberate Mary. They restored the mass and mustered some 7,000 men. Finding, however, that the majority of Catholics in general were loyal to the queen, they fell back and dispersed, some falling back into Scotland, Spanish Netherlands, and elsewhere. Vengeance was exacted upon the retainers and friends of the fugitives, and executions were held in every market town and village, including the assassination of Murray. Mary wept bitterly over the untimely death of her half-brother, Murray, forgetting for the moment the many injuries he had done her in her exile. [5]

The king's men, as they were called, called also upon Elizabeth to send a strong English army to their support, which she did. The two armies, in a chastising raid the night of Murray's murder burned 300 village and 50 castles, according to Cecil's diary. Elizabeth sent the earl of Lennox, father of Darnley, to be ruler over Scotland. He could do nothing however; therefore the armies of Sussex and Mumsdon entered anew with 1200 foot and 400 horse to complete the submission. This was in the year 1570. [6]

In 1570 Elizabeth was excommunicated by Pope Pius V. He had invited her to the Council of Trent in 1550, but his patience was at an end; "though his obstinacy might provoke, his prudence taught him to suppress, his resentment." When he heard of the failure of insurrections in Scotland, he prepared a bull to pronounce her guilty of heresy and to deprive her of her "pretended right to the crown of England. " [7]

On April 2, 1571 Parliament met at Westminster to settle indebtedness on the recent insurgence. In response to the Pope's bull, a bull was enacted to isolate English Catholics more from the pope and the Continent. It was declared high treason to claim any other succession to the crown "or to publish her as heretic, schismatic, tyrant, infidel, or usurper, or to deny parliament's role in descent of crown." Another bull declared that all persons must attend the Protestant church regularly, receive the sacrament in the form the law required, and to those Catholics who had exiled, they must return in six months after warning to retain their properties.

After these enactments the house and people were zealously Protestant. Many of the Catholic lords in the upper house of course demurred to the extent of the rule but would have had no courage to oppose it. However, Elizabeth voluntarily gave up her bill of forced taking of the sacrament— a heretic thing in Catholic ages— but Catholics were excluded from the house of Commons.[8]

In this era the Puritans imbibed the strict notions of Calvin—that the Church of Christ ought to be separate from and independent of the state—which doctrine also declared an overthrow of the queen's supremacy. Their most heinous offense was fraternizing with the Puritans of Scotland and with John Knox, an inspired apostle who had written against "the monstrous regiment of women." Yet three of the four bishops in her council were inclined against conviction of Puritanism, the earls Bedford, Bacon, and Walsingham, while Leicester intrigued with them underhand in view of furthering his own ambitious projects. All the while, Thomas

Cartwright, president of divinity at Cambridge, professed the unlawfulness of any church involvement in state government except Presbyterianism. [9]

It was a season of discontent, but Elizabeth, always a pragmatist, avoided confrontations by a studied toleration.

Elizabeth's Privateers

It is not difficult to trace why Drake's achievements were neglected by Elizabeth I. After her excommunication in 1570, what had been England's surface support for Catholic Spain and Italy in wars against France no longer had a basis in religious affiliation. She would no longer be subject to Philip II's expectations. But that was a secret battle. She would fund her privateers and undermine his control over the Netherlands, but on the surface she would avoid animosity.

Hawkins and Drake's misadventure at the port of San Juan de Ulúa in 1568 may have provided her with the incentive to fund her privateers, as well as motivation on their parts for retaliation. This is a story of prime importance in understanding the evolution of Drake's epic journey of piracy and claim, an episode that was formative in Drake's ambition to wreck vengeance. John Hawkins was a wealthy landholder and a relative of Drake. He made three voyages to the coast of Africa, beginning in 1562, and bartered articles of trifling value for numerous lots of negroes. Then he crossed the Atlantic to Hispaniola and returned with large quantities of hides, sugar, ginger, and pearls.

This trade was, however, illicit in 1568, and Hawkins was surprised by the arrival of the Spanish viceroy with a fleet of twelve sail from Europe. Hawkins lost his fleet, the treasure, and the majority of his followers. Out of six ships, only two escaped. Then one foundered at sea, and the other, a bark of fifty tons commanded by Francis Drake, brought back the remnant of adventurers to Europe. The two larger vessels, engaged in human trafficking in an age of religious fanaticism, belonged to the queen: It was not unusual to indulge in this most lawless of passions.

Drake attributed his late disaster to the perfidy of the viceroy. This incident, Drake's first encounter with the Spanish, should be remembered as absolutely formative of his hatred of the Spanish and desire for revenge. He had actually been welcomed into port before the attack. He later consulted a naval chaplain who determined that the loss to which he had suffered from a Spanish commander might be justly repaired by the plunder of Spanish subjects in any part of the globe. His conscience was satisfied.

On a subsequent foray into the Gulf of Mexico he plundered Nombre de Dios and captured more than one hundred small vessels. Then he made an expedition by land in the company of the *cimarrones*, or fugitive negroes and a band of French adventurers, and intercepted a convoy of mules laden with gold and silver. This treasure satisfied his rapacity for the moment. To secure it he hastened back to England, pretending that he had recovered it by way of barter from the natives. He later made three predatory voyages to the West Indies in 1572. If the first two were unsuccessful, the last amply indemnified him for his previous disappointments. [10]

The above acount, by the historian Charles Knight, continues with the following quote:

"During this brief expedition from the summit of a mountain on the Isthmus of Darien [now called Panama], Drake had for the first time descried the great Pacific Ocean, Feb. ll, 1573, and in a transport of enthusiasm falling on his knees, he called God to witness that if life were granted him he would one day unfurl the English flag on that sea, hitherto unknown to his countrymen." [11]

Following the above cited account is a footnote by L. Van Ranke from his *Englishe Geschichte*: "This was an important moment in the history of the world."

In England Drake was not unmindful of his vow. When it came time to plan the journey that is the main subject of this study, Walsingham, Hatton, and some of the other councillors applauded and aided his efforts, and Elizabeth herself staked a sum of one thousand crowns on the expedition. In Chapters 7, 8, and 9 we will recount the immense preparations that he underwent, both logistic and scientific. It will be seen that the queen and these councillors were aware and gave authority to his aims which involved great precision and risk.

Yet Drake's voyage, its aftermath, and the historical legacy of Drake are full of elusions and duplicity. In illustration, we will here to present the "official" account of Drake's voyage which has persisted throughout the past four centuries and impeded for the first two any further colonization of America on its west coast. This version is as the historians of the nineteenth century presented it to the world after it was at first prohibited by Elizabeth and then profoundly edited by others in the interum.

We have given what may have been her ostensible reasons for not admitting she had given license to Drake to make a claim for England above Spanish claims in California, but the real reasons were deep inside her womanly breast. He was not one of her favorites and she had no need to honor his magnificent labor in carrying out what should have been a fulfillment of her foreign policy against Spain. She had forsaken the Catholic claim to the church of England, but not the pope's claim to the new world. Her favorites might come to do so, but not Francis Drake. She would go to any extent to promote the obvious deficiencies of Leicester and Essex on missions they were totally incapable of accomplishing while placing Drake, her greatest seaman, in subordinate positions and, at times, in disgrace.

After the destruction of the trading ships of John Hawkins and Drake at San Juan de Ulúa in 1568 there is no doubt that Elizabeth aided and abetted them in their pirating against the Spanish. The chief scene of these irregular activities was Spanish America. Formerly its ports were officially closed to foreign trades. The colonies were not unwilling, however, to purchase goods the Spanish did not provide. English trade merchants found themselves indeed welcome and took pains to avoid the detection of Spanish ships. The debacle at San Juan de Ulúa was a primary turning point for Drake and is pertinent to our story. Thenceforth he was fully involved in attacking and robbing Spanish ships, towns, and treasure caravans along the American coasts, which was quite in line with European practice before international law.

The practice was disapproved by Cecil, though he himself had seized Spanish treasure in the channel. "But if England had not taken the aggressive she would have been forced to accept exclusion from the trade of every continent except Europe, to abandon her maritime and colonial ambitions, and to bow her neck to reconquest of Spain and Rome as soon as the resistance of Holland collapsed." [12]

Drake's Voyage, as Edited

It has been said that Drake's third and troublesome voyage was the true beginning of the Elizabethan Age, yet for at least two hundred years historians could only present it as a grand attempt to further enrich himself. In the 25-volume *Historians' Histories* published in 1904, which the writer has access to, only the following much-edited account, in addition to various dismissive summaries, is given.

From the eighteenth century *Comprehensive History of England* by C. Macfarlane and T. Thomson, we learn that he sailed Nov. 15th, 1577 with five ships and one hundred and sixty men, and crossed the

Atlantic to the coast of Brazil, passed the Strait of Magellan, and reached the small port of Santiago on the Spanish main. No resistance had been prepared where no enemy had hitherto been known. From Santiago to Lima, the towns on the coast and the vessels in the harbors were taken and plundered. His last and richest capture was made at sea, Mar. 1st, 1579 — the *Cacafuego,* a Spanish trader of considerable value.

But the alarm had been raised; a squadron had been stationed at the strait to intercept his return, and Drake took the bold resolution of stretching across the Pacific Ocean to the Moluccas. Thence, after many dangers and adventures, doubling the Cape of Good Hope, he returned to Plymouth in safety, Nov. 3rd, 1580, after an absence of almost three years. His arrival was celebrated as a triumph. He came indeed stained with bloodshed and rapine, but in the estimation of the people these blots were effaced by the glory of the enterprise; and England hailed with joy the return of her adventurous son, the first of mortals who had in one voyage circumnavigated the globe.

Though Drake had sailed with five ships, he returned with only one — the *Golden Hinde*, but it was laden with treasure to the amount of L800,000. Of this sum, one-tenth was distributed among the officers and crew; a portion was given up to the Spanish ambassador, who claimed the whole in the name of his sovereign; and the rest, of which no account was ever received, was believed to have been shared among the queen, the commander, and the royal favorites. Four months, however, were to lapse before she would give to Drake any public testimony of her approbation.

His ship had been placed in the dock at Deptford that it might be preserved as a memorial of his daring adventure. Elizabeth condescended to partake of a banquet which he gave in the cabin, and before her departure conferred on him the honor of knighthood.

When Philip complained of these depredations, they were feebly vindicated on the grounds of his having secretly aided the queen's enemies and sought to excite rebellion in her dominions. But if the plea of retaliation is to be admitted at all, we must seek out the original aggressor, rather than to lay the blame on the unjustifiable conduct of the English adventurers. At length, however, Elizabeth, as the ally of Holland, engaged in open wars with Philip; and the lawless pirate was immediately converted into an officer acting under the royal commission. The skill and intrepidity of Drake were thus successfully employed in legitimate hostilities for the service of his sovereign" [13]

Brief as this story may seem, and anticipating our expanded story based upon all that has been discovered in the past century, it seems incredible that scholars in the 21st century are still perpetuating its brevity and discrediting Drake's achievement, as we shall see in our final chapters.

A WAR VESSEL OF THE FIFTEENTH CENTURY

Chapter 7

A Troubled Voyage

Naval Power of England

W e have seen the scant attention and erroneous legacy given to Drake through the centuries as a result of Elizabeth's cover-up of his true mission in contrast to the celebratory honoring of her favorites. We should keep in mind also that Drake's aim was a colonial expansion, as was Raleigh's, and she dealt the former with a complete denial and the latter with a failure to support. All the while she was promoting in Leicester what turned out to be an attempt at predatory exploitation of her ally in the Netherlands, a topic to be covered in Chapter 10.

Drake's true voyage must be explained in its entirety since recent evidence has come to light which supports it. It was possible, however, only with the supremacy of the navy which had begun much further back in English history, but he was one of the most important sea captains to establish the protocol upon which it flourished. Begun by Henry VII, it was greatly expanded during Tudor times, but with a breakthrough in Drake's time regarding the discipline on board ships which was directly responsible for Drake's success in accomplishing his true mission and, extended further, the reason for success against the Spanish armada.

Historians have been slow to analyze the reasons for the superiority of the English navy, which was due to Frobisher's, Drake's, Hawkins, Raleigh's and other's efforts to overcome the class separation of duties aboard ship. It was left, remarkably, to Trevelyan in the 20th century to describe what the English failed to acknowledge. Because it is so very well analyzed, it is best to capture his own words, and it is essential information to explain a critical incident on Drake's voyage which, had he mishandled it, would have led to mutiny and a failure of his enterprise:

"Since ancient times the Mediterranean had been the main arc of sea power on the periphery of European coasts. Suddenly the Cape route and revelation of the American continent had changed all this.

"Spain and her small neighbor, Portugal, were the first to explore the new situation on a grand scale. They planted South and Central America with their own people, enough at any rate to close them to Anglo-Saxon settlement... While Europe pursued her religious wars, Francis Drake and the Protestant sailors he led became the servants of the English Monarchy and the heroes of the English people, turning England's main thought and effort to the sea. Spanish ships were to little avail against Drake's broadsides. They served to carry out emigrants and bring back silver and gold, but they were not warships, and fell easy prey, therefore, to English pirates. Spain, in fact, began to build ships capable of fighting England only when on the eve of the outbreak of the regular war. The Armada was not the last, but the first of her ocean fighting fleets.

"The English, though their population was small compared with that of French or Spaniards, had a large sea-going community, accustomed for centuries to sailing the stormy tidal ocean of the North. And ever since the reign of Henry VIII they had possessed a royal fighting navy built and armed on modern principles... Spain's ships, a fleet of slave-rowed galleys and its traditions were those of the Mediterranean. The Spanish tactic was to get in close and board the enemy, like the ancients. Soldiers despised the sailors. "

Here Trevelyan applies the English navy's superior manner of managing the cooperation of soldiers and sailors on board ships to Drake's voyage itself:

"While the Spaniards with their feudal prejudices and Mediterranean methods of sea-warfare subordinated the sailor to the soldier even when afloat, Drake worked out the proper relation to be observed between the military and maritime elements on board ship. When he quelled the party of insubordination among the gentlemen adventurers on his voyage around the world, he laid down his golden rule to prevent 'stomaching' between the gentlemen and the sailors: 'I must have the gentlemen to hail and draw with the mariners.' Starting from that point the gentlemen gradually learned their place on board the English man-of-war, in each departure, and they became mariners themselves...

"Drake, who was first the greatest of privateers and afterwards the greatest of Royal Admirals, established as no one else could have done a complete understanding between the Royal Navy and the merchant adventurers who carried on the unofficial war with Spain."

Another aspect of Trevelyan's unique writing is his understanding of what the relationship among soldiers (including gentlemen of the nobility) and ordinary sailors said about the emergence from feudalism occurring in England which was not happening in Spain and other countries where the clergy and monarchy maintained a rigid control over the class system:

>"For indeed the technical difference between the personnel and tactics of a Spanish and an English ship represented something more profound—the difference of social character between Spain and the new England. . . Private enterprise, individual initiative and a good-humored equality of classes were on the increase in the defeudalized England of the Renaissance and Reformation, and were strongest among commercial and maritime populations. The most energetic spirits of the gentry, the middle, and the lower classes were taking to the sea together in a rough camaraderie, for purpose of war and commerce. In Spain the ideas and manners of the people were still feudal, though in politics the king had become absolute. Discipline, as Drake would know, is needed on board ship, but not feudalism and class pride. The hierarchy of the sea is not the same as the hierarchy of the land."[1]

Trevelyan's description is of great importance in understanding how Drake handled his men on the great voyage of discovery and circumnavigation.

The Plan

Another 20th century historian, Samuel Eliot Morison, best identifies a key influence upon Drake as he planned his voyage. John Dee, among others, helped acquaint him with the scientific and geographical knowledge he would need to carry out his mission:

>"Dee seems to have been generous with advice to the Muscovy Company, and to navigators such as Frobisher, Drake and Davis. All the world including Queen Elizabeth came to his house at Mortlake on the Thames to admire his library and collection of instruments. Certainly no intellectual did so much for English discovery as John Dee. He was one of those 'stern men with empires in their brains', like Peckham, Carleil, and Hakluyt, who laid the intellectual foundations of the *British Empire*, an expression which Dee is said to have coined." (emphasis in italics) [2]

Introduced in the above is Richard Hakluyt, a geographer much a part of Elizabeth's inner circle of specialists—of whom we will have much more to say in the aftermath of Drake's voyage—who had for years encouraged Bristol merchants to undertake voyages of exploration to America. He was one of the promoters of the Lincoln Company, established for that purpose in 1507, and he was in the process of publishing numerous volumes of such voyages.

Early in his writings he suggests that "America begs sister England to rescue her from being overrun by the cruel Spaniards, reminds her that Cabot next after the great Columbus showed his sails in the temperate region, and begs Elizabeth to 'stretch thy sceptre where its regal sway befits thine honour.'" [3]

He explained that England's late entry into maritime exploration up to that time (1578), citing George Best's *True Discourse of Frobisher's Voyage*, was due to two reasons: 1) lack of liberality in the nobility and 2) want of skill in navigation, but states that in the previous quarter century England's mariners had made great advances in scientific navigation and in scientific instruments. [4]

Queen Elizabeth accepted the *Discourse* Hakluyt offered but ignored its sound advise. Relations with Spain were already too unstable to launch a state-sponsored colonial enterprise. Later Raleigh would be left alone to make his colonizing effort in Virginia, and the possibility of Philip II bringing the war home to England caused the mighty effort that Hakluyt wanted to stimulate to be shelved for nearly thirty years. [5]

Another contemporary historian, David Cressy, has said of Drake's voyage and mission:

"Whether the mariners and gentlemen on board knew it or not, they were embarked on a dangerous, provocative and highly secret penetration of the Iberian American Empire. They were bound on an odyssey of piracy and discovery which had profound religious and diplomatic significance in the Europe of the Counter Reformation. With clandestine royal backing, and support from the most bellicose faction at the Elizabethan court, Francis Drake was leading his fleet in a Protestant English challenge to the Catholic Hispanic monopoly of the rich Pacific Ocean." [6]

It is not the intention in this account of Drake's voyage to give complete details. This has been magnificently done by the two contemporary writers, Bawlf and Gitzen, previously cited . The intention is to recall significant interplay among the planners, the queen included, the members of his team of voyagers, and its aftermath in order to explain why his achievement was ignored by history until the present century. As we sketch these details we will describe those incidents most indicative of what was a conspiracy to cover up his achievements, both before and after. In the aftermath we will cite contemporary researchers whose discoveries have augmented the much-edited story of Reverend Francis Fletcher, finally published in 1628 as *The World Encompassed by Sir Francis Drake*. [7]

We have quoted in our initial chapter from the title page of Fletcher's journal, which plainly told the purpose of the journey. His statements put to rest any thought that the sole purpose of their undertaking was to plunder an adversary's wealth and circle the globe to do so. Here are other excerpts of that page:

"If a surveyor did a good job. . . measuring bits of land which was already delineated. . . how much more . . . are their famous travels. . . to be eternized, who have bestowed their studies [in] an endeavor to survey and

measure this globe almost immeasurable." And, as we might again quote:
" Whose Land Survey You? for as much as the Maine Ocean by right is
the Lord's alone, and by nature left free, for all men to deal withal, as very
sufficient for all men's use, and large enough for all men's industry."

Drake's Background

We begin to follow Samuel Bawlf's excellent book about Drake's
secret voyage with the telling of Drake's background. Drake
was the eldest son of Edmund Drake, a yeoman who had lived
in the valley of the River Tavy near Plymouth on land leased from Lord
John Russell, who came into its ownership after Henry VIII's confiscation
of Benedictine abbey lands. Edmund was a tenant farmer and sheep shear-
er related to ship owner and privateer William Hawkins, father of William
and John Hawkins, at whose residence Francis may have acquired some
elements of social deportment.

Edmund, also schooled as a preacher in the Protestant faith, was
driven from his lands by church strife, and when he returned from the
north he settled in Kent on the River Midway near the mouth of the
Thames where with his family of twelve sons he lived in an abandoned
ship, eking out a living preaching the new faith to the seamen.

The river was where Henry VIII's ships were laid up for repair, and
young Francis became involved with his Hawkins relations in profiteer-
ing adventures in the mid-60's, where he swore a vengeance for Spanish
assaults upon what had been a legitimate trade, previously described.

Francis married a Plymouth girl, Mary Newman, and after a seven
month stay there acquired two ships, the *Dragon* and the *Swan*, and set
sail for the Caribbean in what he described as a reconnaissance. After the
1568 fiasco with John Hawkins at Juan de Ulúa, he again set off in 1570
with the bark *Swan* in what became a plunder of Spanish gold and silver
between Panama and Nombre de Dios, the predominant port of the Spanish, as previously reported. In these exploits he engaged a group of *cimarrones*, escaped negro slaves of the Spanish, to accomplish his task. Some
of his cache was discovered, and they were driven out. Then his two brothers died in a pestilence which left thirty of his men dead. Leaving some of
the plunder hidden in other caches nearby, he returned with his new wealth
and was able to refurbish and man three ships handsomely. It was at this

time he built his magnificent personal ship, later named the *Pelican*.

In 1575 Drake was recommended to the employ of Walter Devereux, earl of Essex, by his relative William Hawkins and began ferrying troops and intercepting rebel shipping in Ireland, taking time out to recover his cache in Nombre de Dios. At the same time Thomas Doughty was also employed by Essex as messenger between the enterprise and the court in England, a man to watch, as he will be at the core of Drake's difficulties on his long voyage of discovery. Drake did not know that Essex had once discharged Doughty for falsely inciting a serious incident, reporting that Leicester was trying to undermine his reputation at court, a charge which was denied and reconciled by Cecil.

Essex was in Ireland to colonize a district in Ulster, with Elizabeth's help, that they should each furnish an equal share of the enterprise. It is said that everyone in the court was dazzled by the project, "though they had no other view than to remove him from the presence of the queen." Elizabeth's young maid in waiting of her privy chamber, Lettice Knollys, who was married to Essex, was in the depths of a flirtation with Leicester at that time, an intrigue previously recounted. The possible reasons for Essex's failure in Ireland and his death, begin to emerge. He had mortgaged all his estates in England and proposed plans only to be defeated. Once he obtained leave to return home, but was sent back with the empty title of earl marshall. Essex's enterprise was in the process of failure, but it is significant to our story that he undertook to recommend Drake's services to Walsingham, Elizabeth's senior councillor. In 1576 he died of dysentery, though some say he was poisoned by Leicester. [8]

Aware of Drake's capabilities, Essex had recommended his service to Walsingham as one who could carry out the plan that Grenville had initiated in 1573 which had been scrapped when Cecil convinced Elizabeth it was bound to incite hostilities. A window of opportunity was then occurring, and Drake met with Walsingham, drew up a map, a plan, and eventually met with Elizabeth to draw up his company and give signature to an agreement for the voyage, an agreement without spelling out the details which no one could acknowledge. They envisioned an initial plan for a voyage to extend the English jurisdiction to the west coast of America.

She counseled Drake that his plan, which, though discussed, could not be put to paper; and any who might do so "they should lose their heads thereafter." As Drake later recalled during the fateful incident of mutiny during his voyage, "Her Majesty gave me special commandment that of all men my Lord Treasurer Cecil [Burghley] should not know it." He was her councillor who most sought peace with Spain at all costs, whereas Walsingham, compounded by the influence of Leicester, was always open to aggressive moves.

The plan was not followed up at that time due to problems in the Netherlands. It would be early in the year 1577 that a window of opportunity was again occurring, and Drake met with Walsingham, drew up the final plan and eventually met with Elizabeth to draw up his company and give signature to an agreement for the voyage, which, we again stress, was without spelling out the details which no one could acknowledge.

Commitments were made and the crew drawn up. Among the assignments Doughty was given the title of captain of shore procurement, etc. Later we will learn that Doughty, as secretary to Hatton in the court, was meeting with Cecil, who was hoping he might learn something about the voyage which Elizabeth was keeping secret from him. There was a final farewell meeting of Drake with the queen, and she bestowed upon him gifts of a sea cap and a green silk scarf, among other items.

Their initial departure met storms and destruction, as the ship *Marigold* was run ashore, and their voyage was delayed for two weeks. While they were reconnoitering, an incident occurred of which Drake was not told.

Drake had dismissed a procurement officer, James Stydye, in charge of lading whom he found wanting, before the second attempt at voyage, and we here report Doughty's comment to shipmate Edward Bright in Drake's garden. He told him that he was equal in command of the voyage and that Drake should have consulted him before dismissing the officer. This remark was not passed on to Drake until after the voyage encountered difficulties with Doughty.

Details of the plan involved the deceit that Drake's destination was Alexandria. Even the crew on board ships were not privy to their true mission. Gradually it developed that they would stop at various ports along the coast of Africa, which was Portuguese territory.

Drake's initial voyage included five ships—the *Pelican*, the *Elizabeth*, the *Marigold,* the *Benedict,* and the supply ship *Swan*—164 men and boys, and a dozen gentlemen, among whom Thomas Doughty was the most prestigious. Drake's immediate retinue included his cousin John who was a talented artist; his negro servant Diego of the *cimarrones*; his brother John Drake, 14, who had served as his page in Ireland; his brother, Thomas Drake, who would pilot the *Marigold*; Thomas Moone, who would command the *Benedict*; and John Winter, captain of the *Elizabeth*.

The Journey

A fter bad weather first drove them back, their second attempt was on Dec. 13, 1577, when they departed and experienced numerous adventures on the coast of Africa. At Cape Blanco they captured a fishing crew with several ships, retaining them to supply fish for some time. When they released them they exchanged the *Benedict* for one of theirs which they called the *Christopher*.

Their most significant encounter was at Santiago on the Cape Verde islands where they defeated a Portuguese ship, the *Santa Maria*, adding it and its not unwilling captain, Nuño da Silva, to their fleet. This was a great asset to the voyage, since da Silva had been sailing the Brazilian coast since childhood, had all the maps and knowledge of sailing conditions along the coast of South America that Drake would need, and was not adverse to Drake's plan to enter the South Seas. The *Santa Maria*, which they renamed the *Mary*, was a 100 ton vessel bound for Brazil with trade goods, 150 casks of wine, and fully provisioned and watered for the voyage.

It was February 1, 1578 when they put the crew of the *Mary* aboard a newly constructed pinnace to return them to Santiago. They were then two months crossing the Atlantic, weeks in the doldrums without winds at the equator, and in escapades along the coast, always in search of fair winds, fresh water and supplies, which cost them one man and numerous injuries among the natives on the coasts of Brazil and Argentina. In addition, there were many troubles in keeping the ships together and, especially, threats of mutiny, which we will relate, emanating from Thomas Doughty, the gentleman, among others, taken aboard to add prestige to the journey.

Though excessive details would unnecessarily augment the narrative, characters will be identified as they emerge. As mentioned previously, most significant was the inclusion of Sir Francis Fletcher, who would be the chaplain and would keep a journal of the voyage. Many have written of the voyage in recent years, finally accessing documents long neglected, but Fletcher's telling is the source Bawlf has drawn upon most which we use in telling the story. [9]

Initially, there were fifty men aboard the *Pelican*. The gentlemen dined with Drake in the stern-castle, and the sailors slept in whatever crevice they could find in the hold with the stashed supplies and the three dismantled pinnaces which Drake had taken along. Drake's table was the epitome of refinement, with fine china, silver service and an orchestra of musicians, members waiting for Drake to be seated and for him to initiate the conversation. Fletcher was much impressed with Doughty, a man of erudition, who was learned in languages and philosophy. Twice a day they convened with the sailors for religious services. Very often Drake, the son of a preacher, led them in prayer. [10]

The first incident with Doughty occurred after they had sent Drake's new pinnace to see da Silva's passengers and crew safely to Santiago. A dispute arose when Drake's trumpeter, John Brewer, Edward Bright, and others said that Doughty had been pilfering from supplies on the newly acquired ship. John Cooke, a Doughty sympathizer then said it was Doughty himself who had sent for Drake, who then accused Drake's brother Thomas of the theft, namely wine, which was the original charge against Doughty.

Doughty's friend, Leonard Vicary, a gentleman lawyer, eased the situation, as did Fletcher; and Drake solved the problem temporarily by sending Doughty to the *Pelican* while he remained on the *Santa Maria*. Doughty did, however, own up to supplying himself with several items he had taken, which he said the passengers had given him for favorable treatment.

Unbelievable, Doughty assembled the gentlemen and sailors aboard the *Pelican* and gave a little oration regarding his new authority. He said that Drake had sent him as his friend whom he trusteth, that all was forgiven and forgotten (regarding the charge against his brother Thomas), and that there would be no more evil-doing hereafter. Then he said that Drake had committed to him the same authority to execute upon those who were malefactors. Even Fletcher wrote that Doughty was thought to have exceeded his authority, and there were those who went again to Drake to complain.

In addition, Doughty promised rewards to individuals committed to him, and it seemed he was aiming to break away from Drake. Doughty's younger brother John, also one of the gentlemen, began to boast of their powers of witchcraft, which Elizabethans greatly believed in and feared, especially sailors. To make matters worse, when Drake sent his trumpeter John Brown to the *Pelican* on an errand, Doughty seized him and gave him "a cobbey", a paddling on his bare rear end as a joke. Drake sent for him. He arrived at prayers, and Drake commanded him not to board, and then sent him to the *Swan*, the provision ship commanded by John Chester, "in utter disgrace." [11]

Proceeding another month southward they made landfall at 30 degrees, after 63 days at sea. During a sudden fog one of the ships touched bottom, but remained free. Thereafter a violent gale ensued, and the *Christopher* was found to be missing. Two days later it arrived in an estuary they were to call Cape Joy, where they harvested sea lions and encountered Indians whom Magellan had described as "giants."

Out to sea again, this time both the *Mary* and the *Swan* were missing, and they proceeded 800 miles to Cape Hope at 47 degrees since that is where they expected to rendezvous and where they set signal fires to help guide them back. There were skirmishes with the Indians, with Drake receiving a wound in the leg. It was found that the sea lion oil they had acquired was beneficial for their various aches and wounds. They then set off northward to try to find the lost ships.

Finally reconvening, it was learned that relationships had deteriorated into open hostility aboard the *Swan*. Doughty was telling everyone that Drake had owed his advancement to him, that he had a hold on Drake by reason of certain secrets he knew about him, and that he had powerful friends who would reward those who supported him and would punish his enemies. He stated that, indeed, Lord Burghley had approached him to serve as his secretary.

As a row developed in Captain Chester's cabin, John Saracold, master of the vessel, interrupted, "If there were traitors aboard, the general would do well to deal with them as Magellan had," that is, to hang them.

"Nay," said Doughty, "his authority is none such as Magellan had." Later Doughty accused Saracold of keeping the best victuals for the mariners, and blows were exchanged.

At Port Dawn, the next harbor, Drake ordered the *Swan* stripped and burned in order to lessen the problem of keeping the ships together. In the excitement thirty Indians came into view, and Drake offered them trade items which led to a spontaneous dance accompanied with Indian rattles and Drake's orchestra. Drake's prized cap was snatched, but he let it go, anxious to keep a rapport with the natives.

During their two-weeks stay at Port Dawn, Doughty was again aboard the *Pelican* and began again murmuring against Drake, which led to blows and Doughty's being tied to the mainmast. When he was ordered to board the *Christopher* he refused to go and had to be hoisted aboard with a boat tackle. Drake's decision then was to also burn the *Christopher*.

Doughty and his brother were sent to the *Elizabeth* where Drake admonished the crew that anyone speaking with "a conjuror and a witch" would be an enemy of the voyage.

Finally arriving at Port St. Julian, the same where Magellan had wintered, Drake's fleet was down to four ships. Having encountered much delay due to lost ships and trouble on board, Drake determined that they must winter there also, lay plans for crossing the straits, and, most of all, decide what to do about a problem that was threatening the success of their journey. [12]

The Trial

It seems obvious that Drake would not have achieved the secret aim of his journey had he not settled the problem of mutiny from within. Doughty was a member of England's class system of nobles who had no idea of the discipline required to control a fleet of ships with an odd mixture of gentlemen and mariners, especially if any were inclined to sabotage authority of the commander. He could not imagine that a bit of sport and subterfuge would not be acceptable at some level. Other men were to be used as pawns in the banter of play over authority between gentlemen, who may or may not come up winning.

One can imagine the difference in outlook between the two men, Drake having from boyhood been used to tedious journeys of maritime operation where every last morsel of food and water must be shared, and the other, who had always played for sport within the intrigues of court life. Drake was well-schooled in the requirements of the Royal Navy that made such long voyages possible, and here he was saddled with a bevy of knights used to personal jousts, tourneys, and perhaps ribald activity for amusement around the royals. Drake no doubt was given the responsibility of these playboys in order to court the backing of his project. Indeed, Walsingham, Leicester, Hatton and the queen, among others, were all involved in financing the voyage or furnishing ships, and he was obliged to assume the gentlemen they sponsored would go along with the discipline required and not usurp his authority.

In addition, he had a special mission to accomplish beyond that which any man aboard his ships might suspect and, indeed, beyond their imagination. He had to count on absolute authority to accomplish his mission.

Just as history has denied and neglected Drake's true accomplishment, Doughty and any supporters he might gain through his abstinence were ready to thwart him if his actions did not conform to their own aims, which were, as history has assessed, a voyage of plunder and adventure to navigate and encircle the globe. If Drake had not stopped them at Port St. Julian, he would have had even greater problems later on, for this was the same Royal Navy, established by himself, Frobisher, Hawkins, and others in building a classless enterprise which would later conquer the Spanish armada and, indeed, the world.

Our journal does not describe all the events of their winter sojourn at Port St. Julian which lasted from June 20, 1578 to August 10, 1578 in order to concentrate on the above agenda. Though somewhat at the same latitude south as England was north, it was during what scientists have considered the Little Ice Age, considerably colder there and again during the following winter when they would be at latitudes even further degrees north.

Landing at the same entrance past stark gray cliffs as Magellan had 58 years before, where he had crushed a mutiny and left a culprit hanging on a gibbet and two others marooned, they anchored at a low sandy island where they could careen their ships. The next day they went ashore, prepared their encampment, and sent men upstream to find fresh water and perhaps game. In that search, surgeon Robert Winterhay brought along his long bow; the master gunner, Oliver, a harquebus; and others came with swords and shields. Encountering two young Indians, tall but by no means giants as Magellan had reported, Winterhay engaged in some competition with one which he won as to the distance of arrows shot from his bow.

The scene turned ugly, however, when his bow broke and the Indians assumed there were no others. Other Indians appeared, showering them with arrows. In the retreat the surgeon suffered an arrow to his arm and another through his lungs. Oliver, when his weapon failed to fire, was shot with such force that it penetrated from his chest through his back.

Drake ordered his men to flee and was able to retrieve the harquebus, enable it, and fire at the Indian who had first turned hostile. It "tore out his belly and guts" and the others fled. [13]

The Indians were not seen again, though Drake had hoped to trade with them for badly-needed food through the winter. Their sojourn at St. Julian was indeed rather miserable due to the cold, lack of food, scurvy and illness. Much time was spent repairing their boats and sails and endeavoring to survive on shellfish pulled from the bay as there seemed to be no game available nearby.

Nevertheless, the big problem they were to solve if they were to have any success in the voyage began and was pursued immediately. Drake assessed that Doughty did have a following of about thirty men, including some mariners who resented being co-opted into such a trip. There was also a dread among many of proceeding into the Magellan Straits. But Drake felt he had to act with the authority he had, as it was entirely possible that a split would occur with some returning to England. [14]

Therefore, Drake assembled the entire company on June 10th and addressed Doughty with the charges against him, who, of course, challenged him that he had not the authority and that he himself should be tried in England. The written charges from witnesses attesting to his treasonous acts were submitted, and Drake impaneled a jury of forty to determine Doughty's guilt.

Drake initially charged him also with poisoning the earl of Essex, a move to underscore his belief that Doughty was indeed capable and planning to kill him. This led, however, to an outburst from Doughty that he himself had recommended Drake to Essex. Doughty also let it slip that Lord Burghley had obtained information about the "lot" of the voyage from him. This latter drew Drake to his feet in a burst of anger. "How?" he demanded.

"He had it from me," Doughty replied, which, as you know, had been expressly forbidden by the queen. Drake explained to the men the extent of this treachery. Then each of the charges against Doughty en route were read as each witness stepped forward. The lawyer Leonard Vicary tried to appeal to Drake that the trial was illegal, but Drake would have none of it.

The jury returned a verdict of guilty, whereupon Drake called them to the camp where he showed them certain papers proving the queen's involvement and John Hawkin's introducing him to Lord Essex. In a speech Drake asked whether the voyage—wherein the worst man among them in the fleet would some day be a gentleman— could go forward if this man should be allowed to live. "Therefore, my masters," he said, "they that think this man worthy to die, let them with me hold up their hands." The decision was nearly unanimous. [15]

Given two days to prepare himself, Doughty chose to die under the ax. It is remarkable the civility with which he and Drake spent this time, in prayer, with each receiving the sacrament from Fletcher and dining together in Drake's tent.

The traitor was buried with the other two men who had been slain by the Indians and also the bones of Magellan's mutineer Gaspar Quesada. The gibbet which had been over the latter's grave was cut into pieces for souvenirs and two large stones engraved in Latin bearing Drake's name were placed at the head and foot of the grave. It is significant that this ritual was consistent with English practice, in contrast to that of the Spanish.

After this cold and eventful winter, on August 10, 1578, the ships stood ready for sail. Before they left Drake called the men together, reiterated the necessity of his commandership, and impressed upon them the historic consequence of their journey if they emerged successful. He affirmed the worth of each man, but principally he counseled them that they must conquer the mutinies and discords among them.

As he said, "I must have the gentleman to haul and draw with the mariner, and the mariner with the gentleman. What, let us show ourselves all to be of a company, and let us not give occasion to the enemy to rejoice at our decay and overthrow." [16]

As an alternative, he did offer them the *Marigold* if they wished to return. Not a man accepted. Then a choice was offered that they might have wages instead of a share in the profits of the voyage. Again, the offer had no takers. Then, to their surprise, he relieved all the captains and officers of their posts, made changes, and reassigned them. At the end of his speech he reviewed for them the content of his meetings with Walsingham and the queen, stressing that the command had been given to himself alone.

Chapter 8

In Command

The Straits

Reverend Fletcher and John Cooke were the only ones present who recorded the events of Drake's famous journey. Bawlf's *The Secret Voyage of Sir Francis Drake* of 2003 uses their accounts, as well as those coming from Drake's efforts to reconstruct his story, and those others emanating from the Hakluyt Society, which the writer has here abridged. Later historians, however, confounded other voyager's claims with Drake's in order to award them his discoveries, but there is no need to doubt the veracity of those former eye witnesses. The ways that their records were confiscated and warped will be told in the chapter on the aftermath of the voyage and in the reprise at the end.

Taking leave of Port St. Julian, Drake and his fleet waited for a change of winds and finally entered the Strait of Magellan, commonly referred to as "the straits", on August 21st. Drake held a ceremony changing the name of the *Pelican* (Elizabeth's favorite bird) to *Golden Hinde* in honor of Sir Christopher Hatton, the new favorite in Elizabeth's court, perhaps hoping eventually to petition his understanding in the execution of his secretary, Doughty. (Hatton's crest featured a hind, that is, a female deer.)

Land to the south of the entrance to the straits had been called Tierra del Fuego (land of fires) by Magellan because of the bonfires the Indians set when they passed through. Drake carried the 1570 map of Ortelius which gave only a vague approximation of it. When Magellan's ship returned to England in 1522, his records indicated that the strait was

approximately
100 leagues.
There were
several other
attempts to
bridge it be-
fore Drake's:
Loaysa's in
1525 with
seven ships;
Alcazaba's
in 1535; de
Camargo's
in 1540 with
three ships,
one of which
reached Peru;

The Golden Hinde

and Ladrillers in 1557, who made the reverse trip from Chile to Spain via
the straits. The others ended in total failure. [1]

From the Atlantic the strait squeezes into two narrows, then wid-
ens to a lengthy passage through the spine of the Andes called the Broad
Reach which is subject to dangerous squalls. At the end of Broad Reach
at a point called Cape Froward numerous channels branch off with squalls
emerging from many directions.

Drake turned northward to the channel that runs 180 miles before
it reaches the Pacific. Here was the most dangerous passage, its width of
only one to two miles with swift tides and winds leaving little room to tack
(a sidewise turning of the ship in order not to sail directly into the wind)
and few places a ship can anchor. Even after arriving in view of the South
Sea, a ship might be driven back as far as Cape Froward due to strength of
the winds and tide. [2]

Drake had taken his brother Thomas and most of the crew of the
abandoned *Mary*—perhaps ninety men—on board the *Golden Hinde,*
and the remainder of men were divided between the *Elizabeth* and the
Marigold. Before taking the narrow channel toward the northwest, they
came to anchor near three islands, the largest of which Drake ceremoni-
ously named Elizabeth Island and the smaller isles, St. George and St.
Bartholomew. The islands were teeming with flightless birds—now called
penguins— of which they slaughtered some 2,000 to replenish their food

supply. On the 29th day of their journey through the straits they rounded Cape Froward and sailed three days covering thirty miles up the narrows where they found a place shallow enough to make anchor, with glacier-clad towering mountains above them. [3]

At their next such anchorage three days later they made the discovery that underneath the trees, which had been bent and tightly compacted by the snows, were a variety of herbs and edible plants. Drake and his men harvested these, much to the improvement of their diet and health. They encountered also some nomadic Indians, having only shells for scraping skins and moving earth, yet who created beautiful baskets and other containers. On September 6 they emerged into the South Sea. It had taken just sixteen days to clear the straits.

Luck, however, would not be upon them as they attempted to follow the maps in a northwest direction, which actually took them away from the coast 150 miles in two days. Then suddenly a violent wind drove them southwest for three days. In a calm, however, they were able to observe the lunar eclipse that had been predicted on September 18 and to calculate their longitude. In the early morning of the 16th, a difference of six hours, they were about 90 degrees west of England. [4]

The three ships had stayed together thus far; however, on September 28, after storms had raged through the night, the *Marigold* was no longer to be found. On October 1 they turned back and were suddenly driven against the coast, separating the two remaining ships.

Captain Winter took the chance he had been waiting for and headed back into Magellan's Strait, where he and his men spent three weeks at Cape Froward, out of the winds and terror. There was nothing for Drake to do but to proceed. They had agreed to meet at the latitude of 30 degrees in Chile, and most of Winter's crew desired to do so. They would have had plenty of time to convene, but Winter had had enough. On November 1 they sailed for England. [5]

Again Drake was driven far south by winds, where he gathered herbs on an island among others they encountered beyond the land mass that was Tierra del Fuego and sought the recovery of his men whose health was deteriorating. Two of the men died. At this point, however, he envisioned that he had reached the southernmost extremity of America where the oceans meet and flow freely together. Here on this island Fletcher chiseled Her Majesty's name, her kingdom, and the date. The islands were named the Elizabethans, and here Drake took the opportunity of replenishing their supply of penguins. The passage through the islands and around

Tierra del Fuego would later be called Cape Horn, though its discovery by Drake would be disputed. [6]

Chile

D rake's journey north was surprisingly speedy and uneventful, covering 1,000 miles in 28 days, stopping first at an island called Mocha. There, however, they encountered Indians, friendly at first, but who attacked them as they dispatched to obtain water from a nearby creek. All who were thus engaged were struck with arrows and were only able to escape by cutting a rope to release a pinnace they had boarded in their flight, leaving two men behind. They returned, further armed, only to watch the men being butchered by the Indians.

The savages, called the Arancanian tribe, had been at war with the Spanish for years, and Drake chose not to retaliate since the group had suffered enough through the years. [7]

Sailing for a week and another 350 miles they came to anchor at the Bay of Quintere where they hoisted a fisherman aboard and learned that a Spanish ship was at harbor in Valparaiso nearby. He offered to guide them there, where a welcoming party met them, unaware that they were not Spanish. Drake and his crew were able to subdue them and board their ship, the *Los Reyes*, an impressive vessel carrying 1,770 jars of wine, cedar lumber, and four cases each containing 75 pounds of gold.

They were able to take command of the ship and retain its captain, a Greek named Juan Greco, whose charts showed all the bays and ports in the area. Drake returned the rest of Greco's crew to shore, moved 25 of his men on board, and renamed the vessel the *Capitana*. Then he returned their guide to the Bay of Quintere and bestowed gifts upon him and his friends, promising to return with a larger fleet to assist them against the Spanish. This was the first indication in the journals of Fletcher that he was already planning a follow-up voyage with a larger plan. [8]

Five days out of Valparaiso they searched at 30 degrees, the point of rendezvous, for his lost ships. They then searched the coast in vain for five more days. It had been three months since they lost the *Marigold* and two since the *Elizabeth* disappeared. Their search up and down the coast attracted attention, however, and as they stopped to find water they were attacked by Indians. A skirmish followed in which another seaman was slaughtered. Though the Indians then offered a truce, Drake set sail and arrived at the Bay of Saluda, 100 miles north, the next day, where he intended to careen the *Golden Hinde* by transferring its load to the newly acquired *Capitana*. But first they laid out and began construction of a new pinnace, took a week off, and prepared a feast for New Year's Day. It had been a year since they left England. [9]

After completing the pinnace and installing a cannon upon it, Drake took fifteen men and again searched the coast for the lost ships. After two days, encountering stiff winds, he finally gave up the search and the cannons were transferred to the *Capitana*. Then able to move the *Golden Hinde* to the beach he made a thorough repair and careening of his main ship. They again set sail on January 19. Approaching the equator there were few rivers or streams that reached the desert area they were now in, and they had problems locating water.

At a place called Tarapata they encountered a Spaniard leading eight llamas each laden with 100 pounds of silver, which they relieved him of. Soon the wall of mountains narrowed and they entered the harbor of Arica, the principal outlet for the silver extracted by thousands of enslaved Indians from the rich mines of Potosi. In the town there were fifty or so houses with their plantations and orchards, though no one came to challenge their presence.

They encountered a negro who told them that ahead there was a ship laden with silver. Without much trouble they captured two other barks along with their owners, one a Corsican and the other a Flemish. Moving ahead they then found the galleon which was already unloaded, as they had been forewarned of their pursuit. They did, however, tour her out of the harbor to join their ships, now numbering five.

Drake realized then that due to their delays, word had been sent ahead of their coming. He knew that he must move quickly and set afloat the *Capitana* and the two other recent prizes in order that the *Golden Hinde* and the pinnace might reach the next port unannounced. They were nearing Peru. [10]

Peru

Our story progresses, following the accounts as given in Bawlf's researches, one of which was an *Anonymous Narrative,* written shortly after the voyage by one privy to insider accounts but also subject to the queen's edict, which will be discussed more fully in the next

chapter. In it there were over 200 pages on the part of his voyage dealing
with Spanish plunder and barely 10 describing all of the exploration above
Spanish territory which he had been sent to describe and lay claim to.
These encounters in Spanish territory are recounted herein not only to give
evidence of the mastery of his command, but also because he often indi-
cates to those he rescues and releases that he will return and that he has a
larger plan.

Lima, called Los Reyes (City of Kings), at that time was the
second largest city, after Mexico City, of those in the Spanish colonies of
the New World. In addition to the viceroy's palace and quarters of several
hundred colonial officials, clergy, and soldiers, there were 2,000 households, and its viceroy, Don Francisco Alvarez de Toledo was the senior
representative of Philip in the entire region. Lima was six miles inland
from its port, Callao, and had five monasteries, two convents, and two
hospitals. It exceeded Mexico City in the trade of gold and silver since it
also traded in the Philippines and the entire Pacific in addition to carrying
it over the isthmus.

Another privateer, also a friend of Drake's, John Oxenham, in 1576

Conquest of Mexico

had come with 57 men and two dismantled pinnaces which they carried
across the isthmus, intending to raid shipping at Panama and the Pacific
coast. Eighteen were captured, fourteen were executed, and four were
awaiting judgment of the Inquisition at Lima. After plundering the harbor
at Callao, Drake intended to rescue Oxenham and his men.

When Drake made a raid on the ships in the harbor he was able to
install his men on a galley called the *San Cristobal*. The viceroy was alert-

ed, however, but by the time they arrived in Callao Drake had put out to
sea. Four leagues out they were becalmed, and Drake proceeded to transfer
what they wanted from the *San Cristobal* to the *Golden Hinde*, whereupon
he released the captain and set free the Greek pilot, who eventually told
Toledo of Drake's journey through the straits. The viceroy was furious. [11]

The viceroy then questioned Oxenham who told him about Richard Grenville's failed journey and that he knew of no ship that would ever
attempt the straits without the queen's license. He also told the viceroy of
the reputation of Drake who was the only one who could do it. [12]

Oxenham told him that if the queen would allow it, "he would pass
through the Strait of Magellan and found settlements over here in some
good country." When asked how Drake might return, he told him, "perhaps through the strait thought to be into the North Sea."

In the harbor Drake also was able to intercept a bark, piloted by
Benito Diaz Bravo, from whom he took a Negro, a former *cimarrone*, and
18,000 pesos of gold and silver. Drake sent the crew to shore, and retained
Bravo, whom he shut up in his cabin. He told Bravo that, if spared, due to
the hazards of his journey, he "would return within two years with aid of
seven ships."

Toledo sent his son Don Luis out to pursue Drake with General
Diego, a newly appointed admiral, and also a great navigator and cos-
mographer, de Bamboa, with 100 soldiers, 80 sailors on two ships with
newly cast artillery to search for Drake. Drake had set off in search of the
rumored one great prize, the *Cacafuego*, carrying a magnificent load of
gold and silver, of which he had been alerted. It had, however, a ten-day
head start. With his ship at full sail, and stopping to push forward with
the pinnace when they were becalmed, they were able to outdistance their
pursuers and overtake the vessel. [13]

Cacafuego's captain, Juan de Anton, steered close to the *Golden
Hinde*, not suspecting trouble until too late. There was a barrage of arrows;
however Drake had his trumpeter sound and appeared with all his armor
ready. He none-the-less welcomed Anton on board. He then had all the
passengers and crew placed under guard and took Anton to his own quarters to dress a wound on his face.

Aboard the vessel were 1,300 bars of silver weighing 26 tons,
13 chests of silver coins, and 80 pounds of gold. The value was 362,000
pesos, 106,000 of which belonged to King Philip and, in addition, a certain
amount of unregistered treasure later greatly augmenting the treasure. The
transfer of the treasure, by pinnace, took three days to replace the ballast in

the *Golden Hinde*. Meanwhile Anton was entertained by Drake with meals
and orchestral entertainment, and there was an exchange of valuable and
significant gifts. .

Drake advised Anton to release Oxenham and his companions or
they would kill 2000 Spaniards. He advised him of the great loss of John
Hawkins at San Juan de Ulúa in 1568 on a mission of trade in which 300
men were killed, and he had come to collect money due in compensation.
He also had letters of the queen authorizing him to pursue a good route
into the South Sea and that if the King of Spain did not give Englishmen
permission to trade in payment of the duties, he said,"he would come back
and carry off all the silver gifts exchanged."

Then the negro and all other prisoners except da Silva were released to Anton and they bid him farewell. Drake and his small fleet then
steered in a direction north by northwest for the coast of Nicaragua, the
Golden Hinde laboring, its hull fouled with barnacles and seaweed. [14]

New Spain

A t the port of Manta they found Bravo, whom they had released, repairing his ship. His navigator, de Gamboa, concluded that Drake
had already raided the *Cacafuego*, and had proposed to Toledo to
bypass Panama and head for Nicaragua where he might intercept Drake.
His son Don Luis, however, wished to get to Panama so that he might
carry on to Spain with his father's report.

Continuing his journey Drake completed a 600-mile crossing to
Costa Rica and came to the island of Cano where he sent a party in a pinnace for water. There they found lush forests and wildlife and were able to
feast on fresh meat, including alligator and monkey.

Here they intercepted the bark of Rodrigo Tello carrying a 40 ton
cargo of maize, lard and honey. Aboard were two pilots sent by Toledo
to conduct the new governor of Philippines to Manila who were carrying
official navigation charts and sailing directions to and from. Taking control, they realized that they had here acquired a desirable vessel for their
northern tour of discovery, as well as valuable charts for their crossing of
the South Seas.

In command of Tello's bark they proceeded to look for a place
to careen the *Golden Hinde*. With no suitable beach available, they first
stripped the cannons, lifted the treasure ashore, and used Tello's bark to

unload her. Then by drawing the ship into the mouth of a river and ground-
ing her at low tide, they scraped and caulked her sides down to the water.
They also refitted Tello's bark with higher gunwails to suit a longer voyage
and enable her to hold more sail. They were obliged to move swiftly.

A difficulty was encountered when they undertook to set free Tello
and his two pilots, one of whom Drake desired to retain. Alphonso San-
chez Conchero was offered 1,000 ducats to accompany them on the next
leg of the journey, but he protested leaving his wife and wished to write
a letter to Toledo to explain he was being taken against his will. Though
money was sent for his wife and the letter composed, he would later present other problems. At this time a pinnace was loaded with food and water
and Tello and the others were set free to go. They later reported that Drake
had treated them very well. [15]

Their next port was at Realejo where it was rumored the Spanish
were constructing a new galleon. Here Drake wanted Conchero to pilot
him through the shoals at the entrance to the harbor so he could burn the
new ship. Conchero refused, saying he did not know the harbor, and was
finally hoisted off the deck on a rope to jog his memory, though it appears
the ship was not, after all, destroyed.

On April 3 a ship was seen on the horizon. Drake's men boarded
her just before dawn and learned that she was bound for Acapulco with
silks, linens and dishes and that there was a passenger on board who was
a Spanish nobleman named Don Francisco de Zarate. When the latter
was summoned to the *Golden Hinde* he expected death, but was received
courteously by Drake, shown around the vessel, and invited to dinner.
Zarate later wrote a long letter to the viceroy of New Spain, Don Martin
Enriquez, the one who had attacked the fleet of John Hawkins at San Juan
de Ulúa some years before. In his letter to the viceroy he described Drake
and reminded him that it had been he who had raided the port of Nombre
de Dios five years previously in revenge. But he told Enriquez of Drake's
view of the matter and appraised him of the excellent treatment he had
received from him and of the devotion and discipline of his crew.

After entertaining him at dinner there was an exchange of gifts—a
fine sword and a silver brazier being given to him, with Drake receiving of
fine linens and china for his wife—and, it being Sunday, he attended their
religious service and asked questions about the words of the scriptures.
Drake also told him about their voyage and about the difficulties with
Thomas Doughty.

The next morning, in reloading his ship, he ordered Tello's bark alongside and placed six cannons aboard her, six dozen archers, and escorted Zarate back to his ship, including Conchero whom he was glad to get rid of. At their parting Drake took with him from Zarate's retinue a negro woman, "a proper wench named Maria," with Zarate's blessing.

A week later on April 13 they entered the port of Guatulco, which was nine miles from the city further inland of the same name. On shore to welcome them were Gaspar de Vargas, chief magistrate, and Benardino Lopez, lieutenant governor of the province. Realizing that they were Englishmen, they were alarmed and ran into the woods. Coming on shore with twenty-five harquebusiers they intercepted a merchant fleeing his house where they found a cache of gold and coins. The fleeing officers and other captives, including two captive negro men, were taken out to the *Golden Hinde* where they were treated well and entertained. As with Zarate, these officials were to communicate with Viceroy Enriquez their encounter with Drake, who claimed to the Spanish the legitimacy of his voyage, if not to his own queen.

The captives they held were induced to assist Drake in locating a source of water and in loading the ship with firewood under threat that they would burn their vessel. Then they put them all ashore except one of the negroes who wished to accompany them.

It is hoped that the reader has observed and will remember Drake's courtesies and humane behavior toward all he met, including the natives, on his journey. This would be quite in contrast to the slaughter at San Juan de Ulúa he himself endured and, indeed, the slaughter that Cortez and Pizarro inflicted upon thousands of native Indians when they set out to conquer and colonize the New World earlier in the century.

On Good Friday April 16 before daybreak, with the *Golden Hinde* and *Tello's Bark*, they raised their sails to pursue the main goal of their expedition. At the end they left a forlorn Nuño da Silva and his gear aboard the trade vessel, the last captive among those who were not to know the more precise purpose of their voyage, and departed. [16]

HERNANDO CORTES
(1485-1547)

After Drake's departure from Guatulco the letters of Anton and Zarate had their desired effect upon the viceroys of their respective domains,
both alerting them of Drake's achievements and plans, but also the stated
purpose of his voyage. The fleet of Don Luis Toledo had already arrived in
Panama on April 2 telling of the extent of Drake's plunder in the province
of Lima. In addition, the testimony of the Portuguese pilot da Silva whom
Drake released at Guatulco was relayed to Philip of Spain.

San Juan de Anton in his letter to Toledo in Lima quoted Drake's
three possible routes home: the straits, via India, and via a strait around the
northern extremity of America. He also informed Toledo that their losses
equaled 447,000 pesos in gold and silver and 100,000 in further damages.

The letter that Francisco de Zarate sent to Viceroy Enriquez in
Mexico City reported similar information but negligible losses. His reports
confirmed those of Anton as to Drake's stated intention. A letter, however, from the chief magistrate of Guatulco, Gaspar de Vargas, to Enriquez
stirred him to order a force of 200 soldiers to Acapulco where there were
ships to go in pursuit of Drake.

It was de Vargas who later reported to Enriquez the results of their
interrogation of da Silva and the intension to hand him over to the inquisition to obtain information "by other means." Da Silva then confirmed
Anton and Zarate's information, but also offered that Drake, under the
instructions of the queen, gave warning:

"He told Don Francisco de Zarate that if the king would give
the English license to trade in the Indies of the North Sea they would be
peaceable, but if not they would come and plunder in both seas."[17]

Here was the purpose of Drake's voyage laid out in great clarity.
These messages were going directly from the two viceroys to King Philip.
Philip always knew the intentions of Drake's voyage, whereas England
failed to countenance them. For two centuries Spain avoided Drake's
claims whereas England failed to take advantage of them.

Philip was also concerned about ongoing reports from Don Ber-
nardino de Mendoza, new ambassador to the English court replacing
Antonio de Guaras who had been arrested for plotting to free Mary Queen
of Scots, reports of Frobisher's three voyages to the northeast coast of
America which he considered a challenge to their sovereign claims, also
their attempts to find the northwest passage. These reports had come from
George Best and had been printed by a servant of Christopher Hatton. In
them were numerous alterations of the true position of places, latitude and
longitude, distance, etc., evidences of the then current practice of falsify-

ing information. Mendoza reported that none dared divulge anything about Frobisher's last voyage as they were "under threat of pain of death." [18]

Preceding any reports from Anton, Zarate, and da Silva reaching Philip, however, was the arrival on June 8, 1579 of John Winter on the Devon coast with the *Elizabeth,* the first definite report of Drake's voyage up to the time of Winter's separation, including the trial and execution of Thomas Doughty. Through Mendoza this information reached Philip before the other reports, which arrived during the first week of August. Through Philip, however, news of the plunder of 600,000 ducats, including one-third belonging to Philip, caused much elation among investors in England.

We take a moment here for a modern view of the above happenings by a professor of history at the University of Southern California. Peter C. Mancall, who would certainly have had access to the same research as Bawlf and others, wrote a book, *Hakluyt's Promise,* in 2007, published by Yale University Press, which summarized this portion of Drake's journey thus:

"In August his crew suffered a brutal passage through the Strait of Magellan. After sailing northward and reaching the coast of California, the expedition turned westward, reaching the Moluccas in November 1579." [19]

Is the reader not aghast, as we are, that authentic history can be thus ignored? More will be said of Mancall's analysis in our final chapter, as well as of Richard Hakluyt, who, of all people, was the custodian of the various

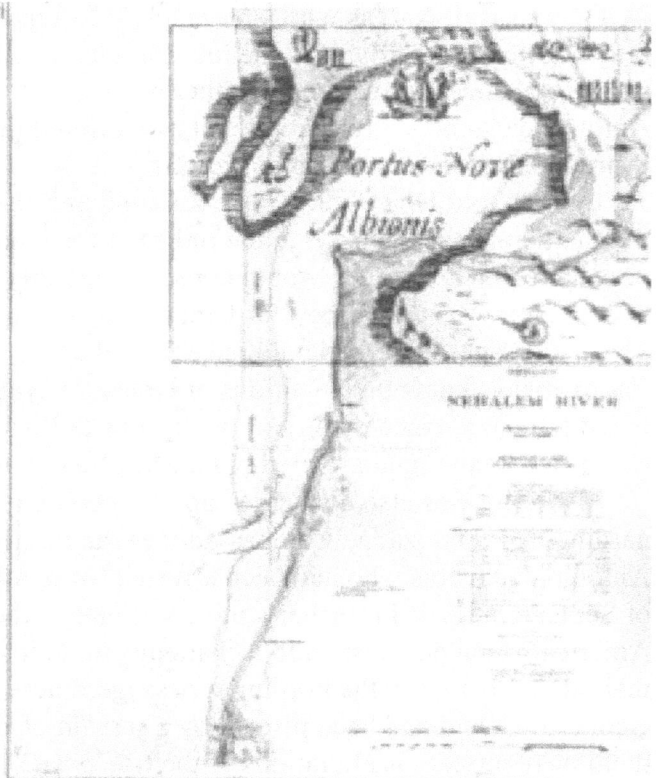

Porttus Nove Albionis

versions of Drake's navigation seeping through official channels and subject to the queen's veto.

We include here also a map borrowed from Google on the internet which, in the same way, presents a modern consensus and ignores all the evidence of his northern journey which has been made available through the Hakluyt Society findings. Drake was on a mission in search of the Strait of Anian for the queen of England, taking him all the way to southern Alaska, and he possessed the queen's "license" to establish a Nova Albion for England above the Spanish claims in California.

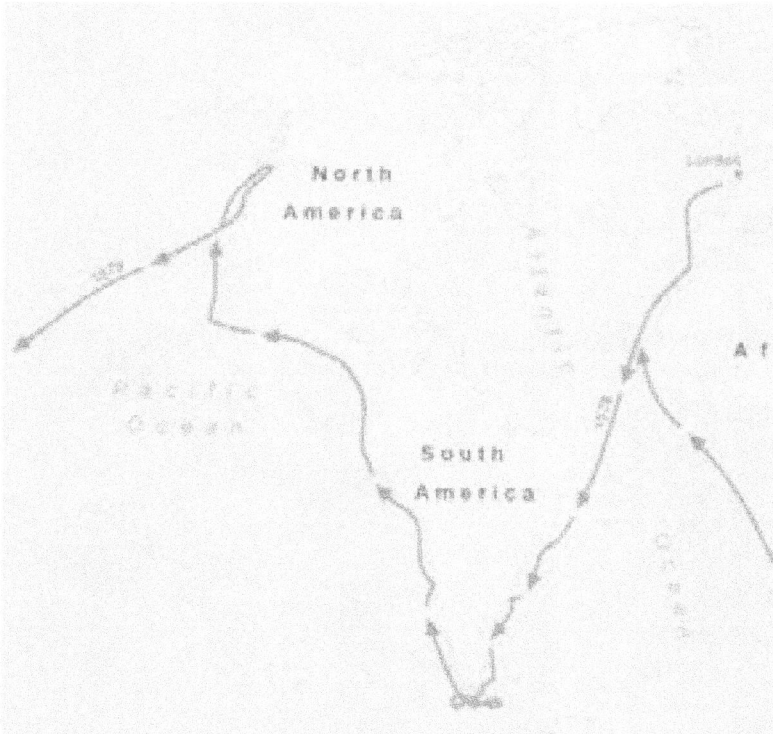

Contemporary map of Drake's Initial Voyage which disregards his Northern Voyage and Sojourn at Nehalem Bay

In anticipation of our next chapter, let us regard the map in the upper left corner of the Hondius Broadside, again produced on page 102, and compare it with the map in the Costaggini *"Survey of Artifacts at Neahkahnie Mountain, Oregon"* of the setting where Drake in 1579 surveyed and made a claim for an English colony in America. Note the actual convergeance of the outlines of Nehalem Bay and be prepared to agree that nowhere else could Drake have accomplished his task except in that setting.

Be prepared to follow Drake's activity there as presented in the next chapter.

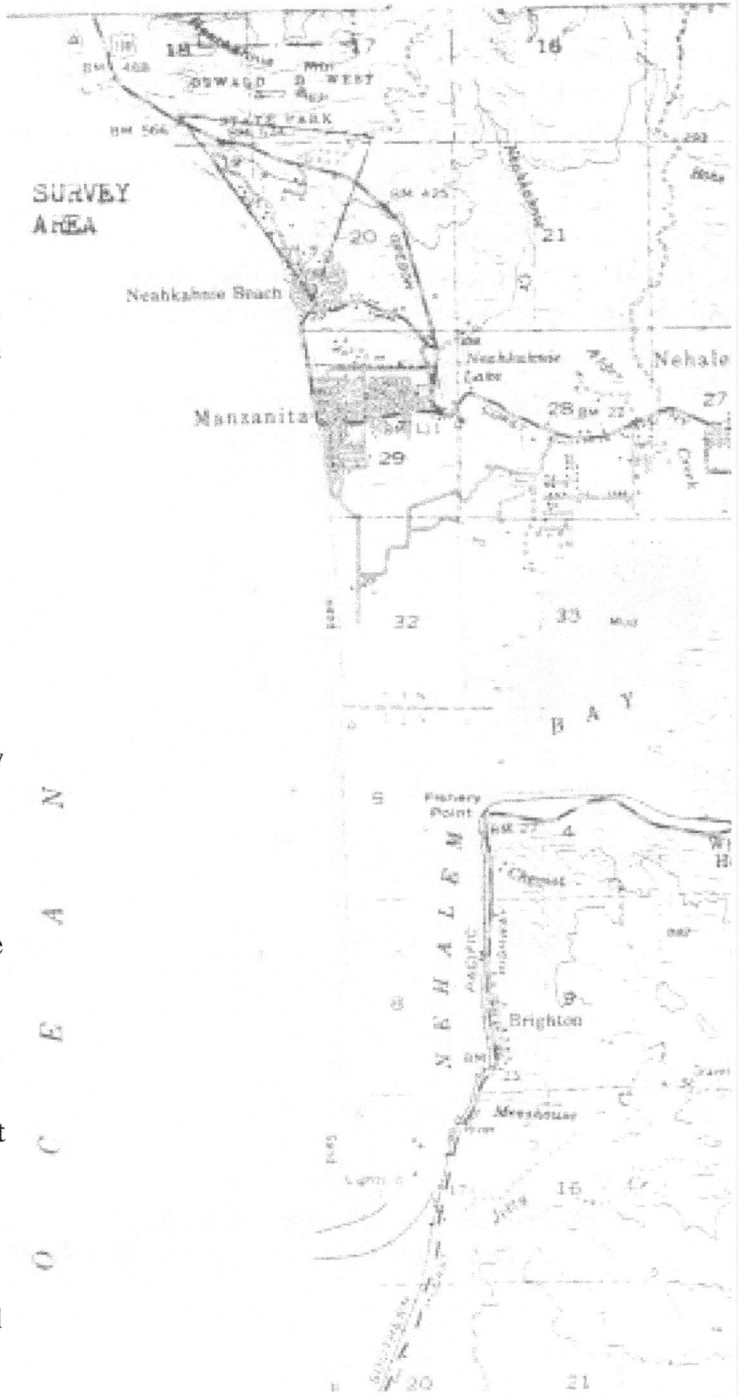

Phillip A. Costaggini map showing survey location at "point of position"

Chapter 9

The Lost Labors

Guatulco to Nehalem Bay

Until the 1628 publication of *The World Encompassed by Sir Francis Drake* there was but little account of how Drake spent some seven months between the time he left Guatulco on April 16, 1579 until he was sighted by Portuguese merchant ships south of the Philippines, bound for the Moluccas. The world "encompassed by Sir Francis Drake" was the subject of the book, not its author, as we know, but was what remained of Francis Fletcher's journal, published by Nicholas Bourne in conjunction with Drake's nephew and heir, also named Sir Francis Drake. Bourne was the son of the William Bourne whose method of triangulation Drake copied, which will be further identified. That was forty-eight years after Drake's return, long after its import would have affected the political relationship between Spain and England. Since two generations had elapsed, little notice was taken that would erase the cloak of secrecy which history would preserve.

Prior accounts of his voyage through the 1590s eliminated all of his voyage in search of the northwest passage and the claim for New England and gave but few pages concerning the Pacific crossing. In our last chapters we will trace what is known about the early releases of Hakluyt and others in their writings and maps. They were under the rule of Elizabeth not to mention Nova Albion or the search for the Strait of Anian and could use only a code—minus-ten degrees—for any revealed latitudes. In spite of this they were able to exchange much information to assist later navigators by the use of cryptograms, i. e., codes for actual distances.

In telling Drake's story and keeping its details in a chronological sequence, we will again use Bawlf's and Gitzen's research into Fletcher's edited descriptions, as on the initial portions of his journey, and to explain what is now known of this enormous gap. Their research, in addition to the *World Encompassed*, includes the other sources mentioned in Chapter 1: the Hondius Broadside, the Niccola van Sype and Edward Wright maps, the depositions of John Drake and Niño da Silva, and various other papers submitted to the Hakluyt Society.

My one inquiry at Powell's in Portland, Oregon netted me a glimpse in their rare books room of a 1589 original, Hakluyt's *Principal Navigations, Voyages and Discoveries of the English Nation*, which had been rescued and rebound from the Hagley Hall Christmas Eve fire in 1925, priced at $14,000. That was the first edition by that title, the second and third editions being published in 1599 which have now all been incorporated into the Hakluyt Handbook, published in 1972 which I have been able to access through an interlibrary loan. It was in the third edition that the Edward Wright map was finally published which confirms the latitude where Drake made his claim for England, to be described further Chapter 14.

Not having access to other sources, I give credit to Garry Gitzen, whose conclusions about the relics at Neahkahnie Mountain and Nehalem Bay I highly respect. Proceeding, I would describe Drake's northern voyage principally through Bawlf's interpretation of Fletcher and others who have analyzed Drake's maps and, later, the survey at "point of position" through that of Gitzen. It is here given briefly, in order not to add unduly to this neglected portion.

Drake had learned from Rodrigo Tello's two pilots and their secret charts the sailing directions for the voyage to the Philippines and back and that the circulation of winds north of the equator were the reverse of those off South America — clockwise rather than counterclockwise. Taking advantage of this information he first sailed due west, picking up those trade winds and sailing 1000 miles before turning northward. He then sailed northwest and then north by northeast another 3000 miles to latitude 44 degrees, altering then to east by northeast, altogether 5000 miles in forty-eight days, making landfall at 50 degrees on the backside of what is now Vancouver Island.[1]

Due to bad weather he later referred to this landing as "Cape of storms" or "Cape of worries." Some Indians came out to meet them, members of the Nuu-chah-nulth, a tribe observing the "potlatch" or gift-giving feast, in which the first gift is presented to the most honored guest. In later centuries it was learned that in one branch of that tribe at Checleset Bay, the first gift was taken down to the sea to dedicate it to the "great chief" of the bearded men who visited them in his "floating house" long before the visits of Captain Cook and the Spanish two centuries later. [2]

Experiencing some difficulty with fog, Drake picked up a fresh wind and made rapid headway to the northwest arriving at the outer shores of an island at 52 degrees where they encountered excruciating cold, causing the men in general to complain bitterly. Catching a wind toward the north the next day they altered their course eastward and made landfall at the present Queen Charlotte Islands at 53 degrees, 150 miles west of their original landfall. Drake later referred to this coast as "Frozen land" and "Coast of objections" for it appears that from this point onward they were still immersed in a protracted winter. [3]

Rounding a cape at latitude 54 degrees they beheld a long line of snow-capped mountains disappearing into the horizon. From there a broad passage led eastward, a passage now called Dixon's Entrance, and the mountains appearing in the northeast were the islands of southern Alaska. It is thought he may have encountered the Haida tribe, which, in the intervening centuries have been known to trade in highly valued commodities and to erect totem-poled villages. As Bawlf remarks in his story, "when Drake's narrative was adapted from the journal [Francis Fletcher's] everything concerning the voyage north of 48 degrees was omitted except for the passages concerning cold weather." East from Dixon's Entrance Drake would have seen Prince of Wales Island cloaked in snow. "Fletcher was perplexed that with the sun so near the summer solstice, it seemed powerless to remove the snow." [4]

Again it must be remembered that this was at the height of the Little Ice Age. Oral history among the Tlingit Indians 200 miles north of Dixon Entrance at Glacier Bay has it that their village was being swept away by glaciers at that time and that they were forced to move to the shores of an adjacent strait.

Beyond the present Prince of Wales Island Drake saw a second mountainous coast and referred to a cape there as "Cape of good fortune." Around the cape he saw a large opening toward the north, now called Clarence Strait, which leads northward some ninety miles. There they encountered an impossible barrier at 57 degrees where a river extends across the strait nearly blocking it and causing the channel to virtually drain at low tide. There was no possibility of the *Golden Hinde* getting through.

Rounding the southern tip of Prince of Wales Island, however, they discovered a twelve-mile wide passage leading northward, directly toward the Arctic sea. Here, at Admiralty Island, at 57 degrees was the spot where Drake determined he had found the Strait of Anian. Here is where he made a pen and ink insertion on the world map of Ortelius with that assertion. [5]

He proceeded no further, needing to continue his commitment to Elizabeth to establish a site for the future colony of New England, careen his ships, and be back in the strait by the beginning of September in order to reach the Atlantic Ocean before the arctic winter closed the passage. [6]

Here Bawlf's interpretation raises the question for the writer and for posterity whether he did indeed return to attempt such a feat. First of all, what happened to Tello's Bark and twenty or so men? And what consumed six months or so of his time after departing, as they say, for the Moluccas? I believe we shall never know.

Departing Admiralty Island he performed the arduous task of mapping the inner passages of Puget Sound, including all the rivers and islands of the area, at first designating the inner shores of Vancouver Island as his Nova Albion until the hostility of the Indians drove him further.

Eventually his maps and descriptions guided others to replicate them and claim his discoveries, e. g., Robert Dudley, of the Cape Flattery and Gray's Harbor area, and Juan de Fuca of the straits erroneously attributed to him. It has even been suggested that de Fuca might have been one-and-the-same Benito Diaz Bravo, whom Drake encountered in Peru and to whom he expounded upon his plan that he "would return within two years with aid of seven ships." It would seem that all along Spain had been more aware of Drake's journey and its extent and aims than England ever was privy to.

We proceed now to his point of arrival down the coasts of Washington and Oregon to 45 degrees, Neahkahnie Mountain, where he was to accomplish those other elements of his original plan.

Point of Position

B oth Samuel Bawlf of British Columbia and Garry Gitzen of Nehalem Bay are dedicated to the prodigious work of Wayne Jensen and Don Viles in the discovery of the monuments found on Neahkahnie Mountain and their interpretation in their survey by Costaggini. It is interesting at times to find that their opinions, which basically converge, do at times differ. Bawlf is an academic historian with interests in many fields, and Gitzen is a local amateur, completely devoted to the findings which indicate that both the surveying and the careening of Drake's ships took place over his five-week landing and stay at Nehalem Bay. They both espouse the findings of the original researchers which, it should be noted, included Bob Ward, to be identified, but differ on the bay of Drake's landing. Bawlf is of the opinion that after the survey Drake sailed 60 miles south to Whale's Cove for the careening.

If the writer might put in a word, there is no way Drake could have accomplished such a detailed task of the immense survey he accomplished at Neahkahnie without an anchorage inside the bay nearby, nor could he have hidden and careened his ships without entering an estuary. The bay at Whales Cove 60 miles south is too shallow and exposed even for the careening, and there were no large groups of Indians near the steep-banked cove.

In Bawlf's words: "When settlers began arriving in Oregon in the mid-nineteenth century the Tillamook Indians told them of a place on the

Manzanita Beach below Neahkahnie Mountain

coast where strange men in ships landed many generations before and left some things on a mountainside." [7]

Continuing with Bawlf's words:

"The place was Neahkahnie Mountain, thirty miles south of the Columbia, which was regularly burned by the Indians in order to provide new forage for game they pursued in hunting. It was there and on the beach that the settlers began to find and unearth stone monuments inscribed with strange arrows, words in Latin and other symbols. By 1890 these were investigated for buried treasure. No treasure was ever found, only an Elizabethan coin which was found on the beach after a storm. "

In regard to his sources, he states,

"In 1980 an English engineer named Bob Ward resolved to investigate the assertion in the '*Anonymous Narrative*' that Drake's careenage was situated at 44 degrees. Examining the coast at that latitude, Ward found a small bay—indeed it is the only one on the entire coast—that matches Drake's drawing." [8]

Representing the British point of view, Bawlf took Ward at his word and may never have sailed up the river into Nehalem Bay. Neither does the bay at Whale's Cove match the Hondius Broadside at all in its particular details. As an academic with resources into British archives, however, Bawlf has done a splendid job of putting together the documentary aftermath of Drake's voyage.

Gitzen, however, has pursued local legend with a passion, following up the lifetime work of Jensen and Viles, collecting and digging out from the mountain and charting the historic relics. On the beach at the foot of the mountain, they first investigated a large pile of rocks, called a cairn, ten feet in diameter and two feet high near which was a monument inscribed with symbols and the number 1632, now called the "W" rock.

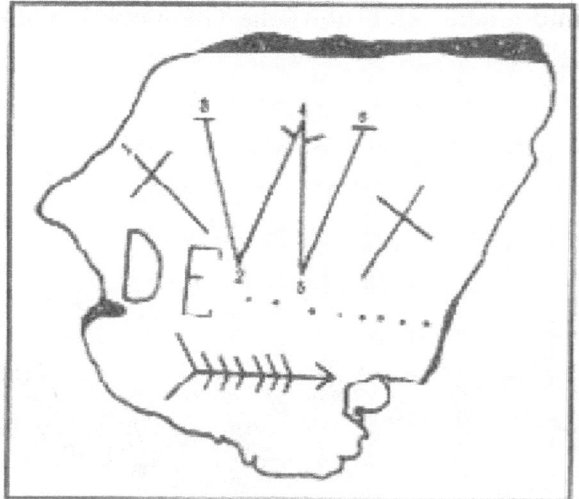

Nearly a mile up the mountainside toward the northeast, they found a similar cairn and beneath some undergrowth a squared stone with a deep grove across which measured an English yard, which they assumed might have been used as a measuring cord. This is now called the "Measuring Rock". As Viles later explained, "It dawned on me that the rocks represented 'shots' or compass bearings, that someone had taken a 'fix' on something, or in other words taken a compass bearing on a specific object or place." [9]

This was only the beginning. Over the years they amassed and recorded some **forty** engraved stones and a library of books, letters, journals, and logs of those who wrote about Drake's journey from all over the world. The relics and the library, now called the Jensen Collection, are now in the care of Gitzen. To repeat as in our original introduction: after their partnership ceased Jensen then engaged Phillip A. Costaggini in 1980 to interpret the survey for his masters thesis in engineering at Oregon State University in Corvallis. Maps of his survey and method of triangulation to determine longitude appear on succeeding adjacent pages. [10]

They learned that Drake had only the navigational instruments of the day, the magnetic compass, the sandglass, cross-staff, astrolabe, and a log and line. They knew he was aware that Spanish ships had not landed north of 38 degrees and that Frobisher in 1576 had charted the longitude on the east coast and established that there was a magnetic variation of the north pole.

Whether he was aware of Gemona Frisius's 1530 *De Principils Astronomiae & Cosmographiae* who described using the stars for triangulation and Copernicus's treatise on the solar system in 1543 is not known, as these books had not yet been translated into English. Certainly their implications were known, and Dr. John Dee, who was a Frisius student and Elizabeth I's appointed court astrologer, would have put him in touch with the latest navigation techniques. Dees was an advisor to the Muscovy Company to explore the sea route over Russia, who trained Frobisher and certainly encouraged Drake in his venture. . . His goal was "to trade and explore the new world," [11]

It was William Bourne, friend of Dees, whose triangulation survey would have made the most significant contribution to Drake's method. Drake's survey, when it was finally analyzed by Costaggini, was very similar in method and technique. The monuments established the points of triangulation required by the method in order to establish longitude. .

Aside from the survey itself, the method of laying claim to territory used by Drake was prevalent only among the English. The Portuguese set up stone pillars; Balboa assembled a heap of stones; and at Port St. Julian Magellan set up a gibbet, or wooden cross. Frobisher, however, "heaped up stones on high mountains" and stacked rocks into cairns in Nova Scotia in 1575-6 and in his second voyage in 1577 just as Drake was to do.

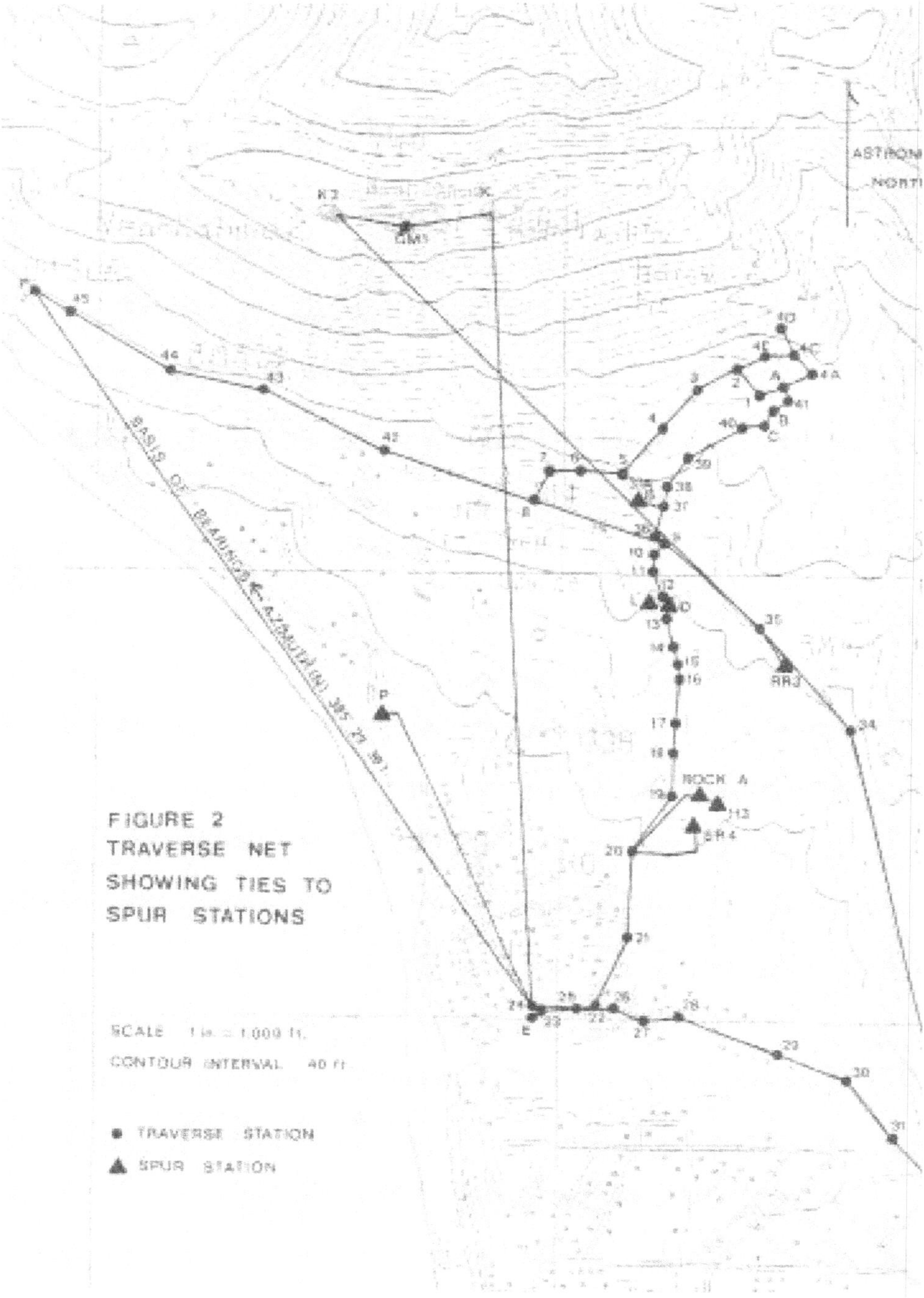

FIGURE 2
TRAVERSE NET
SHOWING TIES TO
SPUR STATIONS

SCALE   1 in. = 1,000 ft.
CONTOUR INTERVAL   40 ft

● TRAVERSE STATION
▲ SPUR STATION

Phillip A. Costaggini map showing relics found in "point of position"

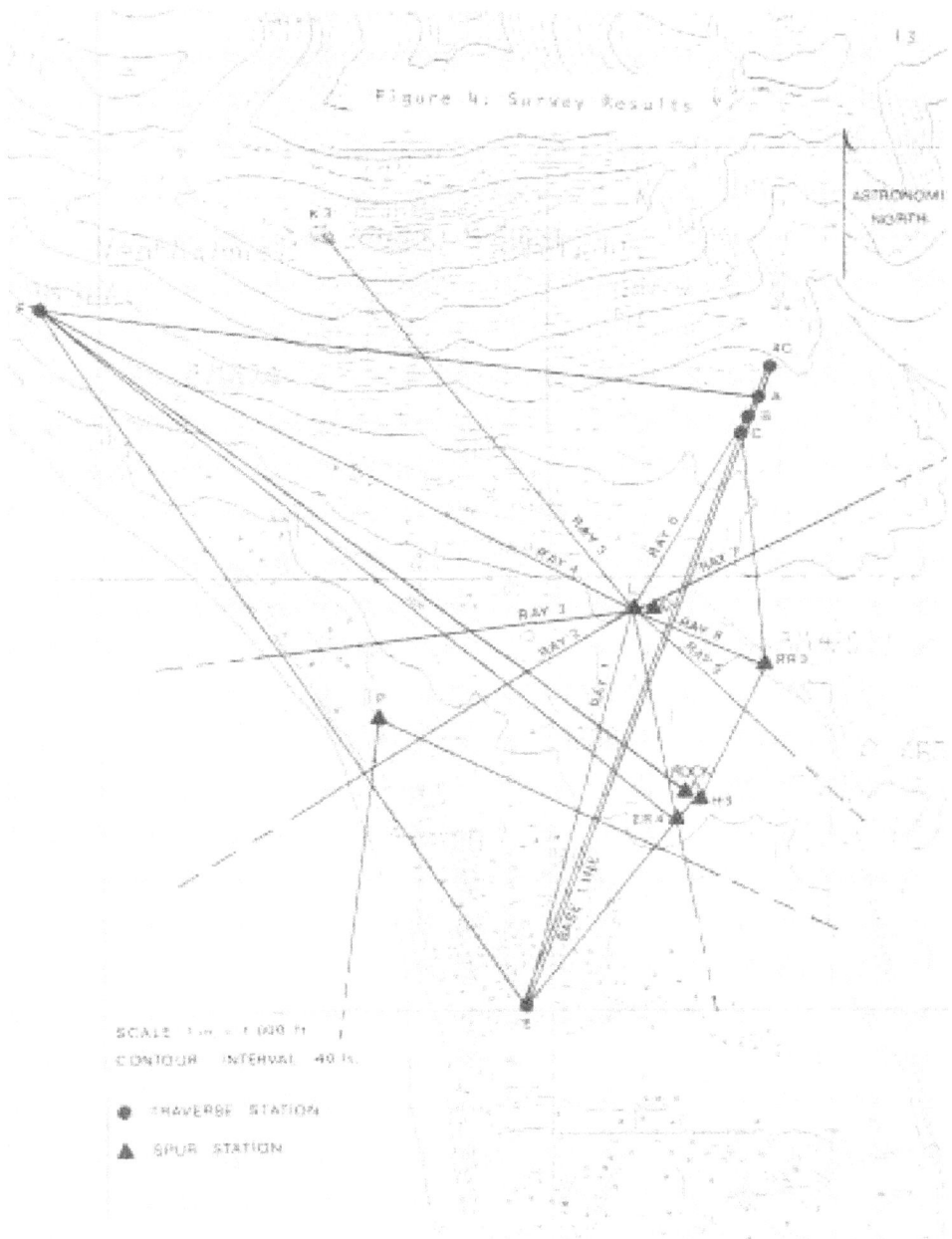

Costaggini's triangulation survey establishing longitude

The English method included also the setting up of an engraved
plack on a sturdy post or tree in addition to the cairns and engraved stones,

which Fletcher recorded they left upon the site. Sir Humphrey Gilbert in 1583 in Newfoundland also recorded setting up a survey and lead plack. [12]

Bawlf reported in his research that evidence of Drake's survey was "the most important artifact of Elizabethan science yet found in North America." [13]

Gitzen has remarked that "although Jensen and Viles' specific interpretations of all the marks on the stones may not always be correct, their conclusion of a Drake land claim was correct. Research of these markings has led to a direct link to the Copernicus system published in 1543 as well as to other 16th century mathematical symbols then in vogue with the Queen's augur, John Dee."[14]

In the building of the cairns and monuments, it seems likely that the Indians would have taken great interest and assisted in the work of carrying on the survey. From Fletcher's journal we learn "they are a people of a tractable, free, and loving nature, without guile or treachery. . . sending the arrow neither far off, nor with any great force; and yet are the men commonly so strong of body, that, which two or three of our men could hardly bear, any one of them could take upon his back, and without grudging carry it easily away, up hill and down hill an English mile altogether." It would seem the above is "a definite reference to the monument markers and cairns which they would have carried for Drake's men in surveying Neahkahnie Mountain." [15]

Tillamook Indian Culture

Other significant aspects of their culture were noted by Fletcher which do not occur among the Milvok Indians 300 miles south in northern California. When the multitudes of tribes came visiting Drake and his men, they were proceeded by their *Hy'oh*, their king among them, who was of a large body, with a goodly aspect, and carrying a 'power stick' of black wood. In addition to the shell necklaces which came from trade with the northern Salish, they used and prized a "fireweed", soft as silk, a plant that appeared first after a burning had taken place and when it went to seed produced a plume of down much prized as a symbol among their chiefs. [16]

In addition to the *pet'ah*, wapato root, the *ta'bah* tobacco plant, and their manner of constructing canoes, the Europeans observed in their vicinity what Fletcher called a "conie", a land otter of considerable size, evidence of their salmon runs in the spring, and certain waterproof baskets indigenous to the area. Though their dwellings were of a particular round house dug into the dirt and entered through the roof at the time Drake visited, it is now thought that they adopted Drake's longhouse, which was prevalent among them when Lewis and Clark visited the area, a practice not found among the California Indians. [17]

Another name for the *pet'ah* or wapato root is "arrowhead plant" due to the shape of its leaves above ground that can absorb or ward off the sun's rays as required. It was the tubers growing in the soft mud that were harvested. Lewis and Clark were able to purchase it from the Indians during their winter on the Columbia River in 1805-6. They named the present Sauvie's Island near the present city of Portland "Wapato Island" for the great quantities that grew there. The Nehalem Indians had a trade route on the Nehalem River whose counter-clockwise circular loop pass-

Map courtesy of the Salem Statesman Journal

es a short distance from there, returning to within 14 miles of its original source, which one can see on the adjacent present-day map. [18]

Nehalem Bay is between Rockaway Beach and Manzanita on the map; one can see also the large bay at Tillamook and the small one at Whale's Cove between Depoe Bay and Lincoln City. Again it is evident that Nehalem Bay is the only one that conforms to the *Portus Nove Albionis* on the Hondius map shown in Chapter 1.

Fletcher also described the dress wherein the Oregon Indians wore fur garments down to the waist and the women wore rush skirts, also necklaces of shells of great value found only in the off-shore waters of Puget Sound which found their way down to Nehalem. [19]

In regard to Drake's transfer of the name Nova Albion from Vancouver Island to this spot, Fletcher had this to say: "This country our general named Albion, and that for two causes: the one in respect of the white banks and cliffs, which lie toward the sea: the other, that it might have some affinity, even in name also, with our own country, which was sometimes so called." [20]

His description of dedicating the land to England is also given:

"a plate of brass, fast nailed to a great and firm post; whereon is engraved her graces name, and the day and year of our arrival there. . . underneath was likewise engraved the name of our general & c. The Spaniards never had any dealing, or so much as set a foot in this country; the utmost of their discoveries, reaching only to many degrees southward of this place."

This in the 1628 document ought to have settled for posterity the legitimacy of the English claim, which, at least at that time, they had every right to follow through upon, especially as the Spaniards seemed to honor it. When the Spanish carried on their explorations two centuries later, they skipped that jurisdiction, and explored only above the English claims. In any case, regarding the plate of brass adopted by California as proof of Drake's landing which proved to be a hoax, **there would be no significance of Drake making a claim on what was Spanish territory** (boldface added). [21]

And finally, there are no Indian legends among those in California about men appearing in ships with wings whom they regarded as gods or supreme beings. We leave Drake's departure, the heartfelt farewells of the Indians as they lit fires on the mountain to say goodbye, and especially his three-day sojourn fourteen miles below Nehalem on the St. James Islands for another telling at the end of our book. The date given was July 23, 1579, though as previously stated, the date may have been August 23 in order to help cover for the northern journey which preceded it.

We do not know what became of Tello's Bark. In the John Drake deposition for the inquisition in Lima where he was taken after capture on another venture a few years later, he said they left it at Nehalem Bay. But there are also about twenty of the crew missing who did not cross the great South Sea with Drake. One is inclined to think that after the tremendous labor Drake had been through to accomplish his task, he had either taken them with him to try to cross the Strait of Anian and lost them there, or he might have directed them to go through alone as a final triumph of his journey.

He must have felt such supreme confidence at one point, having accomplished so much, that he felt Elizabeth would honor his success in starting a colony; would, in addition, have been willing to launch another voyage to further dedicate it; and especially to rescue the twenty mariners who stayed to complete the purpose of their journey. That was not to be, as we will see.

Elizabeth was in the midst of a tiff with her favorite, the earl of Leicester, over his secret affair and then marriage to Lettice Knollys, and was considering marriage to the duke of Enjou, next in line to the king of France. If she could not honor her long-time confidant with a victory of some sort, she would in no wise honor a commoner such as Drake, whom she had sent on a mission nearly impossible to achieve, but certainly one that she had no mandate to acknowledge.

The Moluccas

W hether Drake departed on July 23 or August 23 and whether he first attempted to return by way of the Strait of Anian we will never know. We do know that according to the journal "the entire voyage through the Indies until he departed the south coast of Java allegedly consumed an incredible six months", a total of 139 days to cover in the extreme perhaps 3,000 miles, 20 miles per day,. Yet Drake was a superb sailor who had demonstrated how quickly he could move. [22]

It is difficult, therefore, to track his voyage and expenditure of time in the crossing, but one can at least attempt to account for whatever encounters and activities remained after his records were edited. His first recorded encounter was with a Portuguese carrack in November 1579 on the seas south of the Philippines where he was bound for the Moluccas.

The carrack at first attempted to arouse those on the *Golden Hinde* as they drew near but observed only two men on deck who declined to respond. As they followed them the *Hinde* returned decked out with flags and pennants, whereupon the Portuguese began firing upon them. Drake had turned their stern toward the carrack, making a narrow target, and was able to get away.

They had a pressing need for food, however, and also needed a map through the archipelago. At the first landfall they were besieged with a hundred canoes offering coconuts, fish, potatoes, and fruit in trade. Their numbers were too many, however. They climbed aboard snatching and stealing everything they could lay their hands upon. Drake and his men were barely able to eject them, whereupon hundreds more appeared. Not allowing them again on board, they found themselves barraged with stones and had to fire one of their cannons, killing about twenty of them. [23]

They came thereafter to Mindanao, southernmost of the Philippines where at an island two native fishermen offered to lead them to the Moluccas. They arrived there after a few days. They came to the first of four small islands near the equator which are considered the main islands of trade among about 70 islands spread over hundreds of miles. These four had been ruled by sultans for centuries until the Portuguese in 1521 conquered Tidore, and then Ternate, and themselves monopolized the spice trade.

Ternate was reconquered by the sultan Babu, and at Drake's approach he sent war canoes out to defend the island against what he thought were the Portuguese. Drake sent a velvet cloak as a present to Babu, who, upon finding that they were English, inaugurated a huge pageant for their welcome consisting of three banks of rowers, the sultan finally arriving in a royal *cavacoa* rowed by 80 slaves.

Drake fired his cannons in salute and the orchestra struck up a tune to welcome him. What ensued was a royal entertainment, a grand welcome, and the trade Drake had been seeking. [24]

Thus a truce came about between Drake and the sultan. It seems that Babu was concerned that the Portuguese would again conquer his island, and he greatly desired English support. Drake assured him that within two years he would "decorate" the sea with English ships for whatever need Babu might have. He bestowed upon him numerous gifts, and, in exchange the sultan agreed to supply Drake with six tons of cloves and gave him a "rich ring to give to Queen Elizabeth." [25]

From Ternate Drake headed toward Java, 1,000 miles to the southwest edge of the Indian Ocean. On his second day from Ternate he came to anchor at a small wooded island in the Banggai Archipelago where he was able to unload the *Golden Hinde* and pull her ashore for careening. Inhabitants of nearby islands began supplying him with fish, fruit, and other fresh foods which greatly revived the health of Drake's crew.

The providence of the islands, therefore, led Drake to a painful but much needed decision. He decided to leave Maria and the two Negro men who had accompanied them from the Americas, who would remain on the island, provided with provisions and what they would need to sustain themselves.

The anonymous account later revealed that after he left Maria and company on the island and proceeded toward Java he unfortunately struck a subterranean reef and was driven hard aground. The next morning he and his crew waited in vain for the tide to lift them off, whereupon they prayed for divine intervention. To relieve their load they threw overboard many provisions, eight cannons, and three tons of the cloves. Finally at four o'clock in the afternoon the *Golden Hinde* suddenly slid off into deep water. Finding no leaks aboard they determined that it was a reef they had struck, not an offshore rock. Drake was exceedingly angry with Fletcher at one point, however, who contended that their mishap was in retribution for the execution of Doughty.

Because of the delay in Drake's own account of their journey in the *World Encompassed*, which was not published until 1628, there were many discrepancies concerning Drake's journey through the East Indies. Nor did that much-edited journal explain the loss of so much time. Many accounts that came forward had radically differing dates in their attempts to come within the requirements of the queen to cover up their possible search for the straits of Anian. The only date that can be agreed upon is January 9, 1580, which was when they had the mishap on the reef. [26]

After the mishap, and according to the 1628 account, contrary winds drove them far to the east toward Timor, finally reaching Java after a voyage of two months. The problem with this is that there were much shorter routes, and it was the monsoon season when the winds should have been in their favor. In addition, locations were described which have never been found, the entire voyage through the Indies taking an incredible six months.

It is thought they might have visited Bali and Lambok, the last strongholds of the Hindu religion in Indonesia from his description of the people, people who later said they remembered his visit. It may be that this was the island he called Barativa. [27]

Uncontested are the accounts from the *World Encompassed* that he visited the port of Cilacap on the south coast of Java, sent gifts to their local Baja, and spent two weeks receiving a succession of chiefs from neighboring areas. [28]

Being entertained and welcomed they were able to fill their water casks and take on board hens, goats, fruit, coconuts, sugarcane, and seven tons of rice. Evidently there were two Portuguese spies among their visitors, for they learned afterward from the villagers that there was a great ship on its way to approach them. Needless to say, Drake gave the order to set sail, and it was from there that they began their trip across the Indian Ocean to round the Cape of Good Hope. This was over the equator where their supply of water was critical. Fortunately when there were storms they were able to lay tarps and collect rainwater.

It took a month and another 3,000 miles to arrive in Sierra Leone on the coast of western Africa. There they found that the mangroves, trees with long interlacing roots growing on the muddy banks of streams, had magnificent oysters growing at the roots. The natives supplied them also with lemons and other fruits. Drake is thought to have been one of very few navigators who knew the value of whatever green vegetables and fruits they might find to protect the men from scurvy, which took many lives of seamen.

They then set sail and did not land again until they reached Plymouth, at least by some accounts. There are, however, two letters which exist among the French which indicate that they spent time at La Rochelle for careening, where those he visited gave correspondence to that effect. Drake was simply elongating his stay at various locations. And, as remarked earlier, we will never know what happened to Tello's Bark and twenty or so missing men. [29]

Instead he was the first European captain to sail a ship around the world—Magellan's being the first *ship* to do so—sailing more than 40,000 miles. It is agreed that "he was at that time the finest English commander of a fleet of sailing vessels, skilled in navigation, and also devoted heart and soul to God, Queen Elizabeth I and England." [30]

— Chapter 10 —

The Aftermath

Drake's Return

There had been a crisis in Elizabeth's court over Drake's voyage. Cecil was an enemy to the expedition, but Walsingham had been quite willing to take shares in the greatest piratical expedition in history. As for the queen, when she finally gave assent to the voyage, it was the following aim that was uppermost in her mind. "Drake!" she exclaimed, "So it is that I would gladly be revenged on the king of Spain for divers injuries that I have received!" She had applied to the right man.

Word came by Panama of Drake's successes "and so loud was the outcry raised by the Spanish ambassador, that if Drake had failed to return home safe and rich, the victory at court might have rested with Cecil's more timid policy, and the victory in the world policy might have fallen to Spain and Rome." [1]

Drake's first question as he and his crew approached the harbor at Plymouth: "Was the queen alive?" As previously related, he then waited four months to be brought into her presence to relate his story of the achievement of their goals, at which time she condescended to accept his invitation to a banquet on board the *Golden Hinde*. The French ambassador being present, she obligingly conferred a knighthood upon her servant Drake. It was the most important one ever conferred by an English sovereign, for it was a direct challenge to Spain and an appeal to the people of England to look to the sea for their strength. "In view of this deed, disapproved by her faithful Cecil, who shall say Elizabeth could never act boldly. Her bold decisions are few and can be numbered, but each of them began an epoch. . . After the accolade at Deptford, events drifted towards open war as fast as Philip's slow spirit could move." [2]

We briefly recall that in 1579 Elizabeth was contemplating a marriage to the duke of Anjou, future king of France, due to her anger with Leicester over the Lettice affair, but the unpopularity of that marriage with the people led to her being again reconciled to Leicester.

In 1581 there was posited a joint rule of Mary and James in Scotland, but because of an assassination plot against Elizabeth, Mary was deserted by her son James. By 1584 the breach with Spain expanded over Elizabeth's support of the Netherlands, and the prince of Orange was assassinated. Spain began an open enterprise of building huge ships, preparatory to war.

In 1585 Elizabeth sent Drake with a fleet of twenty-one sail to the West Indies, where he burned the town of Santiago, plundered those of Santo Domingo and Cartagena, and razed two Spanish forts on the coast of Florida. In this expedition he lost 700 men to sickness and brought back to England the survivors of a party in Roanoke, Virginia that Sir Walter Raleigh had sent out from England.

At the same time, Thomas Cavendish—a gentleman of Suffolk who had dissipated half his property, sold the remainder, then built or purchased three small vessels—sailed in quest of adventure to the Spanish Main. Like Drake, he made the circuit of the globe, but unlike him, he added little to the stock of general knowledge. Again we have the prognosis of history as told by the nineteenth century historians: "The object of both was to enrich themselves at the expense of the Spaniards." [3]

The foregoing maritime expeditions, however, caused no immediate reaction from Spain. It was the subjugation or independence of the Netherlands that was to be decided in the next confrontation; and there, as it turned out, Philip had little to dread as long as the conduct of the hostile army was entrusted to the presumption and incapacity of Leicester,

At one point harmony had been restored, and Elizabeth sought to restore peace with Philip. Leicester, however, sought a continuation of the war. But it was foretold that the Spanish squadrons would unite and invade, and this fear wrought so powerfully on the fears and feelings of Elizabeth that Drake was dispatched from Plymouth to watch the harbors of Spain, and to oppose the Spanish fleet if a merger was attempted.

But that officer had no intention to confine himself to the letter of his instructions. He hastened to Cadiz, bore fearlessly into the harbor, dispersed by his fire the Spanish galleys, and sacked, or burned, or captured, or destroyed, no fewer than eight sail, partly ships of war, partly merchantmen, either recently arrived from the east or equipped to proceed to the West Indies. From Cadiz the conquerors returned by the coast of Portugal. In the waters of the Tagus they insulted the marquis of Santa Cruz, the admiral of Spain, and at sea their labors were rewarded by the capture of the *St. Philip*, a carrack of the largest dimension and laden with much valuable merchandise.

It is in this confrontation that Drake is quoted as saying that he had "singed the Spanish king's beard!" This triumph at Cadiz and this capture of the rich merchant ship were of permanent importance. The English ever after that time more cheerfully set upon those huge, castle-like ships which before they were afraid of and afterward also set up a company of East Indian merchants in a gainful traffic to the Orient. [4]

Upon Drake's arrival home after the battle at Cadiz he was received with gratitudes by all but his sovereign. Elizabeth trembled lest so great a loss should awaken in the breast of Philip the desire for revenge. In answer to a letter from Farnese, duke of Parma, the Spanish commander, she assured him that Drake had been sent out for the sole purpose of opposing any attempt at invasion, that orders had been forwarded to him to abstain from every act of hostility; and that as he had disobeyed her commands he should suffer for his presumption on his return.

Elizabeth then sent her minister Lord Buckhurst to signify her displeasure. Farnese affected to be satisfied, but prepared to play a similar game. Cadiz had not been the only problem. The threat of England's assistance in the Netherlands was imminent.

ALESSANDRO FARNESE, PRINCE OF PARMA
(1545-1592)

The Siege of Antwerp

A t this point in our story we note that little is said in the volumes on English history in the *Historians' History* about the Battle of Antwerp of 1584 in the Netherlands which preceded England's involvement in 1585. In the volume on the history of the Netherlands, however, we learn much from our historians about the status of Spain in the European world at that time leading up to that battle, after which there was indeed a question of whether Netherlands should turn to France or to England for assistance against the Spanish.

William the Silent, the "Prince of Orange", as history calls him, had been murdered on the 10th of July 1584 by a single obscure fanatic, who achieved a victory — by the offer of gold from Philip 11 — greater than had the armies of Spain in the low countries for a decade. One by one the provinces had finally succumbed to Spanish invasion, and the Prince of Orange had been their one hope of leadership to sustain them. At this late period in the life of Philip he exerted a final fanaticism in support of the Catholic church, and thousands of so-called heretics were burned in each of the conquered provinces.

We wonder what would motivate a sovereign to such invasion and murder. Is this the same Philip who once married Mary Tudor and wooed her sister, Elizabeth? The historian Grattan describes Philip at this stage in his life:

"A small, dull, elderly, imperfectly educated, patient, plodding invalid, with white hair and protruding under-jaw and dreary visage, was sitting day after day, seldom speaking, never smiling, seven or eight hours out of every twenty-four, at a writing table covered with heaps of interminable dispatches, all to be scrawled over in the margin . . . in a big schoolboy's hand and style. . . interminable epistles which contained the irresponsible commands of this one individual. . . and the destiny of countless millions of the world's inhabitants. . . [It was a] system of government against which the Netherlands had protested and revolted. . . to put an end to which they had been devoting their treasure and their blood for nearly the length of one generation. . . which. . . had just brought about the death of the foremost statesman of Europe.

"The industrious Philip. . . had just sent three bullets through the body of William the Silent at his dining-room door in Delft. 'Had it only been done two years earlier,' observed the patient old man, 'much trouble might have been spared me; but it is better late than never.'

"Philip stood ruler, by divine decree, of all America, the East Indies, the whole Spanish peninsula, the better portion of Italy, the seventeen Netherlands, and many other possessions far and near, and he contemplated annexing to this extensive property the kingdoms of France, of England, and Ireland. The holy league. . . was to exterminate heresy and establish the Spanish dominion in France. . 'The holy league,' said Duplsis-Mornay, 'which has overleaped so many lands and seas, thinks nothing inaccessible.'" [5]

The Seige of Antwerp showing the indentation of the country

This age of Philip was also the age of Luther, Calvin, Walsingham, Sidney, Raleigh, Queen Elizabeth and William Shakespeare. It was not an age of blindness, but of glorious light. This king firmly believed that the heretics of the Netherlands, of France, or of England could escape eternal perdition only by being extirpated from the earth by fire and sword, and therefore, felt it his duty to devote his life to their extermination. Still more, he believed that his own authority lay over the bodies of those heretics.

At that period our western civilization was in the balance. Where might France, the Netherlands, the British Empire and the Americas be today if Philip had succeeded? We proceed now to the battle of Antwerp, wherein the Dutch did not succeed in overcoming the strategies of the Alessandro of Parma, the adroit Spanish statesman and general who was devastating, one by one, the provinces.

At Antwerp he constructed a bridge over a narrow part of the river Schelde in order to prevent traffic to the city and thereby cut off means of survival from her imports. It was a mighty stream, bridged and mastered in the very teeth of winter, a spectacle capturing the attention of Europe for seven months, and on the result of which it was thought depended the fate of all the Netherlands and, perhaps of all Christendom. [6]

Numerous plans were devised for the purpose of breaking down the bridge, among which Giambelli, an engineer of Mantua, undertook to blow it up by means of two fire-ships, laden each with six or seven thousand pounds of powder. One of these, taking fire before it had approached sufficiently near the works, proved useless, but the other, named the *Hope*, of about eighty tons' burden, exploded with fatal and terrific effect. About eight hundred Spanish soldiers were mingled in one horrible and promiscuous slaughter. The shock was so violent that it was felt at the distance of nine miles, and the waters of the Schelde inundated the surrounding country.

Unfortunately, the vessels of the Netherlanders were left in ignorance of the rupture of the bridge till Parma had time to repair it, which he effected in two or three days. Here we must inform the reader that the war between Spain and the Netherlands was to last a total of eighty years and was only into its second decade at that point. We will see now the efforts of England thereafter to affect a change in the balance of rule there and the obscene character of the queen's favorite, Leicester, in his attempt to make himself ruler there while assisting the provinces.

The Netherlands Fiasco

Spain had gained a near complete control of the Low Countries, after twenty years of war to combat the spread of Protestantism. When Charles V abdicated from the empire which had controlled Spain and most of Europe, he left Philip II ruler over Spain and Netherlands. Philip would then lose control because of his fanatic application of the Inquisition to those enlightened states, as we shall see.

It is estimated that between 50,000 and 100,000 lost their lives to the most gruesome forms of torture and burning on the continent, St. Bartholomew's massacre in 1572 being one of the most flagrant events. In 1585, however, the Reformation had opened the minds of men to that intellectual freedom without which political enfranchisement is a worthless privilege. Manufacturing, however, had progressed to a high perfection, and the opulence of the Netherlands was unequaled anywhere in Europe at that time. In addition, the invention of the printing press had led to an enlightened and reading public unwilling any longer to be subjugated. [7]

Some contemporary historians of England skip the details of Leicester's fiasco in the Netherlands, and it is necessary to go back into the *Historians' Histories* of 1904 to glean the treachery that he inflicted there in the Netherlands history. Through historian T. Knightly we review more of that event and its result: "On the 10th of July, 1584, the great prince of Orange was shot by a man. . . who said he had been kept for some time in the Jesuit's college at Treves which was endorsed by the duke of Parma, Philip's man in Netherlands." William, Prince of Orange, had been among their most valiant defenders of the fourteen provinces, and his assassination triggered the offer of sovereignty to Elizabeth. Instead of accepting the responsibility of the rule of Netherlands, she agreed to offer her armies and Leicester, for if the Dutch were subdued, England would certainly be attacked. [8]

The details of their agreement were very well spelled out—5000 men and 1000 horse—in exchange as security the English would have garrisons in Flushing, Rammehans, and Briel, and two fortresses in Holland until the debts were liquidated, with no demands of control or sovereignty after the engagement and only a repayment of her monetary outlay. The latter elements Leicester invalidated immediately. He first sent Sir Philip Sidney with an army to establish a presence. Sir John Norris also arrived with a command of English forces.

Then Leicester, totally without military experience, landed at Flushing in December 1585, with 50 ships, accompanied by the earl of Essex, his stepson, and a company of nobles, knights, and gentlemen to the number of 500. He immediately organized tourneys, banquets and processions in order to draw attention to himself and his contingents. The states duly bestowed the title of governor and captain-general of the United Provinces upon him, gave him a guard, and treated him nearly like a sovereign, which greatly angered Elizabeth, who had pledged not to interfere with the political or civil government of the country. At one point Leicester falsely accused a Dutch officer and demanded legal counsel.

It soon became obvious the lamentable condition of the English soldiers, unpaid and starving, which fed the hopes of Parma and Philip that they would yet take the place. Having no pride whatsoever, Leicester began bragging in Delft that his family—through Lady Jane Grey and family— had been unjustly deprived of the crown of England, causing a shudder in all who heard him.

Meanwhile, the English were singularly impressed with the opulence and stately appearance of the country and its inhabitants whom they had come to defend and began to feel like those protected rather than as their "protectress". Although the Netherlands had been at war with Spain for twenty years, their commerce had continued to thrive and their resources to increase. Leicester's next fiasco was to undermine all of their legal protections by enacting an embargo essential to their trade and continued progress.

Philip moved slowly in light of these developments for he had "planned his invasion of England, in most of its details, a necessary part of which was the reduction of Holland and Zealand." [9]

First there was a siege at Grave; next Venico and Naues fell to Parma. Leicester then took the field without forces sufficiently strong to encounter Parma. It was during the siege of Neuse that Leicester commanded Sidney to undertake the invasion of Flanders. Without waiting for an assault, Sidney was enjoined to sally out with his body of musketeers and cavalry, wherein he met his death, in a great show of bravery.

All of a sudden, Sluys, a fort of the first consequence, garrisoned partly by Englishmen and partly by Hollanders, was besieged. "The earl arrived, assembled his forces, and made three unsuccessful attempts to defend the fort. Sluys capitulated, July 30, 1587, and the earl in a few days became the execration of the people. From the conflicting reports of Leicester and his opponents, it is difficult to form a correct notion of the proceedings." [10]

Nonetheless, Leicester was held to account for the debacle which had resulted from the inadequacy of his command. They charged him with aspiring to the sovereignty of the provinces. Leicester, on the contrary, complained bitterly of the ingratitude of the Hollanders. Nevertheless, his influence with Elizabeth was apparently gone. She believed he had neglected her instructions.

He was recalled from his service, threw himself at her feet, and conjured her to have pity on her former favorite. Though Elizabeth relented, the question before the counsel would be: "She had sent him to the Netherlands in honor; would she receive him back in disgrace?" Coming before the privy counsel, instead of kneeling at the foot of the table he took his accustomed seat. When her secretary, Lord Buckhurst, began to read the charges against him, he arose and inveighed against the baseness and perfidy of his accuser, who was then ordered to consider himself a prisoner in his own house, which lasted until the death of Leicester. It is apparent that Elizabeth could not bear to subject her former favorite to his just punishment. [11]

Hatton, Latest Favorite

Leicester was Elizabeth's oldest favorite and confidante, but was no longer called to her side. For some time she had courted the proximity of the somewhat younger, more dashing Sir Christopher Hatton. Certainly Drake never had a chance of entering her private circle. It is even said, but we don't agree, that Drake squandered his new wealth in an attempt to buy approval from rich and powerful people. [12]

We give the above late 19th century historian's opinion as typical of those who had adopted history's assessments. His attempts to buy approval, however, would have been totally out of character, He was well-aware that he had been chosen for the journey of circumnavigation and to extend the English claims in the New World, solely because of his experience as a pirate. A further proof of their social distance is in the fact that Thomas Doughty whom he beheaded was Christopher Hatton's secretary. Elizabeth and Hatton had received a bounteous return on their investments from that voyage and wanted nothing more of Drake except his expertise in war and navigation.

In 1587, the queen was able to satisfy the ambition of this latest favorite, Hatton, who had been for twenty-five years a member of her privy chamber. It was observed that over time she gradually assigned to him a much more valuable present on occasions than to others and that she spent hours at a time with him in private. It became the general belief that he occupied that place in her affection which had formerly been assigned to the earl of Leicester. In 1577 she had conferred upon him a knighthood. It was observed, to his favor, that at times he employed his authority to shield the poor and friendless from oppression.

One who caused Hatton some jealousy, however, was young Sir Walter Raleigh. In 1582 Raleigh received some distinct work of royal favor. Hatton was offended, withdrew himself sullenly from court, and shut himself up in the country.

With an exchange of correspondence, involving a play upon pet names she gave her favorites, Hatton suffered himself to be persuaded by the queen to return. When, however, he was elevated to the lord chancellorship, his ambition was sufficiently gratified, and Elizabeth was perhaps loosened from the constant attendance of a then old and querulous servant. Remarkably, both Leicester and Hatton had grown old, and there would yet be young Essex, after the death of Leicester.

A word about Raleigh's ongoing assignments under the auspices of Elizabeth: It is said that in 1579 he was stopped by the council from taking part in a voyage planned by his half-brother, Sir Humphrey Gilbert, and in 1583 he risked L2,000 in an expedition in which Gilbert perished. It is said by our historian, however, that "he was one of those who were dissatisfied unless they could pursue some public object in connection with their chase after a private fortune." We learn in our chapter on martyrs, none-the-less, what a tremendous price he paid as years went by. [13]

Later, on February 16th of 1587, after the trial and execution of Mary Queen of Scots—the order for which Elizabeth at first signed and then tried to avoid responsibility for—she decided to distract the attention of the public by holding the public funeral for Sir Philip Sidney, as we described briefly in Chapter 1. He was the much-lauded poet and statesman and the hero of Leicester's siege in the Netherlands, which fiasco she could not bring herself to acknowledge.

As you may recall, brave comrades of Sidney in his battlefields were there, and there was the ambitious Leicester, who had not yet resigned the scheme of being sovereign of the Netherlands. But the people gazed upon Drake, the great mariner who had circumnavigated the world and carried terror of the English flag though all the Spanish settlements. His story had not been revealed, but his presence helped satisfy their curiosity and lent prestige to the empty pageantry of that day. [14]

There were many things in the reign of Elizabeth which are opposed to our ideas of freedom. It was essentially an arbitrary government. But the people were thriving, they were living under an equal administration of justice; and the feudal system was gone. The people had arms in their hands and they were taught to use them.

It was certain at that time that Spain was making plans to invade England. The people, by Elizabeth their queen and her ministers, had taken the life of the Catholic Mary Queen of Scots, but that queen had had the scheme of bringing back to England and Scotland the faith for which Philip was exacting the horrors of the Inquisition. The day to decide which of the two principles, Catholic or Protestant, would rule the Christian world was fast approaching. [15]

England's final defiance to all comers, the execution of Mary, Queen of Scots, was the volition of the people rather than of their sovereign. Without these events the Reformation would be over and war, civil war in England, backed by Spain most likely, would have occurred.

Elizabeth's worst error was to avoid responsibility for Mary's death by ruining her Secretary Davison, upon whom she shifted blame. Knighting Drake was her best action, so to speak. Mary's execution united England to resist. The limitations imposed on the scope of the war against which Drake and Raleigh fretted, may be counted among the blessings of a reign on which the Englishmen have reason to look back as the most fortunate as well as the most wonderful in their history. It was to the glory and maritime excellence of men such as these that they were able to succeed.

At the end of Elizabeth's reign four million people, not wealthy nor populous enough to seize Spain's possessions or to found an empire of their own, were able, by a fluke, to pave the way for the Stuart epoch and the path of the Puritans. In that way lay a greater future for Anglo-Saxons.

Elizabeth signs Mary Queen of Scots' death warrant

Before dealing with that great and fortunate victory over the Spanish Armada, we digress to further explain the composite evil from within the heart and soul of Spain at that time which was leading to her demise. We must go back in her history to understand what had led her to expel her most productive people, the Jews, the Moslems, and then her own people through the onset of the Inquisition.

— Chapter 11 —

Spain and the Inquisition

"Letters of Marque"

Certain historians take no account of the trade embargo which Spain had placed upon her possessions in the New World and the atrocities she performed in order to enforce it. In assessing the alleged rapacity of English privateers they write as though Spain's embargo did not exist, and that the plunder that finally took place had no claim to vengeance for unprovoked attacks and losses of the English in their attempts to bring much-needed trade to the Spanish colonies.

We remind the reader of Francis Drake's ventures to trade in the New World with his cousin John Hawkins before their third and fateful journey in 1568 into the Caribbean where they had never been before. We repeat this story for emphasis that indeed vengeance and a challenge to Spain's hegemony was due.

Driven by a series of storms from returning to England after trading slaves and commodities in outlying parts, they sought entry into the principal port called San Juan de Ulúa. This time they were in dire straits due to their leaky boats and lack of provisions. To complicate their predicament, the new viceroy from Spain arrived and a major battle occurred. Of eight English ships and some 400 men and boys, they escaped finally with but two ships, Hawkins on the *Minion* and Drake on the *Judith*, and, losing contact in the battle, arrived home separately.

Following the debacle of Hawkins defeat at de Ulúa there was no longer a reason to seek a fair trade with needy Spanish colonists. Elizabeth began to issue *"letters of marque"*, her permission to exact a recompense for their losses. These were fully authorized and controlled by the queen in conference with her councillors. No sea captain would dare venture into Spanish territory without the required "license" from the queen, who expected to use her own resources to outfit the expedition and to obtain her share in the profits.

We begin again to wonder how this had all come about. Spain at the time of Columbus and the pope's bull which established the demarcation line had not been at that time so aggressive and hostile toward the rest of the known world. Jews and Moslems lived there peaceably and there was little diligence in persecuting the people for their lack of orthodoxy.

Yet we know that Columbus's discovery of the New World, in 1492, coincided with Spain's expulsion of the Jews from Spain, where they had co-existed with Catholics and Moslems for seven hundred years, perhaps more peaceably than anywhere else in Europe. We might wonder what caused their sudden expulsion, followed closely by that of the Moslems, in a country that had benefited from their special talents and contributions for so many centuries. Even more ponderous, one wonders why they suddenly conceived that the pope's demarcation line now gave Catholics an ascendancy they had not had before.

We first look at the extraordinary vile treatment of the Jews in other countries before their expulsion from Spain. The guilt was perhaps stronger in England, where they had been expelled centuries before. The tool Spain used to claim the New World was the church which expelled them, which England had already done. Spain in essence was following in England's footsteps, and since the treatment of the Jews is one of the greatest scourges of mankind it may be well to review that history.

England's Expulsion of Jews

It is ironic that the Old Testament upon which monotheism and Christianity is based is actually a history of the Hebrews and their beliefs. We might also be persuaded by Paul Goodman in *History of the Jews* that "an uncompromising adherence to ethical Monotheism and to the moral purpose of human life is the imperishable Jewish contribution to the foundation of civilization." [1]

As he wrote in 1904, well before the holocaust:

"This people, whom the historians and geographers of ancient Hellas deigned to notice as a strange Syrian tribe, had already produced one of the most remarkable literatures of all time as well as a body of men who were later on acclaimed as the ethical and religious leaders of mankind. While in their most flourishing political state the Israelites formed only a petty Asiatic kingdom, the descendants of those who served the Pharaohs and whose national existence was wiped out by Nebuchadnezzar the Babylonian, about 2500 years ago, yet they still represent one of the most active and progressive human groups of today." [2]

Of the Spanish epoch Goodman says: "It is a pregnant indication of the vitality of the Jewish people that, at repeated periods in history, after adverse circumstances seemed to have entirely overwhelmed it, it rose superior to all obstacles, and played again an important part in the affairs of the world.

"While Christendom, enthralled by countless superstitions, had sunk into a deadly torpor, in which all love of inquiry and all search for truth were abandoned, the Jews were still pursuing the path of knowledge, amassing learning and stimulating progress with the same unflinching constancy that they manifested in their faith." [3]

Their superiority in philosophy and of their physicians and financiers, was second only to the Moors in the cultivation of natural science, and they were the chief interpreters of Arabian learning into western Europe. A principal transfer came about when they were captured by pirates and sold into various quarters of the world, where they became heads of new Jewish centers of learning, hence the arrival of Moses law at Enoch and the revival of Talmudic studies and Hebrew letters at Cordova, within the Moorish caliphate which preceded them into Spain. In the struggles of the Moorish kings and the breakup of the caliphate, Jews were forced to flee from one part of the peninsula to another wherein they came under Christian rulers at a time when there were tolerant treatment and equitable laws. [4]

After the Black Death of 1348-51 Jewish communities who were swept away by fire and sword found refuge in Poland, where they escaped the religious convulsions and religious fanaticism that tore central Europe into innumerable bleeding fragments. In a society of nobles and serfs, Jews were an advantage to

A JEW OF THE MIDDLE AGES

the country and were long recognized for their special abilities. Poland, especially, became an asylum for the Jews. [5]

The acceptance of Jews as having a useful place in the history of Spain was short-lived, however. The crusades introduced among the Jews that era of darkness which was to envelop them for centuries. When unable to make headway ousting the Muslims (a variant of Moslems) from Istanbul, the crusaders enacted a wholesale massacre of the Jews, broke their economic prosperity, and drew them entirely into money-lending and petty trading as part of a new relationship between East and West. [6]

This exclusion from the soil and every honorable profession or handicraft drove the Jews into those professions which, under abnormal conditions, lend themselves to extortion and exert a pernicious effect on both parties to a transaction, especially when used only by emperor and king, baron and bishop, to draw substance out of the people. [7]

Many Jews came over in 1070 with William the Conqueror as slaves and could rely only on being ransomed by brethren-in-faith or welcomed as honored guests. Richard the Lion-hearted attacked, murdered, plundered, and burned the houses of Jews whose wealth he then used to finance his crusade. [8]

King John imprisoned all Jews and extorted by the most violent means the wealth possessed by them. His tactics were copied by barons, other kings, and those Jews in Parliament. In England 298 Jews were executed in 1278. [9]

In October 1290 about 16,000 were exiled. Thereafter England spared further persecutions, because no professing Jew openly settled there until the middle of the 17th century. [10]

Moslems in Spain

To understand the Moslems, who adopted Islam as established by their prophet Mohammed in the seventh century A.D., it is necessary somewhat to understand the Arab race. Like the Hebrews, it had been in existence since recorded time and had a character of its own.

Arabs were known as Bedouins, or nomads, and it was said that the "son of the desert likes to reap where he has not sown." Thus, one wave of Arabs would slowly overtake another. Rome destroyed Damascus where they held sway in the year 106 A.D. but found that the Arabs were in no way suited to monarchy. The Bedoin has too strong a sense of independence. He is averse even to peaceful enterprises for his own profit, if they call for discipline and subordination. He could, however, keep his own savage kinsmen far more effectively in check than regular imperial or royal officials could.

At that time two new names for the Arabs came into existence, Saracens and Taits; and the name Saracen continued in use and was applied to all Arabs in the time of the Roman emperor Ptolomy. [11]

They were known only as a savage race notorious for hindering the march of caravans or levying heavy tolls upon them. In the Bible they were known for their traffic in incense, gold and precious stones. Yet those in the area of Yemen who were conquered by the Persians in 570 A.D. were thought to have acquired the art of writing at that time and a certain Christian influence. [12]

Christianity had a following among early Arabs, who had a tradition of a yearly festival at Mecca, certain persons even preaching a monotheistic faith more or less Christian. Therefore, it was fertile ground for Mohammed at the beginning of the seventh century to receive his own direct message from Allah. [13]

After his death in 632 A.D. his newly-founded Islam split into two factions: the Shiites who followed Ali, one of his sons-in-law, and the Sunnis who followed one of his fathers-in-law. In essence both follow the five pillars of Islam, revering Allah as the only god and Mohammed as his Prophet, praying five times a day, fasting during Ramadan, giving to charity, and making a pilgrimage to Mecca. Through the ages their differing precepts have varied regionally.

A SARACEN

The frequent wars between Rome and the Persians significantly weakened both Christians and Moslems at this time. As with the decline of Rome elsewhere, large areas were ravaged in Palestine, Syria, and Egypt. The Persians were then torn asunder by succession and the Moslems were under the rule of Heraclius.

When the Romans were defeated in 636 A.D., Islam, which had only slumbered, reawakened with true Semitic fury. Koreish led Islam from victory to victory. [14]

Thus began an era when the Arabs began to have a great influence in Europe. Spain, not yet united by Aragon and Castile, was especially an area of tolerance, where all the learning of the east found a fertile ground. The crusades did indeed bring greater misery than ever upon the wretched land of Palestine, but on the whole they affected the nations of Islam far less than those which adhered to the church of Rome.

The attacks of the Mongols were the first shock which destroyed the fairest flower of Islamic civilization. The destruction of Baghdad in 1258 inflicted a terrible burden on Arab culture. The Mongols annihilated the flourishing civilization of the East by destroying the great cities there and massacring their inhabitants. A remnant of Arab culture found refuge in Egypt, whither happily the Mongols did not penetrate. Yet even this conquest actually promoted the spread of Islam. The Mongols settled among the Moslems and soon went over to Islam themselves. The greater part of Asia Minor had already been won over by the Seljuks to Turkish nationality and the faith of Islam and from thence arose the empire of the Ottoman Turks, for centuries the terror of Europe.

At the very time when Islamism, after a protracted struggle, was thrust forth from Spain after 1492, the fierce and fanatical worshipers of the God of Arabia bore the banner of his prophet far on the way towards Europe. And while warriors fought for the glory of Allah, Arabic learning was zealously pursued in

THE ALHAMBRA

the theological schools of the Ottoman empire, as it had been in the Middle Ages. In Spain's dispersal of the Moslems to other parts of Europe the great simplicity of the religion of Mohammed made it possible to effect the restoration of its pristine purity in a far higher degree than the mighty efforts of the sixteenth and subsequent centuries could effect a return to primitive Christianity. [15]

Persecution of Jews in Spain

Christian Spain bore from the very beginning of its history an unenviable distinction in religious bigotry, and this expressed itself most emphatically in the case of the Jews. For a while they did not fare so badly, since their language was Spanish and Sephardic religion did not interfere with their becoming very useful citizens.

After the conquest of Granada, however, and the continued presence of the Moors in the peninsula, Spain began to focus on a takeover of religion over all of Spain. The easiest, and most profitable move they could make was the expulsion of the Jews, whose property would enrich them in their quest for supremacy among nations. Pressures of the church had already assimilated many of them into a professed Christianity, and their speech and thought refinements had become barely indistinguishable.

This was perhaps the reason for first developing the Holy Order, a system of courts with judicial power to distinguish heretics who secretly were still committed to their Jewish faith. The Jews were therefore the first to go, all those not professing Christianity or deemed to be heretic. They were given a certain time to sell all the worldly goods they could not carry with them—though gold was forbidden—and to depart. As we have indicated, England was not available to them, and they scattered all over Europe, Africa, and the middle east. [16]

As background to this, in February 1413 through November 1414 there had been a public disputation by Pope Benedict XIII on respective merits of Catholicism which outlined the falsehood of Judaism, therefore commanding the conversion of 35,000 Jews who wished to integrate and preserve their lives and property. Having thus assimilated, one can imagine the degree of betrayal they felt. "The deeper the Jews of Spain became embedded in the nation, the more painful was the wrench which tore them out with their very roots." [17]

It was under Ferdinand and Isabella that the Inquisition was organized: "the vilest organization ever devised for the enslavement of the human mind." This began before their expulsion, when Isabella became convinced by her mentors, including Torquemada, that it was her duty to the church to establish the Holy Order and to begin questioning the extent of the Jew's conversion to Christianity. Thousands paid their last penalty at the stake, where hundreds observed their last auto-de-fe (act of faith) and where gory bullfights are still the favorite entertainment.

In 1492, 200,000 Jews were expelled "for the sake of the human conscience to which civilized men of all opinions now pay sincere homage," as it was claimed. The reactions of those countries accepting them are most revealing: Don Isaac Abravnel of Italy and sultan Bayazid II of Turkey expressed surprise that Ferdinand and Isabella had impoverished their country and enriched theirs by expelling such useful subjects. [19]

Our story of Drake and his singular assault on the claims of this despotic nation must record that Spain, once a nation with prime standing among nations of Europe, began a gradual decline at this point which did not end when other nations were relaxing their hold on the minds of their people.

An interesting look into history beyond Francis Drake finds that when the Spanish colonies in the New World became aware that the successor to their king, as was the Enperor Charles V — who to them represented their "god" on earth — was imprisoned by another nation and had lost his sovereignty, they began their revolts against Spanish authority.

The Rise and Fall of Spain

Whereas Spain had become obsessed with heresy, Elizabeth's tactic in accommodating Catholics in England during their advance toward Protestantism resulted in no great persecution. As expressed by two nineteenth century historians, "Witchcraft and heresy are two crimes which commonly increase by punishment, and never are so effectively suppressed as by being totally neglected." [20]

In the marriage of Ferdinand of Aragon and Isabella of Castile in 1479 there was now a new Spain, though the government of the two kingdoms was separately administered under separate constitutions long after their time. Spain was at last a nation, fronting the world united, as far as the Spaniards of that time could be united, and the first reign of the new realm was the most glorious of all." [21]

The reign of Ferdinand and Isabella brought a new principle of vitality into a government which had been fast sinking into premature decrepitude. It was an era of reform, and the royal audiences, or chancery, the supreme and final court of appeal in civil cases, was entirely remodeled. No less that 4,000 suspected persons, it is computed, terrified by the prospect of speedy retribution for their crimes, escaped into the neighboring kingdoms of Portugal and Granada. The king and queen were at court in the Alcazar in Madrid every Friday, dispensing justice and providing advocates for the poor. [22]

It is said that Isabella revolutionized the institutions of their country, religious, political, military, and financial; and she consolidated her dominions, humiliated her nobles, cajoled her commons, defied the pope, reformed the clergy, and burned some ten thousand of her subjects. She deported a million more, and of the remainder she made a great nation. Yet, as the great historian Martin Hume has said, "The king and queen who made Spain great were the worst enemies she ever had."

She even took more effectual means than any of her predecessors to circumscribe the temporal powers of the clergy. Laws were enacted which were designed to limit their jurisdiction and restrain their encroachments on the secular authorities. Thus she succeeded in restoring the ancient disciplines of the church and weeding out the sensuality and indolence which had so long defiled it.

Much of Isabella's legislation, it is true, is that of a comprehensive character which shows that she looked to higher and far nobler objects. But with much that is good there was mingled, as in most of her institutions, one germ of evil, of little moment at the time, indeed, but of which, under the vicious culture of her successors, shot up to a height that overshadowed and blighted all the rest. This was the spirit of restriction and monopoly, aggravated by the subsequent laws of Ferdinand, and carried to an extent under the Austrian dynasty that paralyzed colonial trade. Therefore, as time went on Spain was becoming poor in the midst of her treasures. As Martin Hume says, "Spanish gold and silver coin, in a few years, was

QUEEN ISABELLA

plentiful in every country but in Spain itself." [23]

The reasons for Spain's decline were in addition to the exile of Jews and Moslems. They had set up a nation which was destined to make an end of the feudal system which had financed and ruled the country throughout the Middle Ages and before.

The question is asked: "Did bigotry destroy feudalism?" It is another way of addressing the problem of dependency upon wealthy nobles, who depended upon the social structure which included Jews and Moslems. When bigotry, the Inquisition, and the expulsions occurred, which were coincidental with building a great nation from diverse provinces, these provinces were no longer supported and governed by wealthy nobles.

In addition, there had been a simultaneous kingdom in Spain, that of the Moslems, centered in Granada. The fall of Granada excited a general sensation throughout Christendom, where it was received as counterbalancing, in a manner, the loss of Constantinople nearly a century before. It was thought to end 741 years of conquest. Now, it was thought, Christian Spain would gradually rise, by means of her new acquisitions, from a subordinate situation to the level of a first-rate European power.

It was not realized, however, that with the expulsion of the Jews, 160,000 individuals, their deficit might have been repaired except for the Inquisition. In the expulsion of the Moslems in 1499-1503—who might have gone on living among them in a subordinate position—Spain had placed herself on a pedestal from which she could not sustain control.

Without the backing of those nobles, the sovereignty was in a precarious position if its succession should be absorbed by another country. This is exactly what happened. In 1504 Isabella assigned sovereignty to Ferdinand and then through Juana, their defective daughter, to Charles V, her uncle and Holy Roman Emperor, and, in addition, "all the net proceeds and profits accruing from the newly discovered countries in the West."

It was only a matter of time until Philip II, first as regent and then as king, was to engage in continual wars of religion on the continent. He followed so well in the footsteps of the former sovereigns in burning heretics that he is known to history as Philip the Catholic. Thus, the crown of Spain was to devolve on a foreign crown after his death. [24]

Chapter 12

The Invincible Armada

The Spanish Fleet

The defeat of the Invincible Armada is a milestone in our study of Francis Drake. It is to be revealed in this context as a defining moment in English history, where what he had devoted all his labors to, overcoming of the tyranny of Spain, was finally coming to pass.

There has probably never been a more audacious preparation for a major battle than that of Philip II for the Spanish Armada. It was all out there for the world to see, and in spite of Philip's knowledge of the capacities of English seamen, the size of his ships were enormous.

From the 19th century historian Lingard we learn that the ships of the fleet — galeasses, galleys, galleons, and hulks — were so over-weighted they could bear little canvas, even with smooth seas and favorable winds. The galeasses were floating edifices, gorgeously decorated with splendid state apartments, cabins, chapels and a pulpit in each; the galleys one-third smaller, were equally appointed with the trappings of wealth; the galleons alone were about 600 tons rowed by 300 galley-slaves.

There were more than 130 vessels in all, divided into ten squadrons, a total of 19,205 on board, including 8,252 sailors and 2,088 galley-slaves. Besides these, there was a force of noble volunteers, of the most illustrious houses in Spain, with their attendants, amounting to nearly 2,000 in all. There was also Don Martin Alaccon of the Holy Inquisition with 200 monks of the various orders, totaling about 30,000 in all.

Replacing Santa Cruz at their head was the newly appointed duke of Medina Sidonia, a grandee of vast wealth, but with little capacity and less experience. The plan was simple. Medina Sedonia was to proceed with their vast fleet from Lisbon to the Calais roads; there he was to wait for Alexandro Farnese, the duke of Parma, who was to come forth from Newport, Sluys, and Dunkirk, bringing with him 17,000 veterans and to assume command of the whole enterprise. They were then to cross the Channel to Dover, land the army of Parma, reinforced with 6,000 Spaniards from the fleet, and with these 23,000 men to march at once upon London. Not a gun was to be fired.

It seems an unbelievable plan, even an embarrassment to relate. They could not have been ignorant of the Dutch fleets off Dunkirk, Newport, and Flushing. It never entered their heads that 40,000 to 50,000 troops in the Netherlands could be kept in prison by a fleet of Dutch shippers and corsairs. Did the question arise that if the arm of Parma did not arrive, were they simply to go through with their plan of invasion without them?

In the meantime Parma reported to Sidonia that their numbers had fallen off from sickness and other causes so that instead of 30,000 he had only about 17,000. With the 6,000 Spaniards he was to meet from the fleet of Sidonia, he would therefore have only 23,000 for their proposed invasion of London. "When we talked of taking England by surprise," said Parma, "we never thought of less than 30,000. Now that she is alert and ready for us and that it is certain we must fight by sea and by land, 50,000 would be few."

They at last set sail from Lisbon at the last of May 1588 after waiting for a month for favorable weather. The size of the ships of the fleet were so encumbered with top-hamper, so overweighted in proportion to the draught of water, that they could bear but little canvas, even in smooth seas and favorable winds. Such was the machinery which Philip had at last set afloat for the purpose of dethroning Elizabeth and establishing the Inquisition in England.

There were no light vessels in the Armada and no heavy ones with Parma; Medina could not go to Farnese, nor could Farnese come to Medina. Yet it never entered the heads of Philip or his councillors to provide for that difficulty. The king never supposed that with 50,000 soldiers in Netherlands, 300 transports, and very large funds for one great purpose, they could be kept in prison by a fleet of Dutch skippers and corsairs.

After a three-week sluggish journey, the Armada was taken by a tempest and scattered hither and thither. Of the squadron of galleys, one was already sunk in the sea, and two others had been conquered by their own galley-slaves. The fourth rode out with difficulty and joined the rest of the fleet, which ultimately reassembled at Corunna where they remained a month, repairing damages. On July 22 they again set sail.

On Friday July 29 they came in sight of England, where ten thousand beacon fires

A SHIP OF THE ARMADA

had been set to warn every Englishman that the enemy was at last upon them. Neither Howard, who had been appointed lord-admiral, nor Francis Drake were men to lose time in such an emergency, and before that Friday night was spent, sixty of the best English ships had been warped out of the Plymouth harbor. [1]

An anecdote is often told of Drake, who would have been waiting in the port of Plymouth. He was to have been at a game of "bowls", and at the appearance of the Armada was to have insisted, "Let's first finish our game of bowls, and then the Spanish." [2]

We turn here to the historian Motley, who told the story of the Spanish Armada from the vantage point of the Netherlands:

"By nine o'clock, the 31st of July, about two miles from Looe, on the Cornish coast, the fleets had their first meeting. There were 136 sail of the Spaniards by which ninety were large ships, and 67 of the English. It was a solemn moment. The long-expected armada presented a pompous, almost theatrical appearance. The ships seemed arranged for a pageant in honor of a victory already won. Dispersed in the form of a crescent, the horns of which were seven miles asunder, these gilded, towered, floating castles, with their gainly standards and their martial music, moved slowly along the Channel with an air of indolent pomp. Their captain-general, the golden duke, stood on his shot-proof fortress, on the deck of his great galleon, the *San Martin*, surrounded by generals of infantry and colonels of cavalry, who knew as little as he did himself of naval matters.

"The English vessels—on the other hand—with a few exceptions, light, swift, easily handled—could sail round and round their unwieldy galleons, hulks, and galleys rowed by chained slave-gangs. The superior seamanship of free Englishmen, commanded by such experienced captains as Drake, Frobisher, and Hawkins—from infancy at home on the blue water—was manifest in the very first encounter. They obtained the weathergage at once, and cannonaded the enemy at intervals with considerable effect, easily escaping at will out of range of the sluggish Armada, which was incapable of bearing sail in pursuit, although provided with an armament which could sink all its enemies at close quarters." [3]

While Spain's royal fleet did their utmost, which was little, to offer general battle, the English followed at the heels of the enemy, attacked only the rear guard of the Armada, and continued to tease and elude any counter-attack, while the main fleet proceeded slowly up the Channel. This running battle continued up the coast in full view of Plymouth, whence boats with reinforcements and volunteers were perpetually arriving to the English ships, until the battle had drifted quite out of reach of the town.

There is no doubt, however, of the readiness and command of England's greatest generals at that time: Sir Francis Drake on the *Revenge*, followed by Frobisher in the *Triumph*, Hawkins in the *Victory*, Howard on the *Ark-Royal* and some smaller vessels. The English fleet was continually augmented by the high-born nobles who boarded their ships or brought in smaller vessels in order to have their share in the delights of the long-expected struggle.

The grand flotilla of Spanish vessels made their way slowly past the harbor at Plymouth while the English ships gathered from all points. This open confrontation lasted for days before their first encounter on July 31, 1588, two miles from Loone on the Cornish coast. There were 136 of Spanish ships, both large and small, and fifty-seven of English. It was a solemn moment.

The superior seamanship of the English was apparent from the start as they darted among the huge vessels, inflicting much damage with their cannons but out of range because of their slim outlines. Hours into battle both sides had exhausted their shot and metal. The Spanish, however, did not know this as the English continued their pursuit regardless. As Lord Admiral Howard later said, "[T]hough our powder and shot were well-nigh spent, we put on a brag countenance and gave them chase, as though we wanted nothing."

The Spanish held their course, and there was finally a battle at close range between Leyva's fleet, who held the rear of Sidonia's, and Frobisher's. The Spanish appeared to outwin the battle, but Frobisher escaped, robbing them of their prize as they continued indolently toward Calais and at last dropped anchor.

Soon, however, the sixteen ships of Lord Henry Seymore dropped anchor nearby. This was where the Spanish were to converge with the forces of Parma. Further along the coast, as we have remarked, they never appeared. The fleets of Holland and Zealand, numbering some 150 galleons, sloops and fly-boats, lay patiently blockading every possible egress from the lowlands and longing to grapple with the forces of Parma as soon as they should venture to set sail upon the sea for their long-prepared exploit. Although longing to give battle, the Spaniards were forbidden to descend upon the coast until after their junction with Parma.

John Winter—who you remember circled the world with Drake— standing side by side with the lord-admiral Howard on the deck of the little *Ark-Royal*, gazed for the first time on these enormous galleons and galleys with which his companions were already sufficiently familiar. Remembering, in a lucky moment, something that he had heard four years before of the fire-ships sent against Parma's bridge at Antwerp, Winter suggested that some similar stratagem be attempted against the Invincible Armada.

They had no access to the submarine volcanoes that had been employed at Antwerp, but burning ships at least might be sent among the fleet. In Winter's opinion, the Armada might at least be compelled to slip its cables and be thrown into some confusion if the project were fairly carried out. Howard approved of the plan.

On board the Spanish ships there was exceeding impatience. There was London, almost before their eyes—a huge mass of treasure, richer and more accessible than those mines beyond the Atlantic. And there were those men aboard who also remembered the destruction at Antwerp, a great commercial city which fell, the memory of which the world still shuddered. But where was Farnese? Impatience led to distrust.

At twilight the moon became totally obscured, dark clouds spread over the heavens, the sea grew black, distant thunder rolled, and an approaching tempest became distinctly audible. At an hour past midnight it was so dark that it was difficult to pierce into the gloom. The faint sound of oars now struck the ears of the Spaniards as they watched from the decks. A few moments afterwards the sea became suddenly luminous, and six flaming vessels appeared at a slight distance, bearing steadily down upon them before the wind and tide. The men aboard remembered the floating volcanoes and the explosion which had laid so many soldiers dead at one blow and shattered the bridge and floating forts of Farnese at Antwerp.

In a moment a horrible panic spread rapidly among large bodies of men aboard the Spanish ships. Someone shouted, "The fire-ships of Antwerp!" and in an instant every cable was cut and frantic attempts were made by each ship to escape what seemed immanent destruction. Four or five of the largest ships became entangled with each other. Others were set on fire by the flaming vessels and were consumed.

When Monday morning dawned, several of the Spanish vessels lay disabled, while the rest of the fleet was seen at a distance of two leagues from Calais, driving towards the Flemish coast. The lord-admiral Howard now bore away with all his force in pursuit of the Spaniards. The Invincible Armada, sorely crippled, was being pushed by winds from the southwest, and the English came up to them soon after nine A.M., off Gravelines, and found them sailing in a half-moon. Seeing the enemy approach, Medina Sidonia in the center ordered his men to prepare for action.

Combat began about 10 A.M. Sir Francis Drake in the *Revenge*, Frobisher in the *Triumph*, Hawkins in the *Victory*, and some smaller vessels made the first attack upon the Spanish flag-ships. The battle lasted six hours, hot and furious. The well-disciplined English mariners poured broadside after broadside against the towering ships of the Armada, which afforded so easy a mark; while the Spaniards, on their part, found it impossible, while wasting incredible quantities of powder and shot, to inflict any severe damage on their enemies.

Throughout the action not an English ship was destroyed, and not a hundred men were killed. On the other hand, all the best ships of the Spaniards were riddled through and through, and with masts shattered, sails and rigging torn to shreds, and a northwest wind still drifting them towards the fatal sand-banks of Holland, they received a tremendous punishment at the hands of the famous mariners. Before five o-clock in the afternoon at least sixteen of the Spanish ships had been destroyed, and from four to five thousand soldiers killed.

Medina Sidonia reluctantly gave the order to retreat. Crippled, maltreated, and diminished in number as were his ships, he would still have faced the enemy, but the winds and currents were fast driving him toward shore, and the pilots, one and all, assured him that it would be inevitable destruction to remain. The Armada bore away into the open sea, leaving those who could not follow to their fate.

Following the queen's policy, the English never ceased their cannonading until their ammunition was exhausted. Yet, with their munitions in some vessels gone, and their cartridges all spent, they ceased fighting, but followed the enemy who still kept away. And the enemy, although still numerous, and seeming strong enough, if properly handled, to destroy the whole English fleet, fled before them. "Their force is wonderful great and strong," said Howard, "but we pluck their feathers by little and little."

It was necessary on Friday August 12 to hold a conference among the English commanders to decide whether they could continue to follow the slow retreat of the Armada after their failed encounter with their armies. Howard, Drake, and Frobisher agreed they had but a three days' supply of food, very little shot, and were receiving numerous complaints from their crews. Before a decision was necessary, however, on Sunday there arose a tremendous gale from the southeast. As Howard said, "Twas a more violent storm than was ever seen before at this time of year." Fearing to end up on the ill-favored sands off Norfolk, they headed back, arriving within four or five days safely back in the Margate Roads.

It was a far different fate for the Spaniards. With no safe harbor, their damaged ships, leaking, without pilots and competent commanders for the greater part, the great fleet was hurled against the iron crags of Norway and between the savage rocks of Faroe and the Hebrides. The coasts of Norway, Scotland, and Ireland were strewn with the wrecks of that pompous fleet and the bones of those invincible legions which were to have sacked London and made England a Spanish vice-royalty.

Through August a series of storms continued. Of the one hundred thirty-four vessels that sailed from Carunna in July, only forty-three made their escape to Spain, but so damaged as to be worthless. The Invisible Armada had not only been vanquished but annihilated. Of the 30,000 who sailed there were no more than 10,000 who saw their native land.

The Army of Parma

Meanwhile Farnese sat chafing under the unjust reproaches heaped upon him, as if he, and not his master, had been responsible for the gigantic blunders of the invasion. The Hollanders and Zealanders laughed the invaders of England to scorn. Farnese had been reproached for not being ready, for not having embarked his men; but he had been ready for a month, and his men could be embarked in a single day. So soon as he received word at the arrival of the fleet at Calais, he proceeded to Newport and embarked sixteen thousand men, and before dawn he was at Dunkirk, where the troops were rapidly placed on board the transports.

For two long days these regiments lay heaped together like sacks of corn, hoping that the Dutch fleet would be swept out of to sea by the Invincible Armada, and patiently expecting the signal for setting sail to England. Then came the news of the fire-ships and the dispersion and flight of the Armada. Contrary to what is usually told in history books, it is certain that, of all the high parties concerned, Alexander Farnese was the least responsible for the overthrow of Philip's hopes. The duke of Parma was unable to move his troops alone against the Dutch fleets, and their own Invincible Armada had long gone since the fire-storm, battle, and tempest had sent them far out to sea.

Also stranded were the land armies of England, some 75,000 men under arms, 20,000 along the southern coast, 23,000 under Leicester, and 33,000 under Lord Chamberlain Hunsdon, for the special defense of the queen's person. It would have been difficult, however, to bring anything like that number into the field. A drilled and disciplined army, whether of regulars or of militiamen, had no existence whatever at that time. Those who could muster, however, marched through London to the place of rendezvous.

Leicester's jealous and overbearing temper itself, however, was proving a formidable obstacle to a wholesome system of defense. He, having been given the title of General-in-chief was already displeased with the amount of authority entrusted to Lord Hunsdon, disposed to think his own rights invaded, and desirous that the lord chamberlain should accept office under himself. Looking at this picture of England's commander-in-chief, officers and rank and file, as painted by themselves, we feel an inexpressible satisfaction that in this great risk of England's destiny there were such men as Howard, Drake, Frobisher, Hawkins, Seymour, Winter, Fenner, and their gallant brethren, cruising that week in the Channel, and that Nassan and Warmond, De Moor, and Van der Does, the Dutch fleet, were blockading the Flemish coast." [4]

At the armies' rendezvous in Tilbury, however, tremendous were the cheers when the brave queen rode on horseback among them. It was a pleasant sight. The queen did indeed infuse a spirit of loyalty, love, and resolution into every soldier of her army, who, ravished with their sovereign's sight, prayed heartily that the Spaniards might land quickly, for they imagined a speedy victory. So sure were they of a glorious result for England that they began to lament when they learned that the Spanish had fled.

Nevertheless, Elizabeth felt obliged to honor Leicester and Essex in an historic speech to her troops, thus assembled. Those two earls held her bridle-rein while she delivered a stirring speech to the men: "My loving people, we have been persuaded by some that are careful of our safety to take heed how we commit ourselves to armed multitudes for fear of treachery; but I assure you I do not desire to live to distrust my faithful and loving people. Let tyrants fear!. . . I know that I have but the body of a weak and feeble woman; but I have the heart of a king. . ."

Everything in this camp speech was exciting and appropriate except a laudation bestowed on the general, for her lieutenant was none other than that carpet-knight and most inefficient commander, the earl of Leicester. The thought that she could deliver such an honorarium to these two who had given nothing in battle is beyond belief. [5]

The plight of those men who had dedicated their energies and skill to the defeat of the Spanish Armada must be told, however. They were not lauded by their queen, who knew nothing of what they then had to endure. The sailors, by whom England had been thus defended in her utmost need, were dying by hundreds and even thousands of ship-fever in the latter days of August. It seemed improbable that the thousand sailors by whom the

"Abandoned"

English ships of war were manned would have almost wholly disappeared at a moment when their services might be imperatively required. Nor had there been the least precaution taken for cherishing and saving these brave defenders of their country. They rotted on their ships, or died in the streets of the naval ports, because there were no hospitals to receive them.

The survivors, too, were greatly discontented; for after having been eight months at sea and enduring great privations, they could not get their wages. It is also distressing to learn that the leading admirals of the English fleet were at logger-heads: Seymour against Howard, Hawkins and Frobisher at daggers drawn with Drake, for appropriating the ransom of Don Pedro Valdez, in which both Frobisher and Hawkins claimed at least an equal share with himself. Lord-Admiral Howard was also anxious, with his sailors perishing by pestilence, with many of his ships so weakly manned that, as Seymour declared, there were no mariners enough to weigh the anchors, and with the great naval heroes, on whose efforts the safety of the realm depended, wrangling like fisherwomen among themselves.

Our English historian, J. I. Motley, who relates much of the above in his *History of the United Netherlands,* tells it from the vantage point of that country and reminds us that the invasion of England by Spain had been most portentous. He proclaims that the danger at last averted is to be ascribed to the enthusiasm of the English nation, but also to the spirit of the naval commanders and volunteers of the Hollanders, who gave their staunch support, and, finally, to the hand of God. This historian, however, who would tell it like it is, would say that "very little credit can be conscientiously awarded to the diplomatic or the military efforts of the queen's government. Miracles alone, in the opinion of Roger Williams, had saved England on this occasion from perdition." [6]

— Chapter 13 —

The Last Years of Elizabeth

Leicester's Demise

"While England became 'a nest of singing birds' at home, the last years of Elizabeth's reign were years of splendour and triumph abroad. The defeat of the Armada was the first of a series of defeats which broke the power of Spain, and changed the political aspect of the world" [1]

In spite of the above analysis, there could not have been content at home in England with the unequal distribution of honor toward those who had given so much to bring it about. The important services of the lord-admiral and his officers were not overlooked, but in her estimation they could not be compared with those of Leicester. He stood without a rival; and to reward his transcendent merit a new and unprecedented office was created, which would have conferred on him an authority almost equal to that of his sovereign. He was appointed lord lieutenant of England and Ireland, and the warrant lay ready for the royal signature, when the remonstrances of Burghley and Hatton induced her to hesitate; and the unexpected death of the favorite concealed her weakness from the knowledge of the public.

Soon after the queen's departure from Tilbury, Leicester had by her order disbanded the army and set out for his castle of Kenilworth. His progress was arrested by a violent disease which, by natural causes or not, quickly terminated his existence. The queen's tears were real, but another passion induced her to order the public sale of his goods for the discharge of certain debts. For thirty years he had triumphed over every competitor. As a statesman or a commander he displayed little ability, but his rapacity and ambition knew no bounds. He had for many years not despaired gaining her hand in marriage, and we have just seen that only the week before his death she had promised him a much larger share of the royal authority than had ever been conferred on a subject. Yet, if one has rejected every charge against him not supported by probable evidence, there would still remain much to stamp infamy on the character of Leicester. [2]

We continue with summaries of the historian Lingard. The defeat of the Armada had thrown the nation into a frenzy of joy, but when their queen moved to satisfy the religious animosity of her subjects, or to display her gratitude to the Almighty, she sought to punish the supposed enemies of his worship. A commission was issued, and those Catholics who were in prison on account of religion were brought to trial. Nothing was charged of them except the practice of their religion, and many were massacred.

The earl of Arendel was one of those imprisoned, and he suggested among the prisoners that they should join in one common form of prayer to solicit the protection of heaven. One of Queen Mary's priests, William Bennet, was at some point urged to confess that Arundel had bade them pray for the success of the Armada. On this deposition was grounded a charge of high treason. After an hour's debate his peers found him guilty, and he was placed in the Tower.

Burghley and Hatton advised the queen to spare him. She had already taken his father and at length decided not to stain her reputation with the blood of the son. Yet she carefully concealed her intention from the knowledge of the prisoner, who lived for several years under the impression that the axe was still suspended over his head. In 1595 he was taken ill and died at the end of two months. He was buried beside his father in the chapel in the Tower. In her conduct the queen betrayed an unaccountable spirit of revenge. It is not known what secret offence he had given which could never be divulged, but his treatment was typical of the kinds of prejudice the queen could maintain. Her displeasure extended to Lady Arundel after her husband's death. The countess was obliged to solicit permission to visit London even for medical advice, and to quit the capital before the queen's arrival.

From the defeat of the Armada till the death of the queen, during the lapse of fourteen years, the Catholics groaned under the pressure of incessant persecution. Sixty-one clergymen, forty-seven laymen, and two gentlewomen suffered capital punishment for some or other of the spiritual felonies and treasons which had been lately created. Life, indeed, was always offered, but on the condition of conformity to the established worship.

We may now turn to the foreign wars and domestic intrigues which occupied the attention of the queen until the end of her reign. As she began to calculate the expense of the victory, she stood aghast at the enormous amount. The merchants were rated as to their ability to pay, and almost every gentleman who possessed not some powerful friend at court was compelled to advance the sum at which he had been taxed.

The convocation and parliament convened, and the queen received enormous subsidies from all assembled. But now that the terror of Spanish arms was dispelled, men thought of nothing but revenge and conquest, and the house prayed the queen to punish the insult which she had received from Philip by carrying the scourge of war into his dominions. An association was formed, at the head of which appeared the names of Norris and Drake, men who were justly esteemed the first in the military and naval service, and under their auspices an armament of nearly two hundred sail, carrying twenty-one thousand men, was collected in the harbor of Plymouth.

Essex and the Invasion of Corunna

The reader will recall that Letitia, the dowager countess of Essex, had married the earl of Leicester, who introduced her son, the earl of Essex, to the queen. His youth and address and spirit soon captivated Elizabeth. She made him master of the horse, and on the appearance of the Armada conferred the important office of captain-general of the cavalry. And as recalled, she displayed her fondness for him in the eyes of the whole army at Tilbury and honored him for his bloodless services with the order of the Garter. On the death of Leicester he succeeded to the post of prime favorite; the queen required his constant attendance at court; and her indulgence of his caprices cherished and strengthened his passions.

His first lapse of favor, however, occurred when he suddenly disappeared from court, rode with an expedition to Plymouth, and embarked on board the *Swiftsure*, a ship of the royal navy, with the intention of following the fleet which had sailed for the invasion of Corunna several days before. The queen sent papers for his arrest, and finding he had departed sent a copy of the royal instructions to the commanders of the expedition.

This was the expedition in 1589 which Norris and Drake had recently been authorized to undertake to raise a revolution in favor of Don Antonio, who had unsuccessfully contended with Philip for the crown of Portugal. They were first to endeavor to raise a revolution in his favor, and if unsuccessful should scour the coast of the peninsula and inflict on the subjects of Philip every injury in their power. But Drake had too long been accustomed to absolute command in his freebooting expeditions and sailed directly to the harbor of Corunna.

Several sail of merchantmen and ships of war fell into his hands along with certain suburbs and wares, but in vain was a breach made in the wall of the place itself. Three hundred men perished in the attempt. Norris made a march against Andrada, the Spanish commander, at the bridge of Burgos. They finally succeeded but at another loss of many valuable lives. From Corunna the commanders wrote to the queen an exaggerated account of their success, but informed her, however, that they had received no tidings of the earl of Essex.

That nobleman waited for them at sea and accompanied them to Peniche on the coast of Portugal. The English advanced without opposition, but at length Essex, taking the initiative in their advance, encountered small bands of Spaniards in positions best adapted to suppress any rising in the city. The Spaniards were at a disadvantage, but at length sickness and want compelled Norris to abandon the enterprise.

Not a sword had been drawn in favor of Antonio, and the army marched to Cascaes, a town already captured and plundered by Drake. From Caseaes the expedition sailed on its return to England. They were separated the next day by a storm, however, into several small squadrons, but with a fleet of seventeen galleys successively reached Plymouth.

Of the 21,000 men who sailed on this disastrous expedition, not one-half returned; and out of eleven hundred gentlemen, not more than one-third lived to revisit their native country. The queen rejoiced that she had retaliated the boast of invasion upon Philip, but lamented the loss of lives and treasure with which it had been purchased. The blame was laid by her on the disobedience and rapacity of the two commanders; by them partly on each other, and partly on the heat of the climate and intemperance of the men. In public these complaints were carefully suppressed and every advantage magnified; and the people therefore celebrated. [3]

Against Spain the naval warfare was still kept up, and the earl of Cumberland, Sir Martin Frobisher, and Thomas White did much injury to the Spanish trade. The English at this time also first made their way to the East Indies. The year 1590 was distinguished by the death of the able and disinterested secretary Walsingham. The following year the chancellor Hatton died. Burghley, as a means of bringing forward his son Sir Robert Cecil, took the duties of the office on himself. [4]

Sir Walter Raleigh at Court

Raleigh was born at Hayes, in Devonshire, in 1552. He spent time at Oxford, took service with a body of volunteers serving in the French Huguenot army, returning to England perhaps in 1576. During these years he appears to have made himself master of seamanship. In 1579 he commanded an English company in Ireland, where he was distinguished for his service. In one way or another Raleigh's conduct gained the favorable notice of Elizabeth, especially as he had chosen to seek the support of Leicester, with whom he served at Antwerp in 1582.

For some years he shone as a courtier, receiving from time to time licenses to export woolen cloths and other goods, after the system by which Elizabeth rewarded her favorites without expense to herself. He was one of those, we have indicated previously, who were dissatisfied unless they could pursue some public object in connection with their chase after a private fortune. In 1583 he had risked L2,000 in the expedition in which Sir Humphrey Gilbert perished.

In 1584 he obtained a charter of colonization, of which we have mentioned in brief, and sent two commanders to examine an area in the New World, which he named Virginia. In 1585 he dispatched a fleet laden with colonists. They were, however, soon discouraged, and were brought back to England by Drake the following year. Shortly afterwards fifteen fresh colonists were landed, and another party in 1587. All these, however, perished, and though Raleigh did all that was possible to succor them, the permanent colonizing of Virginia passed into other hands.

In 1584 Raleigh obtained a grant of an enormous tract of land in Munster in one corner of which he introduced the cultivation of the potato. To the people of that land, the English colonists were but the counterpart of the attempt to exterminate its original possessors. This view of the policy of England to Ireland was not confined to Raleigh, but it found in him its most eminent supporter.

As an aside, the reader should know that Drake was exposed to and probably engaged in similar exploitation of the Irish when he was in the employ of the earl of Essex in 1572 where he first met Doughty. It is regretted that two such naval heroes as Drake and Raleigh could have been thus engaged, and it is hoped that Drake resolved at the time not to again mistreat native populations, a resolve which he did indeed carry out when he was himself the commander.

Raleigh's enterprise in Ireland was not entirely successful, but he did his best, so far as a usually absentee landlord could do, to make his colonists prosperous and successful, but he underestimated the vitality of the Irish race and the resistance which was awakened by the harsh system of which he was advised at Elizabeth's court. His whole attempt ended in failure.

If he could not succeed in Ireland, he would fight it out with Spain. In 1588 he took on an active part against the Armada, and is even supposed by some to have been the adviser of the successful tactics which avoided any attempt to board the Spanish galleons. In 1589 he shared the unsuccessful expedition at Corunna commanded by Drake and Norris, and for some time vessels fitted out by him were actively employed in making reprisals upon Spain.

As a courtier he was brought into collision with the young earl of Essex, who challenged him, though a duel was prevented. Some passing anger of the queen drove him again to visit Ireland, where he renewed his friendship with Edmund Spenser. He took the poet back with him to England and introduced him to Elizabeth. It was this encounter which led to Spenser's writing of the *Faerie Queene* in her honor.

At the end of 1591 or the beginning of 1592 Raleigh seduced and subsequently married Elizabeth Throckmorton, and was consequently thrown into the Tower by Elizabeth, who could not endure that the fantastic lovemaking to herself which she exacted from her courtiers should pass into real affection for a younger woman of her court. This assessment, which we attribute to the historian Gardiner, we repeat elsewhere.

Because of his imprisonment Raleigh was unable and forbidden to sail in command of a fleet a great part of which had been fitted out at his own cost for service against Spain. The ships, however, sailed, and succeeded in capturing a prize of extraordinary value, known at the time as the *Great Carrack*. No one but Raleigh was capable of presiding over the work of securing the spoils. Thus he was sent out to Plymouth, still in the name of a prisoner, where his capacity for business and his power of winning the enthusiastic affection of his subordinates were alike put to the test. The queen at last consented to restore him to complete liberty though she tried to cheat him of his fair share of the booty. The next year, 1595, the able and enterprising Sir Walter Raleigh again set forth, this time in search of fortune in America.

Hence Raleigh made his first journey to the lands near the Orinoco in search of the fabled El Dorado. In 1595 he sailed in person with five ships for Trinidad. On his arrival he found that the Spaniards, who had occupied a place called San Thome, had been obliged to abandon it. Raleigh ascended the river to the spot, heard more about El Dorado from the Indians, brought away some stones containing fragments of gold, and returned to England to prepare a more powerful expedition for the following year.

In the next year, 1596, however, he was wanted to take the command of a squadron in the expedition sent against Spain under Lord Howard of Effingham and the earl of Essex. It was Raleigh who, on the arrival of the fleet off Cadiz, persuaded Howard and Essex to begin the attack on the Spanish fleet, and who himself led the van in sailing into the harbor. [5]

Before telling the story of the capture of Cadiz which involved Raleigh, we must relate an expedition of that same year which is the last that our hero Francis Drake was to make. Sir Francis Drake and Sir John Hawkins undertook an important expedition against the Spanish settlements in America, and they carried with them six ships of the queen's and twenty more which either were fitted out at their own charge or were furnished them by private adventurers.

Their first design was to attempt Porto Rico where they knew a rich carrack was at the time stationed; but as they had not preserved the requisite secrecy, a pinnace strayed from the fleet and was taken by the Spaniards which betrayed their intentions. Preparations were made in the island for their reception; and the English fleet, notwithstanding the brave assault which they made on the enemy, was repulsed with loss. Hawkins soon after died, and Drake pursued his voyage to Nombre de Dios, on the Isthmus of Darien. He then attempted to pass forward to Panama, with a view of plundering that place.

Unable to break through the Spanish skirmishes, however, they were obliged to return without being able to effect anything. Drake, from the intemperance of the climate, the fatigues of his journey and the vexation of his disappointment, was seized with a distemper, of which he soon after died. Sir Thomas Baskerville took the command of the fleet, and soon after battled a Spanish fleet near Cuba. The Spanish suffered some loss from this enterprise, but the English reaped no profit. The lack of success in this enterprise in the Indies made Baskerville and the fleet decide to return to the homeland, as it was heard that Philip was making great preparations for a new invasion of England and they wished to be a part of the resistance. [5]

The death of Drake in 1596 does not end our story. What was finally set in motion to curb the expansion of Spain and the Inquisition into all the known world, of which he played so great a part, must be assessed as we follow his emerging legacy.

The Capture of Cadiz

A t Plymouth a powerful fleet was being equipped. One hundred seventy vessels, seventeen of which were capital ships of war, and various small vessels were being assembled. Twenty ships were added by the Hollanders. In this fleet were 6,360 soldiers, 1000 volunteers, and 6,772 seamen besides the Dutch. The land forces were commanded by the earl of Essex, the navy by Lord Charles Howard of Effingham, high admiral. Both these commanders had expended great sums of their own in the armament—for such was the spirit of Elizabeth's reign. Lord Thomas Howard, Sir Walter Raleigh, Sir Francis Vere, Sir George Carew, and Sir Coniers Clifford had commands in the expedition, and were appointed councils to the general and admiral.

They set sail on June 1, 1596, and, meeting with a fair wind, set sail, intercepting every ship that could carry intelligence to the enemy. Fortunately they overtook an Irish vessel, by which they learned that that port was full of merchant ships of great value, and that the Spaniards there lived in perfect security, without any apprehensions of an enemy.

After a fruitless attempt to land at San Sebastian, on the western side of the island of Cadiz, it was resolved to attack the ships and galleys in the bay. This attempt was deemed rash by the admiral, but Essex was especially recommending the enterprise. When it was resolved, he threw his hat into the sea and gave symptoms of the most extravagant joy. He was mortified, however, when the admiral informed him that the queen was anxious for his safety, and dreading the effects of his youthful ardor, had secretly given orders that he should not be permitted to command the attack. That duty was performed by Sir Walter Raleigh and Lord Thomas Howard. But no sooner did Essex come within reach of the enemy than he forgot his instructions to keep in the midst of the fleet, broke through and pressed forward into the thickest of the fire.

The enemy was soon obliged to slip anchor and retreat farther into the bay, where they ran many of their ships aground. Essex then landed his men and immediately marched to the attack of Cadiz, sword in hand.

The generosity of Essex, however, not inferior to his valor, made him stop the slaughter and treat his prisoners with the greatest humanity, and even affability and kindness. The English made rich plunder in the city, but missed a much richer one by the resolution of the duke of Medina, the Spanish admiral, who took to setting fire to his ships in order to prevent their falling into the hands of the enemy. The loss to the Spanish amounted to 20 million ducats, besides the indignity which they suffered from the sacking of one of their chief cities and destroying in their harbor a fleet of such force and value.

Essex, like one possessed, insisted on keeping possession of Cadiz, and he undertook with four hundred men and three months' provisions to defend the place till succors should arrive from England. All the others, satisfied with the honor they had acquired and impatient to return home in order to secure their plunder, finally left him on the Spanish coast attended by a very few ships.

The admiral, Lord Charles Howard of Effingham, was subsequently created earl of Nottingham, and this promotion gave great disgust to Essex, who felt that it was a merit which belonged solely to himself. He even offered to maintain this plea by single combat against the earl, or his sons, or any of his kindred.

Never before had the Spanish monarch received so severe a blow in a single battle. He had lost thirteen men-of-war and immense magazines of provisions and naval stores. The defenses of Cadiz, the strongest fortress in his dominions, had been razed to the ground; and the secret of his weakness at home had been revealed to the world. At the same time the power of England had been raised in the eyes of the European nations. Even those who wished well to Spain allotted the praise of moderation and humanity to the English commanders, who had suffered no blood to be wantonly spilled, no woman to be defiled, but had sent under an escort the nuns and females, about 2,000 in number, to the port of St. Mary, allowing them to carry away their jewels and wearing apparel.

But while foreigners applauded the conquerors and their coun-

trymen hailed their return with shouts of triumph, they experienced from
their sovereign a cool and ungracious reception. Her secret orders had
been disregarded. Even reports of the unusual humanity of her favorite did
not assuage her anger toward those who had allowed him to place himself
in danger. [6]

Summary of Elizabeth's Last Years

There were indeed worse battles to come. But our story falters.
Elizabeth's favoritism and the shabby reasons for it have reached
a point to exhaust the reader. With a few summaries we conclude
her reign, for our goal is to create a background and setting from which
we will backtrack to consider the cover-up of Drake's great achievements
when he returned in 1580. Therefore, we consider only the dates and the
categories of events toward the end of her reign, without the usual exposi-
tion. These summaries are edited from those in the *Historian's Histories*,
our principal source.

1590-1598

Elizabeth and parliament: Her arbitrary demands call for large sums
for personal expenditure. Her parliaments are treated with scant respect.
She curtails liberty of speech. Parliament acquires considerably more importance during this period. Puritanism develops independence of charter;
members bring high qualities to bear on their administrative duties.

In ecclesiastical matters, the same arbitrariness is shown by Elizabeth, tenacious of her supremacy. The church becomes Protestant, and
Elizabeth fills vacant livings with Puritan divines. She exhibits contempt
for the bishops, whom she treats as creatures of her will. The divine origin
of Episcopacy is not yet distinctly asserted in the English church.

1570-1583

The Puritans: Indignant at the abuses in the church, they raise
claims of Presbyterianism as a divine institution. Cartwright's admonition
(published 1572) implies superiority of church to state. But the great mass
of Puritans accept the queen's supremacy and acknowledge the Established Church. The advanced Puritans are persecuted for their republican
views. In 1583 the court of high commission attains full powers, and its
proceedings are characterized by much arbitrariness.

1590

Growth of High Church Party: The Church of England asserts its
highest pretensions after Armada. Catholics now enter the national church.

The Puritans are impelled to a more organized opposition. In 1590 associations are formed for introducing all the apparatus of Presbyterianism (synods and classes). The Star Chamber is brought into requisition, but without detracting from the spread of Puritanism.

1588-1596

Increasing prosperity in England: Trade grows together with piracy and war and increase of manufactures. Corn is extensively grown by landed proprietors. Gorgeous court attire prevails and a rise in general standard of comfort. Improvement in Elizabethan buildings over those of Middle Ages is evident, with windows and glass introduced, where previously men lived in fortified castles. Manor-houses take the place of the old castles. Chimneys are now introduced. Comfortable bedding takes the place of the straw pallet or bag of chaff. Pewter platters and tin spoons replace wooden ones. The quest after wealth accompanies the introduction of greater luxury.

1588-1595

Literary development: Spenser and Shakespeare are affected by the spirit of the age. They espouse reverence for the reign of law. Spenser's cardinal virtues as enumerated in the *Faerie Queene*—the laws of purity, temperance, and justice prevail. Shakespeare's moral in his plays, the retribution which follows close on the heels of the transgression of law, whether moral or physical, set the tone for the people. Francis Bacon begins to dream of a larger science than known hitherto—a science based on a reverent inquiry into the laws of nature.[7]

End of the Tudor Reign

House of the Elizabethan Period

Small occurrences complete the background of the England wherein Drake failed to be documented and rewarded for his particular efforts. The details which follow may or may not be important to our understanding of this setting. Some are obvious results of previous trends:

1597 An expedition of Essex and Raleigh against Spain results in failure. Essex loses the queen's favor. Philip makes proposals of peace.

1598 Death takes Philip II of Spain. O'Neil of Ireland defeats the English army. Following the deaths of Sir John Norris and Burghley, Robert Cecil succeeds.

1599-1600 Essex is sent to conquer Ireland. He intrigues with James of Scotland, and with Romanists and Puritans. He fails, returns without permission, and is imprisoned.

1601 Essex plans rebellion and seeks partisans among the disaffected, followed by his trial and death, requisitioned by Elizabeth. Spaniards land in Ireland. The first regular Poor Law is passed and also a withdrawal of monopolies.

1603 There follows the submission and pardon of O'Neil, the reconquest of Ireland, and the death of Elizabeth.

1603-1604 With the accession of James I (James VI of Scotland next in line to the throne), peace with Spain is entered into. The Rye plot to change the government and obtain toleration is discovered, leading to the false imprisonment of Sir Walter Raleigh.

1604 Events include the Hampton Court conference and the triumph of the high church party.

1605 The Gunpowder plot is discovered, followed by the flight of conspirators, their capture and execution. Bacon's *Advancement of Learning* is issued.

1616 Raleigh, released from prison, is allowed to go to South America, and makes his last voyage there in 1617.

1618 Failure results in his execution, based on his original sentence, his martyrdom further explained in Chapter 15. We see the beginning of the Thirty Years' War [8]

In conclusion, we include the summary of the nineteenth century historian Gardiner, in regard to the Tudor Era:

"The whole reign of the Tudors was a reign of kings and queens who, for the most part with great sagacity, personally controlled their own government. Such a state of matters in England has never been since and will never be again. But the traditions of a system of government cannot but remain after such government is no longer possible and this was the real rock on which the ship of state foundered in the days of the Stuarts. Parliament was summoned at his bidding as the state of affairs in his opinion required it. Nay, there were theorists who maintained that England was an absolute monarchy. . . the king might make laws as though there were no parliament at all." [9]

— Chapter 14 —

A Legacy Denied

Upon Pain of Death

You recall in our chapter on Drake in Nehalem Bay that his experiences there were in the original journals of Fletcher as edited by himself and others. From various accounts here given you are aware that those descriptions in their original form were forbidden "upon pain of death" during the forty-eight years following his arrival back in England in 1580 until they were published in 1628. During those years, and especially in the decades before Elizabeth I's death in 1603, all accounts, maps, degrees of latitude, and drawings of his sojourn in northwest America were denied, manipulated, distorted, and invalidated in her attempts to deny the exploration he had inaugurated, that is, his claim, surveying, and mapping of the northwest coast. She would then try to honor a favored nobleman who would complete Drake's attempt to locate the so-called Straits of Anian so that England could access and colonize that area.

What didn't happen at that time was postponed indefinitely. Eventually Russian fur traders discretely discovered the Aleutian Islands and Bering Strait, finally dividing the Asian and American continents, and found that the fur from the land otter brought huge profits in China. This demonstrated only that there was open sea to the north, but not a passage over the north American continent. Only in modern times has that been accomplished, but not as a regular route because of the preponderance of ice nearly year round. In addition, it took more than two hundred years before Spain and England finally got together to settle the sovereignty of the area Drake had explored. In 1792 George Vancouver met with Juan Francisco de la Bodega y Quadra to begin that negotiation. It began amicably, with the naming of Quadra and Vancouver Island, Drake's first Nova Albion, and the rediscovery of Puget Sound and the Strait of Juan de Fuca.

What sponsored Elizabeth's obsession with the finding of the Strait of Anian can never be assessed, for its passage could never be accomplished until the Little Ice Age was over and modern-day global warming made its passage feasible. What was lost, however, was the legacy of Francis Drake, seemingly forever, unless modern efforts can salvage what he accomplished all along which has been distorted through the ages.

That legacy of denial is still with us. This writer watched a recent PBS production about Castle Althorp in England, the ancestral home of Diana, Princess of Wales. Its current owner, her brother Charles, earl of Althorp, showed viewers through the castle which existed well before the Elizabethan Age. There in the great hall, amidst extensive columns of rare paintings and portraits which haven't yet been absorbed into museums due to the wealth of the family, was a rare terrestrial globe of Emery Molyneux which was first produced in 1592. Since we learn that only three of the originals exist in England, we assume that this was one of the copies produced in the subsequent decade when some changes were made. Never-the-less, Earl Spencer proudly showed the television audience the globe and, especially, the northwest corner of America which was virtually blank, not having been explored at that time. Bear in mind, this globe was produced in 1592 and thereafter, in the second decade following Drake's magnificent voyage of discovery. What a shame!

It behooves us to follow, in any case, the record of events and personalities involved in the cover-up of Drake's famous voyage. You have been introduced to Richard Hakluyt, the caretaker of his story during all the years of his life following Drake's return. He was in the employ of the queen and could never allow any admittance of Drake's attempts to find the northwest passage or to make a claim for England on the northwest American coast. We will review for the reader initial elements of his story.

Our information is again coming principally through that of Samuel Bawlf of British Columbia in *The Secret Voyage of Sir Francis Drake 1577-1580*, published in 2003, who cites the research of Penzer, Taylor, Quinn and Skelton, Wagner, Wallis, Nuttall, Sugden and others, whose research came forward after the establishment of the Hakluyt Society in 1846, which, as an academic, he has access to. Direct quotes will be attributed to him, as well as abridgments.

In regard to Hakluyt, custodian for the queen of Drake's story in all its denials and revisions during Drake's lifetime, the 2007 book by Peter C. Mancall, *Hakluyt's Promise: An Elizabethan's Obsession for an English America*, which I acquired recently and quoted once in Chapter 9, does not even mention the Hakluyt Society nor any of the researchers mentioned above which Bawlf has cited. He cites only that the "expedition had problems", notably the execution of Doughty, trespassing on Spanish territory, and, of course, piracy, and that "these dilemmas played to the hands of those who argued that Drake's achievement should be kept a secret." [1]

So much for a summation of Drake, our explorer, cartographer, and statesman and his achievements, in a book published by Yale University Press, one who would have led England to make a claim for colonization of the northwest. We proceed, none-the-less with what Bawlf has learned from the aforementioned writers about what Hakluyt actually did to assist in the cover-up of Drake's story.

Fenton's Voyage

As we will see, Hakluyt and his elder cousin imagined exactly what Drake was about and anticipated a great awakening of discovery in the Americas. Already he was outlining what the right navigator should attempt which ought to have been a great benefit to England. His 1582 publication was entitled *Diverse Voyages to America and the Islands Adjacent* and revealed that Drake was one of his financial backers. "Francis Drake Englishman" was listed for the year 1578 as exploring the "back side of America" and was encouraging the hope of finding a northwest passage.

Also in the book was a map by Frobisher's former partner, Michael Lok, which confirmed what one made by Dee had established, that the Pacific coast of America was just 140 degrees west of England and suggested that both ends of the northwest passage had been reconnoitered by the English, something which had not yet been established. As we shall see, this was something forbidden by the English monarch.

This 1582 publication by an aspiring maritime chronicler and Welshman printed the record of the first voyages to the New World, following in the footsteps of his cousin and mentor, Richard Hakluyt the elder, a lawyer and member of the Middle Temple—which offered instruction to young courtiers—who was deeply interested in geography, and, in 1577, in association with men such as Dee and Gilbert, had written a treatise for laying out a site for England's first colony. The younger Hakluyt was, in his new book, beginning a career that would lead him to become England's foremost advocate for maritime exploration. [2]

Since details of Drake's voyage were forbidden, in it Hakluyt was only at liberty to describe the voyage of Edward Fenton in 1582. We have mentioned that voyage but have not given details of its scientific preparation. When Elizabeth engaged first Frobisher, then Fenton, to repeat Drake's famous voyage, details appeared in Hakluyt's book. The pilot of the planned voyage was Christopher Hall, appointed by Leicester, who had been the chief pilot on Frobisher's arctic voyages in the northeast and had been instructed in navigation by Dee. Fenton's chaplain, also appointed by Leicester whose *Galleon Leicester* Hall would command, was Richard Madox, who kept a diary of the journey demonstrating a sophisticated knowledge of navigation and astronomy, since the subject of longitude was of great importance to the men who were preparing for Fenton's expedition. During preparations for the voyage, he wrote a long entry describing the lunar distance of establishing longitude such as William Bourne had done in his *Regiment for the Sea*, published in 1574. We have seen Drake's replica of that method in his survey at Nehalem Bay and Neahkahnie Mountain.

During the voyage Madox evidently talked with Drake's men, whom Elizabeth had shifted to Fenton's voyage, who indicated that Drake had careened his ship "at 48 degrees to the north," on "the back side of Labrador." The diary entry is important now as the first indication of a latitude for Drake and also a longitude which was not as far west as had previously been indicated. Drake's men aboard the journey included Drake's trusted lieutenant, William Hawkins, nephew of John Hawkins, and a dozen or so veterans of Drake's voyage, including the artist John Drake, age twenty, serving as captain of the *Francis*.

Fenton's expedition set sail on May 1, 1582. It soon became apparent to Drake's men that Fenton was not at all enthusiastic about the proposed voyage. He first sailed to the island of St. Helena in the south Atlantic, proposed to take over the island, seize Portuguese carracks coming and going via the Cape of Good Hope, and send their spoils to England. When that didn't happen, his officers persuaded him to adhere to their original plan.

When they arrived on the coast of Brazil, yet 300 miles from the Rio de la Plata, he called his officers together to consider a return home. All but Drake's men finally agreed to this. Young John Drake was infuriated by this decision and during the following night deserted the expedition in the *Francis*. The expedition continued homeward, first encountering three Spanish ships and sinking one of them, while John Drake continued on to Rio de la Plata. It is not clear what he hoped to achieve with only seventeen men and but a few provisions.

They sailed some distance up the river, as Francis Drake had done, but soon came to disaster and wrecked their ship on the rocks. Sadly, they were captured and enslaved by the Indians. John and two others managed to steal a canoe and escape across the river where they met up with Spaniards and were take to Buenos Aires. John assumed an alias; but a man aboard the vessel Fenton had intercepted arrived and identified him as the "nephew" of Drake. He was then taken to Santa Fe and eventually transported to Lima and the Inquisition. [3]

It is stated that Fenton was eventually imprisoned, having been accused of conspiring with the Spanish ambassador to sabotage the voyage.

The Making of Maps

So what was happening to Sir Francis Drake at the end of his arduous voyage? Having become wealthy, and denied the credit for his principal achievement, he concentrated on the acquisition and administration of his property, since at least Elizabeth fulfilled the required protocol of endowing him with numerous estates as befitted a knight of her realm. His wife Mary died in 1583, after their brief marriage of twelve years, leaving him with no heirs. News of Fenton's debacle and imprisonment reached him, along with the disturbing news of his cousin John's capture and imprisonment in the Spanish Inquisition.

It was time at least for Drake to do what he could to preserve his knowledge of the Americas, as long as it did not disobey the queen's prohibitions. Drake began a decades-long friendship with Jodocus Hondius, who was having Ortelius draw by hand many maps which, of course, had to pass by Walsingham who was still enforcing the official secrecy. The queen's rule was that on these maps there was to be no hint of a northwest passage and that Nova Albion was to be placed in a latitude ten degrees south of its true position. As a result, Drake's maps and routes formed a carefully conceived representation that was intelligible only to those who knew the rules for the true location of his northern discoveries. Of these various maps there was one for the archbishop of Canterbury, which was lost; an Ortelius world map showing him reaching 57 degrees; the Drake-Mellon map of 1584 adding the 1585-86 Caribbean expedition; and the French Drake map. The latter two show a boundary line separating North America from New Spain. Each of these maps had expository and contradictory elements valuable to mariners at the time, but which bring fresh insights into the present.

Despite the queen's preoccupation with secrecy, Drake had hopes of a new South Sea voyage, but he was to be disappointed. His second voyage was first approved by the queen and signed for in December of 1584 when William of Orange was assassinated in the Netherlands, and she foresaw the need to support that theater in every way possible against the Spanish if it could be advanced without open hostilities. Therefore, Drake's second voyage was changed to the Caribbean, since Elizabeth needed more funds to support her favorite, the earl of Leicester, in his command in the Low Countries. Noted also was Drake's second marriage and establishment of a house in London. [4]

We encounter here important developments for Drake in the contacts that Hakluyt was making outside of England. It is best told by Bawlf quoting from Wallis's book and the *Calendar of State Papers - Foreign*, as compiled by Hume:

"While Drake was assembling his fleet, Walsingham was scrambling to round up allies for the coming fight with Spain. Still of the greatest importance was the posture France would adopt in the conflict. Working in Paris, ostensibly as secretary to English ambassador Sir Edward Stafford, but also gathering intelligence about French and Spanish activities in the New World for Walsingham, was the younger Richard Hakluyt. There Hakluyt found much curiosity and speculation about Drake's great voyage. On October 16, 1584, Ambassador Stafford had written to Walsingham: 'I find from Mr. Hakluyt that Drake's journey is kept very secret in England, but here is in everyone's mouths. When questioned about it I have answered as an ignorant body, as indeed I am, except for what I find by their speeches here. It may [be] they hit not all right, but they guess in great part.'"[5]

We follow that in March 1585 Walsingham received a letter from Henry of Navarre— next in line to the throne of France— requesting a chart and a "discourse" of Drake's voyage. This was an opportune time for all involved, for it gave Walsingham the chance to discuss with the future king the possibility of an alliance. It could even have been that Walsingham had Stafford plant the idea to facilitate this opening. In Bawlf's words:

"In any case, receipt of a map 'many coloured and gilded' was soon acknowledged by Henry, and with it presumably he received the discourse of Drake's voyage he
had requested, because later in the year an account of the voyage was also sent to another
Protestant prince, William of Hesse. No doubt the intended message was the same: If the
Protestant princes of Europe were prepared to join the fight against Spain, England had
the man who would lead them to victory on any sea. Thus, it was no longer a question
of no details of Drake's voyage being given out, but rather what information would be
provided and to whom. " [6]

Drake's reputation was well-known and a great asset to England's
foreign policy, but neither account sent to these potential allies has survived; the manuscript account, however, known as the *Anonymous Narrative* upon which they were probably based has. That account, entitled *A
discourse of Sir Francis Drake's journey and exploits. . . into Mare de Sur,*
appears to have been adapted from a deposition taken from one of Drake's
company shortly after their return; but it also does not mention Drake's
northern explorations.

This latter account, as previously mentioned, after devoting some
2,000 words to Drake's voyage from southern Chile to Guatulco, offered
fewer than 200 words about his journey to northwest America and on to
the Moluccas. It is significant, however, that the writer had changed the
latitude twice: first writing 50 degrees, it was changed to 53 degrees and
finally adapted to 48 degrees. This was the same latitude as was given by
Fenton's chaplain Madox and John Drake in his depositions. Neither does
it mention the islands of John Drake's deposition nor the Nova Albion. It
does, however, state that their latitude at careening was at 44 degrees, a
significant offering. It is interesting to note that Bawlf credits Bob Ward,
one of the original assemblers of the relics at Nehalem, with drawing the
altered numerals to his attention in 1995. [7]

With the inevitability that some of this information would find its
way to Philip's ambassadors, Elizabeth's hope to avoid hostilities with
Spain was fast disappearing. It came about that Philip ordered all English
merchant shipping in Spanish ports to cease, in effect, leading to a crisis in
England.

Drake then amassed a fleet of 25 ships, eight pinnaces, and 2,300
men and sailed into the northern Spanish port of Vigo, demanding to know
why English ships had been impounded and whether Spain was at war
with England or not. Seeing Drake's formidable fleet the Spanish governor
denied knowing anything about a war and quickly released the English
merchantmen and supplied him with whatever supplies they needed.

"Then sailing to the Cape Verde Islands where inhabitants fled to the mountains and refused to pay a ransom, he put their ships to the torch and then set sail to the Caribbean. First he conquered Hispaniola on Dec 29, then Santo Domingo, the oldest Spanish settlement in the New World on New Year's Day, and then on to Cartagena. There he landed 1,000 men and conquered that city the following day, February 10th." [8]

Soon, however, pestilence aboard ships took the lives of 300 men. Pursuing his mission he approached the coast of Florida where he razed the fort and town of St. Augustine on May 27th which he considered a threat to Raleigh's colony at Roanoke. Arriving then at the latter, he found the colony destitute and brought its inhabitants back to England.

His arrival back in England was heralded with church bells. The populace proclaimed him the greatest naval genius of the age, and the weakness of Philip's colonial defenses was exposed to all the world.

Imagine his discomfiture, however, upon arriving home after less than a year, to find that a new expedition to the Pacific under the command of Thomas Cavendish had departed only a few days previously. Since Drake had been expected, it is assumed that Cavendish wished to avoid a meeting with Drake and was probably under instructions to do so. Elizabeth had no intention of allowing him to complete his labors while there was any threat of a Spanish invasion.

The veracity of various maps emanating from Drake's association with the map-maker Jocobus Hondius scholars and enthusiasts of Drake's voyage have been debated through the centuries, as well as the legends that were distorted and evaded. Our attention turns again to the three maps produced in the 1590s which might have led explorers astray had they not been informed of their discrepancies. Needless to say, historians have not known of those distortions, and thus the extent of Drake's explorations have been eviscerated and lost.

We turn again to those three maps that Bawlf lists in the latter category with the suggested revisions which have come down to us. The first is the so-called French Drake map which depicts Drake's landing at latitude 30 degrees, on an island which is one of four. In the bottom margin a note states in French that it is seen and corrected by the aforementioned Sir Drake. Yet it is a copy of the one sent to Henry of Navarre which claimed his travel to 48 degrees where, in French he "turned back because of the ice,"

A year later, a finished copy of the map was printed in the Netherlands, with the inscriptions changed to Dutch, which has two significant changes. It has a broad sea passage reaching across the top of America, and the island where Drake "turned back on account of the ice" has been carefully redrawn to become the largest of the four.

On the third map printed in 1587, Ortelius had ingrained a new edition to incorporate Drake's information about a chain of coastal islands which are about ten degrees higher in latitude than they appear on Henry of Navarre's map. On this map Hondius has placed an island noted as "bay of small ships" and added "strong currents" at 54 degrees, "river of the straits" at 49 degrees, "cape of worries" at 48 degrees and further down the coast a "great river." In total, Drake had provided a total of more than twenty distinct place names, though some were somewhat misplaced on the imaginary coast line given to Ortelius in Spanish.

These three are outlined by Bawlf, and he states that "Richard Hakluyt's 1587 map of the new world placed Nova Albion at latitude 50 degrees and depicted the trend of the coast to the north with remarkable accuracy." [9]

This third map is identical in contour to one Gitzen cites in an article, *"Edward Wright's World Chart of 1599"* published in the Terrae Incognitae, vol. 46.1, April 2014 by the **Journal of the Society for the History of Discoveries**. which is included in Hakluyt's second printing of his magnum opus in 1599. However, Wright's map contains an overlay of lines radiating from the 45 degree placement of Nova Albion. Gitzen feels it is particularly significant in identifying Drake's careening exactly where it occurred, at 45 degrees, with a focus on that compass point to guide other mariners, a map that had been neglected through the ages. Helen Wallis, Keeper of the Maps at the British Museum, first drew it to the attention of the Hakluyt Society. [10]

Distorted Accounts

An attempt is made here to mention in the correct time sequence the various written reports of Drake's journey. You recall that the carefully kept journal of Francis Fletcher was taken from him by Drake before arrival back in Plymouth and that, in due course it is reported, all journals and maps were taken from Drake at his first meeting with Queen Elizabeth. There were initially two journals not subject to that scrutiny, first, the *Anonymous Narrative*, thought to have been written by a close associate of Drake's who may have had access to Fletcher's journal, and, in addition, the Philip Nichols's account which he wrote for Drake,

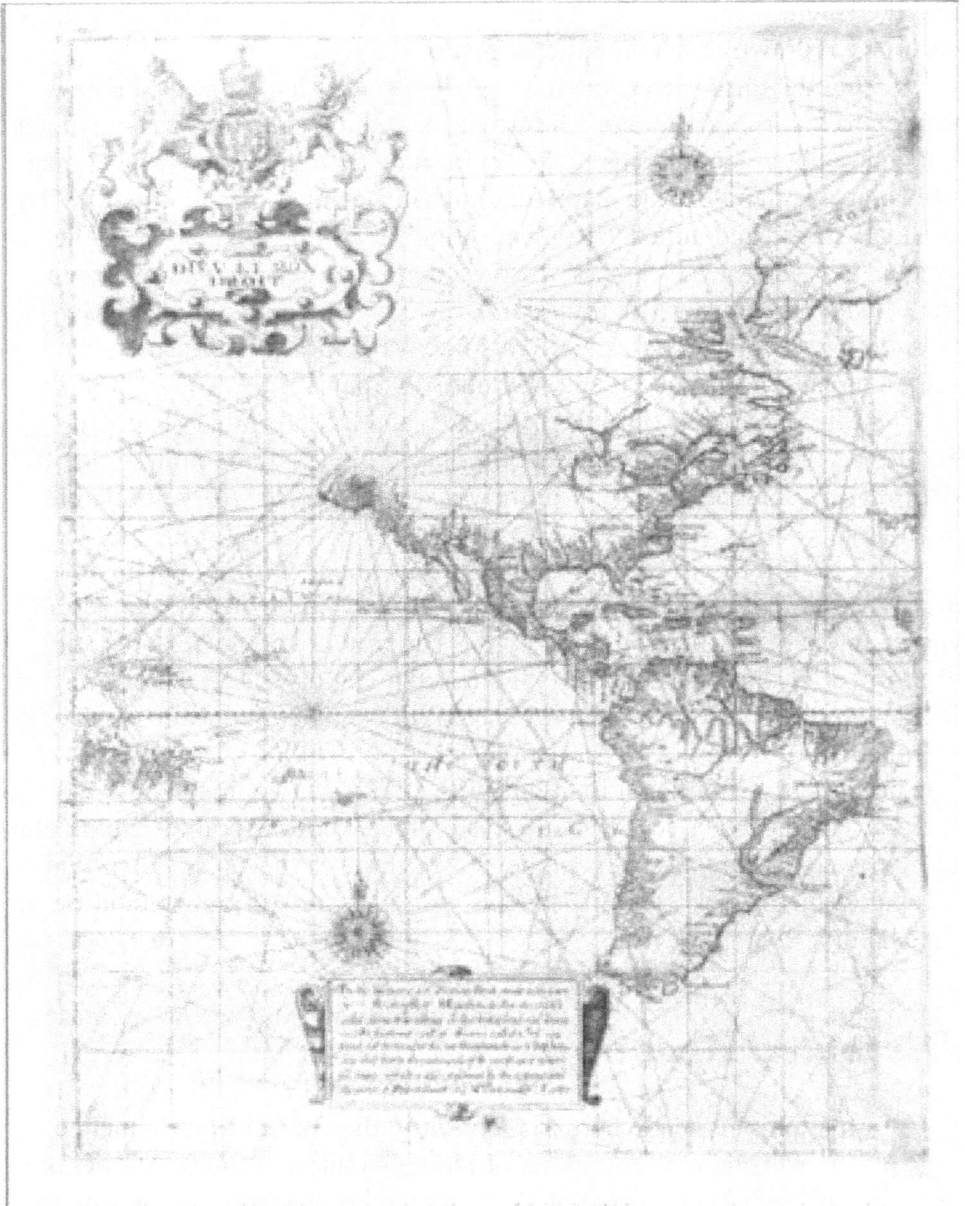

Edward Wright's World Chart of 1599

expecting to make it one of two volumes they wished to publish together. The latter was to be about the 1577 voyage as well as the Isthmus of Panama account during which Drake aspired to establish a colony for England on the great South Sea, two accounts in opposition, since that venture did not come about.

All other accounts, maps and records were taken from Drake and placed, it is said, in the Tower of London. If the queen and Walsingham had access to them for a while, which is likely, they eventually disappeared, possibly in the fire of Whitehall, where they may have been moved. What notes Drake had on the journals is not known. He went on assisting in the drawing of maps with Hondius, as indicated, and, it is believed, continued at various times to rewrite and edit the account as first transcribed by Philip Nichols.

The principal custodian of Drake's story, however, was Richard Hakluyt, who was under the queen's employ, and, it is believed, continued to honor her wishes even after her death. His activities in that capacity are here reported. Bawlf here further describes also the maps listed above:

"Richard Hakluyt was still residing in Paris, although he returned to London at frequent intervals carrying secret dispatches to Walsingham. In April 1587, as Drake was assaulting Cadiz, he printed in Paris a new edition of Peter Martyr's celebrated history of Spain's American empire, *Decades of the New World*. Then in May, before the book was bound, he inserted in it an extraordinary map of the New World. On it were noted Frobisher's Meta Incognita in the far northeast, Raleigh's Virginia on the east coast, Drake's Elizabeth Island at the southern extremity of the continent, and then, far away in northwest America, Nova Albion. As it was the first printed map to do so, it appears that Walsingham had decided to announce England's territorial claims in the New World. Certainly, Hakluyt could not have published the map without Walsingham's permission.

"What was most remarkable about the map, however, was the detail of the northwest coast of America. As on the earlier maps of Dee and Lok, the coast lay, in longitude, just 140 degrees west of England, in sharp contrast to Abraham Ortelius's popularly accepted notion. And on the coast, Nova Albion was placed at its true latitude of 50 degrees north. From Nova Albion the coastline continued northwest and north to 55 degrees and then began to curl westward toward Asia, just as the coast of Alaska does, so that the map bore a closer resemblance to the actual trend of the coastline than any that would be produced for two centuries thereafter." [11]

In 1587, before the attack on Cadiz and the Spanish Armada, Cavendish had arrived back September 9 from his circumnavigation. He had plundered a Manila galleon off the Pacific coast of Mexico, sunk nineteen Spanish ships, and burned Acapulco, then sent one of the two remaining ships toward the "North-west passage, standing in 55 degrees" as he had somehow learned the latitude of Drake's discoveries. His ship of exploration had not returned however, again leaving the existence of the passage in doubt. He did not support Drake's contention that Tierra del Fuego was composed of islands, leaving the impression that Drake's supposed discovery of the Strait of Anian was also a figment of his imagination.

Cavendish's return, however, was immensely celebrated in London, leaving Drake a bit annoyed; however Drake had received assurances from Walsingham that publication of an account of his own great voyage would soon be permitted. That hope was to be put aside, however, since it seems that the Armada, once driven back by initial storms, would indeed make its move toward the Netherlands, where Parma was assembling troops, and then invade England. Hence, all other concerns were put on hold throughout that long season of battle, in which they would produce a preemptive strike against Cadiz. It was decided in the Privy Council, as previously told, that Lord Howard of Effingham would lead the combined forces, with Drake serving as his vice admiral. They set sail for Spain three times, only to driven back by the storms.

During that long season, as we know, it was Spain that was delayed and driven back by unseasonable storms, so that their arrival produced considerable ado as the English quickly assembled their ground and naval forces. In fact, it was a considerable time after the Spanish fleet was finally driven north after their initial confrontation — where the firestorm had been created to disorganize them — that the English knew how badly Medina Sidonia's men had been beaten and had perished on the coasts of Scotland and Ireland. As news and celebrations began to occur in England, the earl of Leicester suddenly collapsed and died. [12]

It is said that Drake was greatly taken back by Leicester's death, since he had been a great support to him in his dealings with the queen and with Walsingham. He knew that without the backing of Walsingham, the balance of support would swing back to Burghley in the Privy Council. Instead of the publication he and Philip Nichols had been promised, Walsingham was now backing a new enterprise which Hakluyt had been planning for years. [13]

It was to be a three-volume set entitled *The Principal Navigations, Voyages, and Discoveries of the English Nation,* sponsored by and dedicated to Walsingham which would be a masterpiece of propaganda for the English maritime service. In anticipation of that project, Hakluyt began packing his papers in Paris, and by the new year he was back in London gathering material for his book which would eventually run to more than 800 pages.

In Bawlf's words we learn a bit more about Hakluyt's actual access to everything extant which pertained to Drake's journey and his actual control over what was to be published :

"For Drake's voyage he already had the use of the anonymous narrative containing the altered latitude of Drake's northern reach, but this compressed Drake's northern exploit into fewer words than Hakluyt hoped to offer his readers. The chief inadequacy in the narrative was the absence of any information about Nova Albion—its discovery, its resources, climate, and people, and Drake's taking possession of it for England. However, editing Fletcher's journal, Nichols had produced a more fulsome account of the voyage, including a description of Nova Albion, and Hakluyt was able to borrow Nichols's draft account to enhance his narrative.

"In the spring of 1589, as Hakluyt continued writing and editing, George Bishop and Ralph Newberie, deputies to the Queen's printer, began printing the first sections of his book, including the title page containing the long-awaited announcement. The third part of the volume, it promised, would contain an account of a voyage to the South Sea and 'Nova Albion upon the backside of Canada, further than ever any Christian hitherto hath pierced.'

"A special medallion had been issued to commemorate Drake's voyage which conformed to the same 1585 map for Henry of Navarre, and these details were supposed to draw the public's attention toward the narrative that Hakluyt was preparing." [14]

The significance of the latter information about the design of the medallion is that by drawing the coast of the North American coast westward, instead of conforming to the Wright map, attention would be drawn away from the possibility of England's seeking the northwest passage.

The promise of an account of Drake's voyage in the third part of Hakluyt's book did not, of course, come to pass. Somehow attention was driven toward the need for Drake in the naval campaign against Carunna which turned out so disastrously for Drake. After that debacle, in February 1589, described elsewhere, the Privy Council sent a note requesting what new enterprise might be recommended "for the greatest annoyance of the enemy." Drake and Norris did not respond except to remind them that they had neither ships nor men that would be fit for another campaign that summer, and it has been suggested that the failure of the expedition was the cause of an apparent falling-out between Drake and Elizabeth later that year. [15]

When that "new enterprise" did not happen, Elizabeth had the story of Drake's great voyage withdrawn. Drake left the court in November and did not actually return for another three years. He had experienced Elizabeth's cold shoulder often before. Hakluyt, at the end of the month, with his book printed and awaiting binding, was obliged to insert a note explaining that he was unable to provide his promised account of Drake's voyage after all.

Why did Elizabeth fail to acknowledge Drake and his immense labors to make a claim for England? His story was not going to be left for posterity, and in time it would be distorted and forgotten. A portion of Bawlf's analysis is here given:

> "In her meetings with Drake after his return from the Pacific, it had been agreed that Nova Albion had to remain a closely guarded secret until the discovery of the northwest passage was completed and the colony was securely established lest the Spanish discover its location and move to prevent these developments. Indeed, it undoubtedly was by her order that the ban on publication had been imposed in the first instance. Therefore, there is reason to believe that she may have been displeased when she learned Walsingham was sponsoring publication of an account of Drake's voyage, including a description of Nova Albion, in spite of the fact that Cavendish's second ship had failed to return and the discovery of the northwest passage had yet to be completed.

> "There may have been some genuine hope that Cavendish's second ship, the *Content*, with its load of treasure, might yet return in the summer of 1589 when the ice had cleared from the supposed Strait of Anian or by way of the Magellan's Strait. By fall, however, that could not have been the case. So when Hakluyt delivered the last part of his book to the printers, Drake's voyage was not included." [16]

One does not know what else might have happened to cause a breach in Drake's rapport with Elizabeth, if it ever existed. She could manipulate the affections of her favorites, but she had no need to appease Drake. Therefore, early in 1590 Hakluyt's magnificent compendium of English voyages and discoveries was released without an account of the greatest voyage of all, **instead recommending to the reader that his account of the Cavendish voyage would satisfy their curiosity about the South Sea**. [emphasis mine]

On April 6, 1590 Sir Francis Walsingham died, Drake's last great friend on the Privy Council who had so well backed Drake's efforts to stand up to the Spanish. There was no longer anyone who would credit him if he should "burn the Spanish' whiskers."

The Molyneux Globe

This chapter began with an expression of regret that magnificent relics yet extant in England in certain museums and castles, e. g., the Molyneux globe-maps produced by Emery Molyneux—with a diameter of twenty-five inches, the most detailed and largest made in the 1590s in England—failed to credit Drake with the detailed map he worked so hard to achieve. There on the globe is a blank contrived shoreline in the Pacific northwest where there should be rivers, inlets, islands and place names which he labored so hard to achieve.

In John Davis's three voyages of 1585, 1586, and 1587, it was well documented where he had explored the strait running north between Greenland and Baffin Island. Davis had taken a twenty-ton pinnace across the Atlantic into the strait to the latitude of 73 degrees, 400 miles above the Arctic Circle. There he saw an open sea extending northwest free of ice, but was unable to go further due to an opposing wind and lack of provisions.

On his return, Davis introduced his sponsor, William Sanderson, to Molyneux, a mathematician and instrument maker who proposed to make a globe to illustrate as realistically as possible Drake's voyage and his own. Walsingham had approved the project, and Jodocus Hondius had agreed to engrave the globe-map. There was convergence also with a Dutch mapmaker, Peter Plancius, who had undertaken to produce one in the Netherlands. Because of the faulty maps that had been tampered with by those carrying out Elizabeth's protocol, his entire coastline was imaginary. He had only the place names somehow gathered from various maps with the accepted degrees of latitude to guide him, which were some 10 degrees in error.

The Molyneux Globe

Molyneux was not to be discouraged, however In 1590 he set sail for the Pacific with a ship and a pinnace. Near the Canary Island, however, his ship suffered heavy damage and he was compelled to return home. Then, when plans were laid to send Thomas Cavendish on a new expedition to the Pacific, Molyneux was encouraged to approach Queen Elizabeth with his first model of the map-globe, which as yet had large areas that were undefined. His much-anticipated terrestrial globe, engraved and colored, was presented to her majesty at Greenwich Palace.

Soon afterward the globe was observed to be covered down to the floor by a taffeta curtain. Consequently it was deemed appropriate for sale only to persons of importance in England and abroad, with a less revealing edition for wider consumption. Therefore, in his second attempt, completed in 1592, Molyneux removed Drake's island of Nova Albion and cut off the coast to the north at latitude 54 degrees. He retained the inscription "Nova Albion," however, straddling the 50th parallel.

The third edition, however, also engraved in 1592, was again judged to be too revealing, and he was obliged to thrust the northwest coast of America some 1,500 miles further west in longitude and to move the inscription "Nova Albion" from latitude 50 degrees, which would have been Vancouver Island, down to 46 degrees.

By the time the third edition was completed, the cost had reached L1,000, an astonishing sum for his patron, William Sanderson. This grotesque globe was parodied by William Shakespeare, who compared a robust kitchen maid to a terrestrial globe in *The Comedy of Errors* and used it to furnish the title of the soon to be Globe Theatre.

The thinly-veiled cover-up of Drake's voyage was notably discussed around England; for example, Thomas Blundeville, a mathematics instructor at the Inns of Court, wrote a treatise on the globe in which he described Drake's track around the world as exceeding 12,010 leagues (36,030 miles), but that he knew there was more to the voyage than had been reported. He ended his treatise with a thinly veiled appeal to the queen to allow Drake to provide a detailed account of his whole voyage, "of all which things," he said,"I doubt not that he hath already written."

With his own five ships, on Cavendish's second voyage to the South Seas, explorer John Davis was to be escorted by Cavendish to California, and from there to make his way to discover the northwest passage. They had made their way part of the way through Magellan's Strait but could get no further due to violent headwinds. They retreated to Patagonia for repairs. Cavendish's ship became separated from the others, however, and he became ill and died at sea in June. His men then turned back for England.

Davis then made three more attempts to get through the strait, finally reaching the Pacific, but had to retreat, with sails in tatters and men dying from scurvy. Taking two months to gather enough penguin meat for the journey home, he was attacked by the Portuguese and Indians and lost thirteen more of his men. In the tropics the meat turned to maggots, and eleven more died.

When Davis finally arrived in Ireland on June 11, 1593, only fifteen out of his original company of seventy-six men remained alive. The news of the failure of the voyage had already reached England. [17]

— Chapter 15 —

The Martyrs

The Final "No"

B etween the years 1589 and 1592 Drake spent most of his time at his
residence at Buckland Abbey, expanding Plymouth's fortifications
and creating a new water supply for the town. There he also spent
much time editing and revising Philip Nichols's accounts taken from the
original Fletcher's journals, hoping for the day when he would be allowed
to publish them.

He was finally invited to the court just before Christmas 1592 and
received warmly by Elizabeth. Apparently all was forgiven and forgotten,
or perhaps her treasury was running low and she wished to initiate a new
expedition of plunder. Drake wasted no time, however, in submitting his
revised manuscripts for her approval. On New Years' Day he wrote to his
sovereign:

"Madam

Seeing diverse [others] have diversely reported and written of these voyages
and actions which I have attempted and made. . . whereby many untruths have been
published. . . so I have accounted it to present this discourse to Your Majesty. . . being the
first fruits of thy servant's pen. . .

[Drake was not apologizing for anything he had done, but trying to
set the record straight. He had written for the ages.]

"that posterity be not deprived of such help as may happily be gained hereby,
and our present age at least may be satisfied in the rightfulness of these actions, which
hitherto have been silenced."

He wrote that he hoped his labor would not be lost and that Elizabeth might at last have been favorably disposed toward publication of an account of his Pacific voyage. Drake's hopes of seeing his own story of the voyage in print, however, were once more dashed.

In Drake's account he took his narrative only to 48 degrees and included Fletcher's description of events at the harbor where they careened. However he still maintained that the purpose of the voyage was to discover the north passage around the extremity of America. He wished, above all, to be remembered by posterity for what he attempted even if he did not succeed in the quest. Therefore he wrote that after a vigorous search no strait was to be found. In Elizabeth's mind, however, the admission that this was his purpose was unacceptable.

It was thereafter determined that Richard Hakluyt should rework the short narrative he had abridged from Philip Nichols's adaptation of Fletcher's journal and eliminate all mention of a search for the northern strait. It was only to say that after departing Guatulco Drake had taken a "somewhat northerly" route for the Moluccas, but that after encountering bitterly cold winds at latitude 42 degrees he turned back. He was to say that Drake then found a harbor at 38 degrees in which to careen his boats which he named Nova Albion.

With permission to publish the revised narrative, Hakluyt ironically neglected to have the printers remove the note in the margin of an old page reading that "the purpose of Sir Francis [was] to return by the Northwest passage" which was included in the carefully edited account.

Hakluyt then published the revised narrative, entitled *The Famous Voyage of Sir Francis Drake,* in his magnum opus, which included the famous and splendid map of the world designed and engraved by Hondius. In the upper corners Hondius had added two more scenes, called broadsides, the one in the left depicting the bay in Northwest America where Drake careened his ships, labeled "Portus Nova Albionis" which matches Nehalem Bay more precisely than any other bay on the west coast.

To a small extent this was a milestone for history, placing the Nova Albion in a bay on the upper coast of America, except that it was now at 40 degrees. Spanish claims were at 38 degrees and that is the claim of California today. It was on Spanish territory.

The Hondius's Broadside map shows Nova Albion placed back at latitude 40 degrees, but a smudged area shows where the map's engraved plate had been scrubbed to erase Drake's track northward to 42 degrees. Nehalem Bay is at 45 degrees, so these manipulations were designed in

1592 only to allay any Spanish suspicions that Drake might have made a claim that wasn't already their own territory.

Further to deny Drake honor for his claims, Hondius had been instructed to include Cavendish's voyage on the map, also to include a note stating that he did not find Tierra del Fuego to be composed of islands as Drake had claimed. A decision had been made to deny Drake's discoveries here as well. Elizabeth had desperately wanted to honor Cavendish for Drake's discoveries in the New World. After all, Cavendish's noble lineage now extends forward through many generations as dukes of Devonshire while Drake has none.

In spite of these revisions, Hondius's map still showed Drake reaching northward to 48 degrees before he turned back "on account of ice," as stated in Drake's revised account and presented to Elizabeth on New Year's Day 1593. Thus an unsuccessful attempt was made to alter the engraved plate back to 42 degrees to conform to Hakluyt's revisions. These changes are not visible on the Hondius map as usually presented; however, in Bawlf's book he presents greatly enlarged evidence of them.

To further confuse history, Hondius reissued the map in 1594 in the Netherlands and again refers to Nova Albion as an island, apparently adapted from a different rendition of Hakluyt's narrative he had made before adjusting it for publication in England. [1]

You are already appraised of Drake's last voyage for Elizabeth during which first his cousin John Hawkins perished, and then he himself, through a combination of storms, failures, and, finally, a pestilence which brought him down in torrid weather. Elizabeth would go on, with her propensity to promote ineffective, haughty, and corrupt nobles until they finally could no longer abide her control of their emotional lives. Before her life ended she tried and executed her latest and youngest favorite, Robert Devereux, 2nd earl of Essex, in 1601 — whom she had made lord-lieu-

tenant of Ireland—for his conspiracies and failures there.

Elsewhere we evaluate her legacy. She left her nation nearly
bankrupt, but at least on the edge of a challenge to absolute authority. Her
successor, James I, tended to carry it on and to appease the Spanish by
beheading Raleigh. Eventually, however, respect for the laws of the land
and a progress towards civil liberty and the life of the mind ensued, and
the Renaissance was on its way.

Spain's Secrecy

There will come, after the years have lapsed,
cycles wherein oceans shall loosen the chains of things,
and a vast land shall be revealed,

—Seneca, Medea

C olumbus was fond of quoting the above. It was in many ways a
disaster to the world that America was discovered at a period when
the Inquisition was filling hearts with a blood-thirst for inflicting
pain, taking life, and suppressing thought in the midst of their devotion
to torture as a fine art, to the avenging of Christ's crucifixion upon the
Jews of their own day, and to the waging upon the sword and heretic race
of Moors a ruthless feud under the alias of a holy war. As great good and
great evil fought bitterly in the soul of Columbus, so they have fought in
the results of his discovery.

In order to hide their prize from a greedy world, Spain took great
pains to keep details of the discovery from other possible adventurers.
Word of his achievements were published in other countries before Ferdinand and Isabella would allow his exploits to reach the ears of their own
people. It is said that Columbus was present in Portugal when the austrolo-
be was invented there, but, as a navigator, he had not even mastered the
ways of calculating the latitude; therefore, there was no great amount of
knowledge to hide. His motivation was based on the ancients, astronomy,
and what little had been speculated about the world's geography. He was
slow to learn his discoveries had nothing to do with India or Cathay.

Thus began a reign of secrecy on the Iberian peninsula, since Spain
and Portugal had received the pope's blessing and their separate portion
each of the new world. Within Spain and Portugal there was a fear of
arousing domestic competitors who would be in competition to the crown.
Outside those countries, reports of Vespucci's voyage, which took place in

1509, were the most widely printed of all voyages to the new world in the thirty-five years after Columbus first sailed west. Sixty editions recalling Vespucci's voyage were printed in those years all over Europe. Yet none appeared in either Spain or Portugal. This suggests the Iberian rulers did not want to threaten their government monopoly by stirring up private competition even among their own people.

Thus, one might ask, does secrecy breed monopoly, or does monopoly breed secrecy? The aim to monopolize any treasure or spoils must be the reason that Spain, for example, would wish to keep secret her advances in the new world. That she had no intention of opening up commerce or prosperity to her own people, let alone to human beings on the other side of the world goes without saying. She would advance troops and horses for the conquering of new world inhabitants in order to enrich the crown and those she would enfranchise, but there would be no charters for colonists to enrich themselves.

A curious parallel to the Spanish experience had occurred on the other side of the earth not many years before. Similarly, the seafaring exploits of the eunuch Cing Ho took the ships of China all over the East, in 1433. That empire then retracted into itself all knowledge of the expedition. As in Spain a decade or so later, in 1480 another Chinese eunuch who had risen to power wished to start a maritime expedition, but the officials of the Chinese war office destroyed the records of the earlier expedition to prevent his carrying out the forbidden work.

We are of course inspired to compare the secrecy around Columbus's voyage with that of Sir Francis Drake. It is indeed odd that it was so necessary to take and prevent access to the illustrated log that he and his cousin had so laboriously produced. It may have been top secret because of the Spanish claims. But their explorations were not on Spanish claims. It should not have taken much time to assess that Spain would not and could not object. Any hostilities she had were certainly in another direction, for example, England's support of the Netherlands, which was much more at hand.

Following the pattern of Spain and China, as it were, in 1589, when Richard Hakluyt published his famous compendium of notable *Principall Navigations, Voyages and Discoveries of the English Nation*—made by sea or over land to the most remote and farthest distant quarters of the earth—there still was no account of Drake's circumnavigation. When the ban was lifted within the next decade and extra pages were bound into his volume to recount Drake's famous voyage, it still did not state his claim for England or present the correct maps and degrees of latitude. [2]

The Passion for Discovery

Before we tell the story of Columbus's martyrdom, we will catalogue the expeditions which did result when word finally got
out to the nations concerning the earth's expanded horizons. The
following summaries, however, are taken from accounts written after the
fact of Spain's extreme secrecy and indicate a growing trend among those
informed of the discovery. Time was lost, however, and real initiative was
taken by informed countries outside the Iberian peninsula.

It was really the Portuguese who began the great passion for discovery. The Cape of Good Hope was discovered by Bartholomeu Dias, a
Portuguese navigator, in 1487. The demarcation line restricted the enthusiasm of the English, then a Catholic nation temporarily, but not for long.
Rapidly — at a time when there were no newspapers and television systems
to spread news — all the seafaring peoples of the Atlantic coast felt the
impetus for exploration, and turned their hopes westward.

The Spanish finally took the lead in enthusiasm and in numbers,
however, till, as Galvano said in Hakluyt's version, "there grew such a
common desire of travaile among the Spanyards, that they were ready to
leape into the sea to swim, if it had been possible, into those new-found
parts." Once his voyage had been made, imitation was so easy that, as
Columbus wrote, "Now there is not a man, down to the very tailors, who
does not beg permission to be a discoverer."

Henry Smith Williams, LL.D., editor of the *Historians History of
the World* made these summaries:

"But Italy had furnished the inspiration, through Marco Polo and Toscanelli, as
well as the men, for many of the best discoveries, though she did not get the credit. In
Genoa was born Columbo (known to the Spanish as Colon) though he was a naturalized
citizen of Venice, whence came also Polo and Cadamosto. In Venice was born the unjustly maligned Amerigo Vespucci, whose name though given only to the part of the continent which he explored soon spread to the whole new world. Florence also lent to France
the true discoverer of the Hudson river, Verrazano.

"To Spain belong by birth and service the brilliantly and bloodily ruthless cohort
of the brothers Pinzon, Ojeda, Solis, Cortez, Pizarro, Ponce de Leon, Grijalva, Cordova,
Pineda, Valdavia, Coronado, Lepe, Alamagro, Alvarado, La Cosa, Ayilog, Gil Gonzalez
Gasea, Perrelo, and others.

"Portugal gave the world not only the famous explorers of the East, but also
Cortereal, Magelahes (known to us as Magellan) who sailed under the Spanish flag in

the most wonderful of all ocean voyages; Cabral, who
gave Brazil to Portugal, Gomez, de Cintro, Jacques, and
Coelho.

"From France came Jean Cousin of Dieppe,
who is claimed as a preceder of Columbus, the plucky
Breton and Normandy fisherman who swarmed over
to Newfoundland immediately after its discovery was
rumoured. Fray Marcos of Nice, Lery, Cartier, Roberval,
Champlain, Villegagnon, Ribaut, Laudoniere, La Salle,
Marquette, Jolet, Gourgues, Hennepin, Frontenae, La
Verendrez.

"In return for borrowing Cabot from Italy,
England lent Hudson to the Dutch when he rediscovered
the river, but bought him back for the fated bay voyage.
She furnished also Frobisher, Drake, Hawkins, Gilbert,
Raleigh, John Smith, Grosbold, Pring, Weymouth, John
Davis, Willoughby, and William Batlin.

"Holland furnished Barentz and Van Horn,
while Juan de la Fuca was a Greek. As a final settlement
of the theory that America was part of Asia, the Russian
Guosedjeff and the Danish Bering proved in the eighteenth century that Asia and America were not anywhere
joined by land.

"The rewards of the discoverers make a sad catalogue. Among those who died
in obscurity and disgrace were Columbus, Gonzalez, and Cortes. The death penalty was
meted out to Pinzon, Grijalva, Ballson, and Pizarro. Among those who perished in battle
or died from the hardships of their career were Cordova, De Soto, Magellan, Vaklura,
Narvaoz, Ayllon, Solia, Ribaut, Roberval, Gilbert, and Hudson. When Bering perished
in 1741 he was—with the exception of those names on the still unfinished death-roll of
Arctic exploration—the last martyr on the still-unfinished of America. But never have
lives and gold been lavished with more profit to posterity, and never have cruelty, avarice,
theft, and oppression borne so liberally the fruit of happiness, riches, and liberty." [3]

The Martyrdom of Columbus

As we pursue the life and martyrdom of Christopher Columbus,
let us reiterate our point of view that his discovery, which should
have been an enrichment for his country if not for the whole
world, instead began a century of steady decline. And lest we regret his
martyrdom too much, we should remember that he himself carried a seed
of that exploitation which would place one of his kind as superior to thousands of natives he encountered in the new world. He died in poverty and
chains, but only one-tenth of the Aztecs survived Spanish occupation and
one-third of the Incas. That is martyrdom indeed.

For eighteen years he sought support first of the Portuguese, then Genoa, and again and again Spain, which would either deny his purposes through the great heads of the clergy or postpone their backing while they pursued their great battles with the Moors in the years before finally taking the Alhambra in January 1492.

He had made a great plea, promising treasures and prosperity by trade with India, virtually laying his whole life and reputation on the line, but was refused. Then he finally fled only to be detained and questioned by a country friar who led him back to the throne. This time he awaited their agreement and then asked for his prize in honor, position, wealth and property as would be appropriate. This denied, he again headed for the door, only to be called back with their reassurances of all that he had asked for.

As we tell his story and its sad ending, we again quote the historian Henry Smith Williams L.L.D.: "as Columbus had made his appeal to Spanish cupidity, by Spanish cupidity he was judged." In all the years that it took for them to begin to realize their profits, they destroyed their man. [4]

This time at the Spanish court, Columbus's hearing was held at the convent of St. Stephen where professors of astronomy, geography, mathematics and other branches of science, together with various dignitaries of the church and learned friars, assembled to question him. Before this erudite assembly, an obscure navigator, a member of no learned institution, destitute of all the trappings that would give him oracular authority, Columbus made his plea.

Typically, instead of geographical objections, he was assailed with citations from the Bible and the Testament, Genesis, Psalms, Prophets, Epistles, and the Gospels. One can imagine which it was that saw reality.

The progress of Columbus's voyage is familiar to most readers. On October 12, 1492 he viewed the island whose light he had seen the night before. The scene of his arrival, the joy of his men, the adulation of the natives is beyond description. His sojourn in the islands and the unprecedented departure of Martin Alonzo Pinzon, captain of the Pinta, there and again at the Canary Island on their return, is memorable. Columbus's return is then marred by the sudden appearance of Pinzon, who is so mortified by his own actions that he goes into retreat and soon dies. One is moved by such regret.

Pinzon's story shows how one lapse from duty may counterbalance the merits of a thousand services, how one moment of weakness may mar the beauty of a whole life of service, virtue; and how important it is for a man, under all circumstances, to be true, not merely to others, but to himself.

One regrets that an unfortunate end also awaited Columbus through no fault of his own. After his first voyage, public acclamations at first had been enormous, in Spanish cities and all across Europe. But his second, third, and fourth voyages were also expected to accomplish miracles, it would seem. There was a great inconsistency in public favor, even when won by distinguished service. No one has ever rendered more incontestable, unalloyed, and exalted benefits to mankind than Christopher Columbus; yet these achievements drew on its possessor more unremitting jealousy and defamation, and involved him in more unmerited distress and difficulty than can be imagined. [5]

His second and third voyages involved him in enormous feats of colonization, distributing the properties due to the men who shared in his victory and overseeing the rules that would control the greed and envy they would prey upon each other. In the colonization of Trinidad and San-to Domingo, each soldier demanded a certain number of islanders to be annexed which caused great complaints against his management.

Prejudice grew, and an arbitrator was sent to the colonies to decide between Columbus and his soldiers. Bobadilla arrived in Santo Domingo in 1500, deprived the admiral of his property, his honors and his command, and sent him to Spain in irons. Ferdinand and Isabella soon intervened, recalled Bobadilla, but to their disgrace, this was all the reparation that was made for so atrocious an insult. To crown their ingratitude, they constantly resisted his petitions and applications to restore his office and his possessions. One would have to discern that the reason was that his award was too magnificent.

Biding his time painfully for two years, they finally agreed to fund him for his fourth journey in order to return to the islands and secure his lands and fortune. Hostility, weather, loss of ships, and abandonment on an island for nearly two years happened to our hero—it is too painful to imagine. When finally rescued, a mock acknowledgment was extended by those in control of his holdings, and he was returned to Spain to die in obscurity. [6]

Thus do we honor our heroes. Columbus spent years and years of land travel and toil preparing the means to invade the unknown sea, found a world there. Then after a brief glory, he suffered ignominy, imprisonment and neglect; and was buried with the chains he had worn.

The year after his death, a suggestion was obscurely made that a certain minor navigator, Amerigo Vespucci, should be chosen as the sponsor for the "New World". In proof of his right to the naming of a quarter of the globe, certain letters of his own were cited to the effect that he saw a coast which he thought to be a continent; this was five years after Columbus made his first voyage. At best the letter utterly lacks substantiation, but evidence which would in a law court hardly establish a claim to an acre of ground has sufficed to fasten the name of a subordinate pilot upon a hemisphere.[7]

The Martyrdom of Sir Walter Raleigh

A summary of Raleigh's early life, so well-covered thus far in our story, is perhaps unnecessary. You recall he had first been imprisoned by Elizabeth I over his affair with Elizabeth Throckmorton but was shortly released to handle the affairs of the capture of the *Great Carrack*, as told in Chapter 13. We also noted his role in the capture of Cadiz and, in outline, the events of this chapter.

This second and most notorious conviction took place just as James I was ascending the throne, after Elizabeth I's death. Raleigh had had a rivalry with Robert Cecil in which Cecil triumphed in being taken on as secretary of state by James with whom he had been in secret communication. Raleigh was deprived of his office, that of captain of the guard, and within a few months was under a charge of high treason. There had been evidently two plots against James, attempts to restore Anabella Stuart to the throne, who had perhaps equal claim: the "Bye" plot initiated by the clergy, which aimed to destroy a protestant crown, and the "Main" plot by acquaintances of Raleigh, but of which he was unaware. .

The conduct of the attorney-general, Sir Edward Coke, during his trial was such as made even Cecil remonstrate against his unfairness. Coke began by declaring that the treason of Raleigh was "the treason of the Main, the others were the Bye," and then went on to mix him up with both treasons. "I pray you, gentlemen of the jury," said Raleigh, "remember I am not charged with the Bye, which was the treason of the priests." Cole informed the jury that all these treasons closed in together, "like Samson's foxes", and went on to associate Raleigh with every charge against other conspirators of whose proceedings he knew nothing.

When Raleigh spoke, "To what end do you speak all this?" Coke proceeded to call him a monster and to say that all that the others had done "was by thy instigation." When he came to the words about "destroying the king and his cubs" which rested upon a declaration of one of the priests, Raleigh spoke out, " Do you bring the words of these hellish spiders against me?" Coke retorted, "Thou art thyself a spider of hell." Such was the rhetoric with which the attorney-general of that day sustained the dignity of English justice.

The charges against Raleigh rested solely upon the accusation of Lord Coddam, which was said to be "no more than the barking of a dog." His conviction was obtained on the single deposition of Lord Coddam, who was already convicted, was not examined in court, and known also to have already retracted his accusation. Raleigh's contemporaries felt that his conviction was most unjust.

SIR WALTER RALEIGH
(1552-1618)

He was led to the block, subjected to mock preparations, then led away again, and finally imprisoned in the Tower for twelve years, during which time he wrote his famous *History of the World*. [9]

Raleigh's trial was remarkable for the blatant enunciation by the judges of the harsh principles which were then in vogue amongst lawyers, and the reactions questioning it were the first signals which from that moment steadily set in favor the rights of individuals against the state. [10]

We endeavor to tell the horrendous plight of any man accused by the crown in the fifteenth and beginning sixteenth centuries, and also to compare what Raleigh sought to found for England on the Orinoco with what Drake sought to do. Raleigh was granted a limited freedom after twelve years to again pursue his dream of founding El Dorado. He and his family were robbed of their remaining estate by accepting a small recompense in order to invest in the Guiana project, King James even exacting a portion in profits if the enterprise should be successful.

He set sail in March 1617 with fourteen vessels and a commission as commander and governor of the country. His pardon was still not resolved, which he might have done for money. He had kept men and com-

munications going through the years and was welcomed by the Indians
and those he had left in charge.

Treachery was aboard, however, by the very king in whose name
he had gone forth "to make new nations". James had obtained from him
the most minute details of his plans, and soon communicated them to Gondomar, the Spanish ambassador, who sent them to his court in Madrid. The
king had promised Raleigh a free passage through the country; and the
end of hostilities between the countries was thought to afford him a safe
passage to his former acquisitions, but he found it fortified against him.

He was himself weak from sickness which had claimed the lives of
part of his crew. He sent a part of his squadron in the direction of the mine,
but the instructions were not obeyed. The Spaniards attacked his encampment, and a battle ensued, in which Raleigh's son was killed. The passes
to the mine were defended by too strong a force to enable them to accomplish the great object of the expedition

Raleigh returned a sick man. He saw nothing ahead of him but
reproach and danger. In a letter to his wife he said, "I protest before the
majesty of God that, as Sir Francis Drake and Sir John Hawkins died
heart-broken when they failed of their enterprise, I could willingly do likewise, did I not contend against sorrow for your sake." Raleigh conducted
his fleet, with mutinous crews, to Newfoundland, and then sailed homeward.

Gondomar, the Spanish ambassador, was now supreme at the
English court and succeeded in negotiating a marriage between Prince
Charles and the infanta of Spain. Raleigh was arrested at Plymouth. He
was again tried and found guilty. It was decided that he had pretended that
he went to discover a mine, when his real object was to make a piratical
attack upon the Spanish settlements. It was decided to execute him under
his former sentence, by a writ of privy seal directed to the judges, but it,
having been expired, required him to go again before the judges to plead
his case. Reminding them that he was discharged of the original judgment
by the king's commission for his voyage, he was none-the-less judged to
be executed.

He asked for a bit of time to settle his affairs but was brought out
the next morning to die upon the scaffold, in the Old Palace Yard at Westminster. The night before his death he wrote these lines on a blank leaf of
his Bible:

E'en such is Time; who takes in trust
Our youth, our joys, and all we have,

And pays us but with age and dust;
Who, in the dark and silent grave,
When we have wander'd all our ways,
Shuts up the story of our days.
But from the earth, this grave, this dust,
The Lord will raise me up, I trust.

When he came to the scaffold he was very faint and commenced his speech to the assembled crowd by saying that during the last two days he had been visited by two ague fits. "If therefore you perceive any weakness in me, I beseech you ascribe it to my sickness rather than to myself." His speech was of a manly tone defending himself from slanders which had been raised against him. When asked by the dean of Westminster in what religion he meant to die, he replied, "In the faith professed by the church of England, hoping to be saved by the blood and merits of our Saviour."

The execution of Raleigh brought forth indignation. People felt he was sacrificed to Spain, against whose power he had waged no inglorious warfare, and by a king who remained supine whilst two great principles which divided Europe were again preparing for a struggle. Very soon Europe would be in the throes of the Thirty Years' War, 1618-1648, and beyond our story. [11]

How may we compare Raleigh with Francis Drake, or vice versa? According the Bancroft, "The name of Raleigh stands highest among the statesmen of England, who advanced the colonization of the United States; and his fame belongs to American history." Here we pause to honor another man, Francis Drake, though not of the same class and caliber, but one who should belong also to American history. Drake's immense labors to lead the way to colonization were lost, but certainly on a par with Raleigh's first efforts in the Orinoco.

A statement that Bancroft makes in his estimate of Raleigh for the *Historians' History* is to be noted and compared with that made for Drake in Chapter 1. First he evaluates his expeditions: "In the career of discovery, his perseverance was never baffled by losses. He joined in the risks of Gilbert's expedition; contributed to the discoveries of Davis in the northwest; and himself personally explored 'the insular regions and broken world' of Guiana. The sincerity of his belief in the wealth of the latter country has been unreasonably questioned." In Drakes' case, it was never allowed.

But the statement alerts us to perhaps something missed previously in Elizabeth's motivations: **"If Elizabeth had hoped for a hyperborean**

Peru in the Arctic seas of America, why might not Raleigh expect to find the city of gold on the banks of the Orinoco?" [emphasis mine] One had not thought of that motivation for Elizabeth. Spain always agreed that they had no claim beyond the 38 degrees parallel, and she didn't want them to know she might have even greater aims for a colony above that parallel that would inflame them with great jealousy and anger. She wanted to discover gold, silver, and mines there that did not have to be gotten by privateering, and a way northward to bring them back home. Obviously, we will never know why she was so protective of Drake's labors. [12]

Chapter 16

Reprise

A Nod to Posterity

As we summed up the legacy of the Tudor Era at the end of Chapter 13, we may have been remiss in not comparing the mindset of that century with those which followed. Obviously the absolute monarchy did not last forever. Without a view to the future, however, we cannot find a place for Sir Francis Drake in the evolution of the spirit of freedom for mankind. In that leap we therefore skip momentarily much of the seventeenth century when the English people, through their own civil war and support for the European war of 1618—1648, finally restored their monarchy and an empowered Parliament.

We would therefore consider what the so-called "Enlightenment"—the last decade of the seventeenth through the first decade of the nineteenth century— has meant to mankind since that evolution took place. It is thought to have been embodied principally in the writings of Locke and Newton in England and, on the continent, Voltaire, Hume, Diderot and Kant. Their writings are among those thought to be the source of everything that is progressive about the modern world, everything that stands for freedom of thought, rational inquiry, critical thinking, religious tolerance, political liberty, scientific achievement, the pursuit of happiness, and hope for the future.

The definition of "Enlightenment" in the Oxford English Dictionary of 1987, however, is not quite so positive, which attributes its spirit and aims mainly to French philosophers of the eighteenth century "in the implied charge of shallow and pretentious intellectualism, unrealistic contempt for tradition and authority." We would agree, none-the-less, that "everything progressive about the modern world" had also adverse effects, e. g., in the Terror of the French revolution and the revival of occult ideas and practices, even attributing the notion that the Holocaust was a result of Nazi social engineering in an attempt to revitalize mankind.

If one concentrates instead on the spread of democratic ideals and political freedoms which have emerged and continue to be the most persuasive voice in the modern world, we can indeed applaud the enlightened mind, even as we see a backlash wherein a union of church and state is again fashionable even in democratic nations. Even so, one might be inclined to believe that the progress of mankind is still possible when such grievances are settled, if only greed did not threaten our natural world.

Having looked ahead to the Enlightenment and its beneficial as well as adverse effects, we would comment here about the Tudor Age of Elizabeth and the trend of her time. Absolute monarchy was the prime motive of the latter at any price, even if it included a nod of subservience to Philip of Spain and all he stood for. The defeat of the Armada was sheer luck, albeit due partly to the strength of the English navy which in its essence was evolving toward greater equality among men aboard ship. Elizabeth was never trying to defend a better way of life or any universal aims for mankind, which, thankfully, her colonists eventually sought to achieve. Her defense was of her own absolute monarchy.

As to Sir Francis Drake, he may have been one of the first harbingers of the Enlightenment, never to be recognized as such. While just vengeance was sought for the destruction of Hawkin's fleet at San Juan de Ulúa while on a trading mission, he dealt fairly in all his dealings with the Spaniards in the New World. He promised to return and exact freedom at each encounter with the natives who were made slaves under Spanish rule after he had established a claim for England. His was a passionate and liberal mind far ahead of its time.

A Labor in Vain

We have tried to establish in our extensive accounts of the social history of Tudor England, and especially during the Elizabethan reign, the many reasons why Drake's most significant labor, the claim for England at the 45th parallel on the west coast of North America, was not acknowledged. A mindset stemming from Pope Alexander VI's granting of all lands west of the line of latitude 100 degrees west of the Azores seemed fixed in time, even after Protestant England had finally arrived. Elizabeth may have challenged the pope's jurisdiction over religious practice in England, but she hadn't the insight to disclaim Catholic jurisdiction over the New World.

True, there had been significant English explorations there, but always with a nod to Spanish supremacy. John and Sebastian Cabot's voyage of discovery to Newfoundland in 1497, the first European expedition that ever reached the American continent, resulted in no claim contrary to the pope's edict. Their exploration touched the shores of Newfoundland and sailed all the way down to the waters off Florida without the world being aware of any claim. .

The result of Cabot's discovery led to French and English fisheries along the coasts of Labrador and Newfoundland and other attempts to discover the Northwest Passage as a route for travel above and around Spanish claims to the Orient, but no real challenge to their sovereignty. For example, in that of Sir Martin Frobisher in 1567, he may have correctly conducted the rituals of claim to the land, the usual rock cairns and monuments conducted elsewhere, but these claims were carefully kept from challenging the overall Spanish claims.

What began as a hands-off policy gradually led to a strange set of modifications after they did finally make a formal claim to the territory. That of Sir Humphrey Gilbert (1583) in Newfoundland led to such a modification, where settlement within six miles of the shore was curtailed, discouraging any real English settlements. What had begun as a limited claim became also a tool for exclusion and trade monopoly against the French. They wanted no interference with their fisheries and their seasonal factories for the smoking and salting of their harvest. By 1650, a century and a half after its discovery, the

Sir Humphrey Gilbert
(1539-1583)

total population of Newfoundland was under 2000, a population which was somewhat expanded during the summer season.

Note again that it was Sir Martin Frobisher, Sir Humphrey Gilbert and Sir Walter Raleigh who were given exclusive patents for laying claim and colonizing, not a commoner such as Francis Drake, who with his cousins, the Hawkins family, had learned the hard way how to manage crews, sail in bitter weather, and fight the Spanish who would deprive them of their harbors for trade and replenishment. Elizabeth only knighted Drake to impress the French viceroy and in a final open defiance of Philip II, but she would go no further by challenging the papal claims.

With such flagrant granting of favors to the nobility one has to imagine what would have happened if Drake had allowed Doughty, and the other fifteen "gentlemen" sent by Elizabeth on his legendary voyage, to usurp his authority while it was underway. It was men like Drake, and indeed Drake primarily, who were establishing a precedent for command and authority which would make it possible to defeat the Spanish Armada in 1588. If by chance Drake's labors could have been carried out under Doughty's authority after the mutiny, the latter might have emerged as a noble she could acknowledge as worthy of the claim she secretly had commissioned Drake to accomplish.

She sent her "favourites", Leicester and Essex, on commands they were not in skill nor endowment able to carry out—to Ireland and to the Netherlands—to her dismay. What might she have done to reward Doughty, who was as equally scheming to discredit Drake as she was? Once she did plan a repeat voyage, but instead gave it to Fenton, as we have related, another favorite of the courts, who did not have the courage or command to carry it through.

It was only when Elizabeth needed him, because of his mastery in command of vessels, that she called for his help, as we have outlined: another voyage of plunder to the Caribbean, another to capture Cadiz, and another as a commander against the Spanish Armada. In these, however, she placed him under the superior command of one from the nobility. After the Armada she sent him again to capture the remainders of the Spanish fleets and discredited him for lack of complete success. He was sent again to plunder Spanish ships in 1596, still under her displeasure, when he died in the Caribbean.

Thus we must conclude two additional reasons the queen discredited Drake: in order to promote her favorites and other contenders for positions of nobility and, in addition, her propensity to avoid controversy and reluctance to take direct action. Because she discredited him, Drake's legacy, except for the trail of evidences to the contrary which we have uncovered, has been that of a consummate pirate, motivated only by his own profits.

We have traced those evidences contrary to the above assessment—which have come about within the past century, and which to some extent are accepted in the contemporary world by those willing to look at them. But what they will not acknowledge is that his survey and the careening of his boats did not take place on Spanish territory in California, but that he laid a claim for England at the 45th parallel, and the vestiges of his story which confirm that location are much resisted by the academic community.

We have listed in Chapter 1 the unassailable proofs that Gitzen has established—Fletcher's *World Encompassed,* the Hondius map, the van Sype map, the deposition of John Drake, and the Edward Wright World Chart of 1599—which confirm the above.

There are many reasons therein to support this claim. First, there was the labor involved: five weeks to build a rock fort, establish a relationship with the natives whereby he could describe their life-sustaining patterns which exist nowhere else on the coast, and to perhaps receive their help in building the rock cairns and monuments. Fletcher's descriptions of their encounters and of the flora and fauna of the area could match no other location.

This peaceful encounter was unique in the New World. Drake was a Protestant, the son of a preacher, and would have taught them only by example, unlike the slaughter and enslavement of New World natives which had been introduced by Cortez and Pizarro in Mexico and South America.

There are vestiges of Drake's contact with the natives in the memory of Oregon natives which have been related to researchers in the 20th century in Oregon. The last speaker of the Chinook language described the legends of the great "whale" ships with wings, the men they felt were gods, and their manner of worship, with hands clasped and raised toward heaven. Another tribal memory—which converges with what is known of the tsunami in 1700 which created a mile long sand spit and encompassed the small island Drake described—is of a storm that blackened the sky, laid waste the land, and piled huge banks of sand upon the land, as can be seen at Nehalem Bay. Its effects can also be seen at the mouth of the Columbia River, 60 miles north, which "great river" Drake clearly saw and which was undiscovered thereafter for 200 years because of that extensive sand jetty.

In identifying Nehalem Bay as matching the one Drake drew from memory, which was placed in the upper left corner of the Hondius Broadside map of 1593-95, there are two major dilemmas. We know that Drake's original maps were confiscated by Elizabeth and disappeared after being placed in the Tower of London.

The first dilemma may be easiest to understand, as long as one accepts the changes that might have resulted after the major tsunami and other ravages of time and human intervention. The landmarks and cartoons (drawings of actual sites and events) are all there as in the original Broadside: the island area now filled in with sand, the approximate area of the Indian encampment, the Alder creek where the fort was established now ending in salt marshes within the bay which is 3/4 miles away, the three hills to the east above the bay, and the rocky point at the south rim which is the same today. The general outline of the bay is remarkably the same. One also must consider the several strips of sand bars now lying across the bay. Also unexpected are the strips of mountain barriers sloping down from Mt. Neahkahnie which would have helped to create a barrier for careening the ships out of sight from the sea which did not appear on the Hondius map.

What must be conjectured, because it is not there, is the river: the Nehalem river which is the whole reason for the estuary being there at all. The river is the sole reason that the bay is carved from the landscape and

Nehalem River showing Hwy. 101 bridge crossing

had the
depths to
accom-
modate
Drake's
ships out
of sight
of Span-
ish ships
which
might then
have been
pursuing
them. Any
perusal of
bays to the
south do
not have
both the
depth and
the seclu-
sion that
would be
required
for Drake
to spend
five weeks
at his
labors.
There is
no reason
to believe
that Drake
would
have gone
south after

Nehalem Bay, Courtesy of the Salem Statesman Journal

the survey,
even as far as Whale Cove sixty miles south, as some would claim,

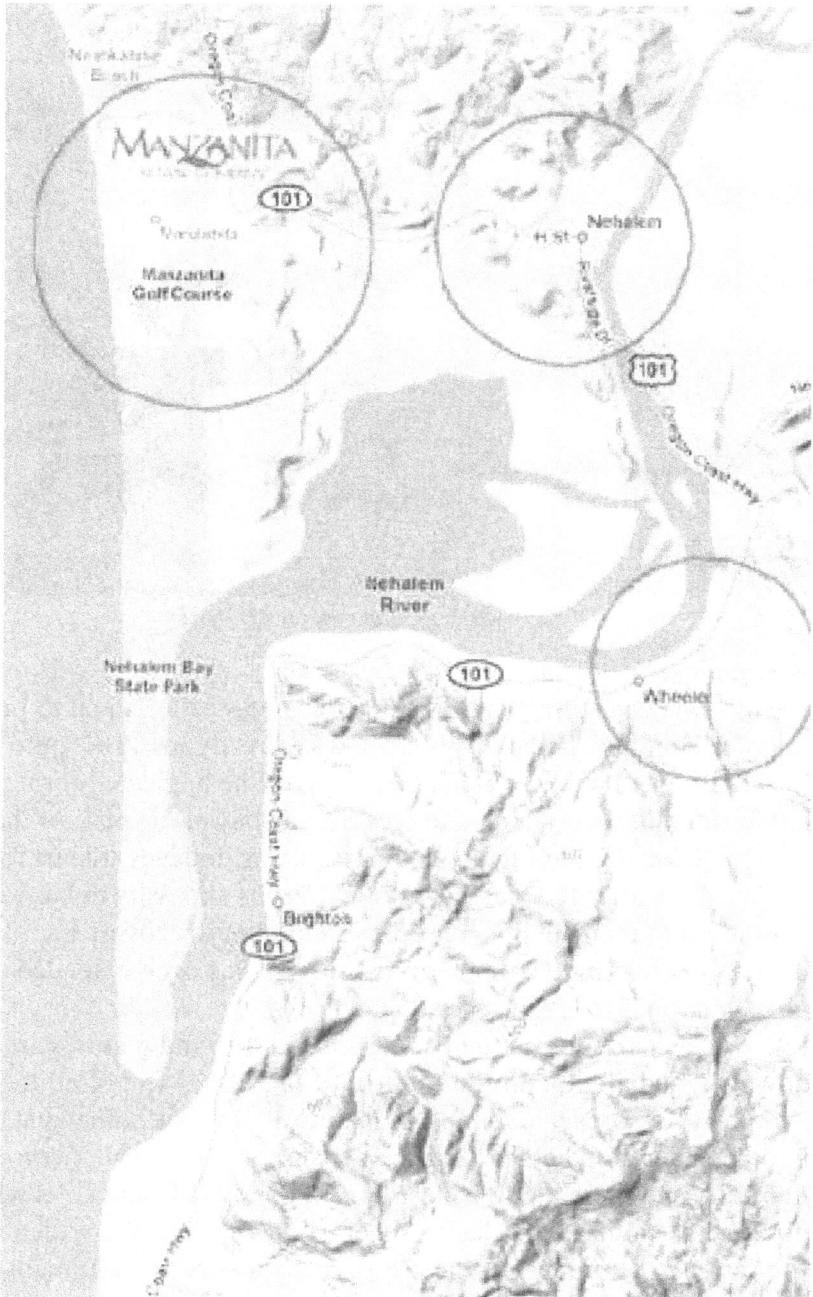

The cliffs of Neahkahnie Mountain

where those factors are missing.

One can surmise that when Drake was called upon to produce the map for Hondius, much of his story was already lost. He could only create the shape as it then was in his memory, and he neglected for no apparent reason the river which had created this bay at the base of the strips of mountainside running down into it. It was, indeed, at least fourteen or fifteen years after the fact and many voyages and wars in between that he was asked to recreate this map. The sand bar now covers the river's exit for another half mile, and the forest service has even extended and planted growth upon it to create a boat launch.

The cartoons on the Broadside and the land features are still there, however, and are not difficult to locate and film. Most of all there are the "white cliffs" of Neahkahnie Mountain, which look somewhat gray in the photos under cloud cover, and the expanse where the survey took place. On the beach there are two clear accumulations of sand spits which would not have been there originally. When Highway 101 was widened and cut further into the mountain, the original upper survey monument was first removed and stored in the Tillamook County Museum thirty miles south of Nehalem. When we inquired recently, however, it was not there or available. Five of the monuments which have the survey markings are,

Alder Creek where Drake's longhouse was located

none-the-less, there in a glass case in the basement. They had been placed on rock cairns in a rough triangle in order to measure a triangulation, and hence, a measurement of longitude. It was believed that fires may have been set at these points in order to view them from afar for measuring the angles and their distance apart. One of the monuments was carved to measure the exact English yard, perhaps to measure rope and hence calculate distance.

The remaining collection of monuments and all the research books and archives accumulated by M. Wayne Jensen, Jr., Donald M. Viles and Garry D. Gitzen are in the latter's keeping at his home in Wheeler overlooking Nehalem Bay, until the time when they will be transferred to the Maritime Museum at Astoria, Oregon, some sixty miles north on the Columbia river near Fort Clatsop, where Lewis and Clark wintered in 1805-06. Interestingly, the latter's journals converge remarkably with that of Fletcher in regard to the native populations, and the flora and fauna of the area.

Here included is a map where Highway 101 crosses the Nehalem River, and also a photo of that bridge as it crosses the river. Alder Creek, in the photo above, is where Drake's encampment was, and it has its source above and to the west of Nehalem. Manzanita at Neahkahnie Beach was where the "W" rock was found in 1895, a sketch of which we included in Chapter 9 from Philip Costaggini's master's thesis at the Department of Engineering at Oregon State University. The place where it was found was used as a point in the survey method of triangulation which Drake used.

Vested Interests

More than enough time has elapsed since November 2012 when the National Park Service designated Pt. Reyes in California as the official landing site of Sir Francis Drake on the coast of North America for a reaction of outrage. Are we so blind to the power of vested interests that we ignore the fact that the NPS is assisting California to increase park attendance by falsifying history?

Garry Gitzen reacted to this false designation in his November 27, 2012 blog on the internet entitled *"An Event That Never Happened"* which I happened to find, and I am sure there has been much further dialogue. It is too much for me to believe that any of the information he cites has escaped the knowledge of those who have perpetrated this hoax. It is a blaspheme that ought to rock the confidence of historical academia. How naive do they think we "non-academics" are?

One can perhaps overlook the outburst of an outsider such as myself, but let us review some of the additional facts that have accumulated since the NPS first considered such an act. These same California groups who finally persuaded the NPS to make the 2012 designation had failed on three separate occasions to gain an endorsement when they pled their case before the California Historical Resources Commission during the 1970s, as Gitzen points out.

We have recounted elsewhere the copper plaque fiasco which took years to be determined a fake in California. Now the NPS wants to protect sixteen sites along Pt. Reyes which they say provide material evidence of early cultural contact pertaining to Drake. However, a few nails and shards of porcelain would not be enough to make such a claim in Oregon, which, on the other hand, has 40,000 documented prehistory sites, none of which are National Parks. There are in addition over 2,200 shards of pottery from these Oregon sites, to say nothing of the forty or so magnificent relics which attest to the survey on Neahkahnie Mountain.

Of all contending sites, only Nehalem Bay in Oregon has received an endorsement as the site of Drake's landing by **any** professional organization. In Oregon there have been two: the Oregon Archaeological Society, as well as the endorsement of the Oregon Historical Society, whose Executive Director of 1955-1989, Thomas Vaughan, C.B.E., in his December 2008 report to the Oregon Archaeological Society Screenings stated that Garry Gitzen "has produced a magnificent compilation which should be in every important historical library and available to every serious student on this subject." As Oregon Historian Laureate, Vaughn went on to say of Gitzen that, "amateur or professional, he will have critics, but they will have a Herculean task to overcome the lucid arguments of this book (*Francis Drake in Nehalem Bay 1579, Setting the Historical Record Straight).*" He goes on to say that the book "has no parallel" and that he is now convinced "that Francis Drake was in Nehalem Bay." [1]

How can we ignore the evidence now so carelessly regarded of the relics of the survey of Neahkahnie Mountain, which may be lost to history without national recognition? Are we persuaded, like Elizabeth I, that such knowledge is of no profit to our status among nations or to historical truth? Archaeologists come and go,. as do relics stashed away in museums whose attendants don't know what they are.

Some time ago a former National Park Service archaeologist, Dr. Aubrey Neasham, said that to solve the questions surrounding the first English landfall in what Drake named "Nova Albion", Oregon ought to form a state commission and that possibly a national Drake commission be created. Another writer proclaimed in an article *"Plaque Records Drake's Arago Visit"* in **The World Newspaper**, August 6, 1977 that "I agree it is about time to have a truly national commission created to finally recognize Nehalem Bay as Francis Drake's Pacific coast landfall." [2]

But, as you can see, this former NPS archaeologist's and a writer's 1977 opinions are already neglected. So when do such opinions become one of the "black holes" of history?

Beyond Reasonable Doubt

Like all detective stories, proof is required, or at least proof beyond a reasonable doubt, not just beyond passionate opinion. In the case of Drake's sojourn in Nehalem Bay there are plentiful documents which now attest to his having labored there. What is missing is an academic assessment by knowledgeable geographers and archaeologists that his recorded descriptions and later map drawn from memory actually

The Gate of the Lions, Mycenae.

match the evidence there. This is not mythology; he was actually there, in that lovely estuary of the Nehalem river, out of sight of Spanish pursuers and with enough time to accomplish his dual purpose: to establish his point of position and careen his boats, with the help and cooperation of his crew and the native tribes.

Sometimes mythology has to be stripped to its bare bones, as happened when Heinrich Schliemann set out to establish that the Trojan War actually happened. It was probably to his advantage that he did not have a host of academics looking over his shoulder. He had made a fortune in business and trade and set out at a late age to accomplish his passion, without the time-consuming and defeatist approval and coordination of other academics. He proceeded according to his own plan. He was well prepared in numerous languages, the study of the classics, and the history that mythology itself had bestowed upon it. Since he did not know nor speak Greek, he acquired a young Greek wife, half his age, through channels which would guarantee him a well-educated helpmate.

First he was involved with other archaeologists in excavations at Mycenae, on the Greek mainland near Athens, to uncover its monuments which had been visible through the ages and to determine the dates, historically, as they pertained to Greek history and culture.

"At Mycenae in 1876 Dr. Schliemann lifted the corner of the veil which had so long enshrouded the older age of Hellas. Year by year since that veil has been further withdrawn, we are now privileged to gaze on more than the shadowy outline of a farback age." [3]

Dr. Schliemann's discoveries at Mycenae have shown a certain likeness between the art of early Greece and that of Asia Minor. Recent researchers have demonstrated that in certain localities, e. g., Cyprus, Crete and most of the Aegean islands, they form in fact a spectrum to be expected on almost every ancient Aegean settlement. Therefore we may assume that Mycenaean civilization was a phase in the history of all insular and peninsular territories of the east Mediterranean basin. It is determined that the Achaean system, that which lies south of the Gulf of Corinth in Greece, fell before the aggressive Dorian invasions. [4]

With the reader's approval I would like to follow through with a brief survey of what is known of the role of Hercules preceding the Trojan War which has those elements which we compare, perhaps somewhat simplistically, with Drake's labors. As previously recalled, this period has been called the "Heroic Age", that is, the period of Grecian history immediately preceding and including the Trojan war. Its duration may be estimated as six generations or two hundred years, a period known to the Greeks through Homer's *Iliad* and *Odyssey*.

In regard to Hercules, however, his actions, or labors, might be separated into two classes: one which carries us back into the infancy of society, as engaged in its first struggles with nature for existence and security, hence a good deal before the pre-Trojan era. The other, which also might be symbolic, would constitute and were enacted in those years where things were settled and mature, where the contest now was between one tribe and another, weak against the strong, innocent against oppressor. His role was to punish wrong, robbery, sacrilege, subduing tyrants, exterminating his enemies, and bestowing kingdoms to his friends. [5]

PAVEMENT OF SOUTHWEST RAMPARTS OF THE WALLS OF TROY

Hercules' labors in the first class above include the Phoenicians, who built temples to honor him in all their principal settlements along the coast of the Mediterranean. Though he was born in Thebes, he was the legitimate heir of the throne of Mycenae from which his father had been ousted. This was also the ground on which the Dorians some generations later claimed their dominion of the Peloponnesus and destroyed Thebes. It is perplexing that his labors in the second class, having some historical basis, are only accidentally connected with his claim to the throne of Mycenae. You will recall also the story in Chapter 1 told by other interpreters of his clash with the mythical Hera, who disclaimed him, drove him mad, and into the terrible crime of killing his wife and child. That story may be but symbolic of his father's loss of the throne of Mycenae. "While overgrowing these hostile dynasties and giving away scepters, he suffered himself to be excluded from his own kingdom. . . It was the fate of Hercules to be incessantly forced into dangerous and arduous enterprises; and hence every part of Greece is in its turn the scene of this achievement." [6]

A recent book also follows one of the labors of Hercules through an ancient route from the southwestern part of the Iberian peninsula into continental Europe and across the Alps into Italy in the course of his contacts with the ancient Celts. This would represent one of the many searches into the legends that are attached to his name. [7]

If we can turn now to the story with some historical basis of those six generations before the Trojan war, Troy had been conquered by Hercules in that fifth generation, but the city had been restored with massive stone walls by Priam, who reigned over a number of little tribes until his son Paris became attracted to Laconia by the fame of Helen's beauty. We know the story of his carrying her away from her husband Menalaus, the king, and of the massive onslaught to rescue her carried on by the king's brother, Agamemnon. Unfortunately, because of its extraordinary defenses, the battle lasted ten years, encompassing many heroic battles and the final penetration of the fortress after the trick entry with the Trojan horse. Thus we have the Trojan War, an historical event, fully credited by Alexander when he stopped by in 333 B.C. to offer sacrifices at the site of Troy. And we have its location fully confirmed in the twentieth century.

"It is the revivifying work of the pickaxe and shovel in the actual ground, as wielded by the excavator and archaeologist that have brought back the repute of Homer." [8]

We continue with Wolf's telling of Schliemann's achievement which gives us additional information: The man who thus championed the cause of the closet scholars and poets and visionaries was himself a practical man of affairs. Having amassed a fortune he pursued what had been an ambition with him all his life, the search, namely, for the site of Ancient Troy. He selected the hill of Hissarik at the site of ancient Ilium and uncovered at least seven different cities of antiquity, each being built above the other at long intervals of time. One of these cities, the sixth from the top, the most ancient but one, he became fully convinced, was Ilium itself. Ilium was another name for Troy, but one in use during later historical times. [9]

Twice before that war which Homer has made so famous, Troy

is said to have been taken and plundered; and for its second capture by Hercules we have Homer's authority. Laemedon fortified Troy with the famous wall said to be a work of the gods. Under his son Priam their realm extended to the Hellespont, the Aegean, and the fertile island of Lesbos and was known to history under the name of Phrygia. But it was to fall under that extended siege of Agamemnon.

In their battles there was a ferocious confiscation of property by the winning side: cattle and slaves, men, women and children in addition to swine, sheep, goats, oxen and horses. But scarcely was a crime more common than rape; and it seems to have been a kind of fashion, in consequence of which the leaders of piratical expeditions gratified their vanity in the highest degree when they could carry off a lady of supreme rank. Pertinent to our story, the king of Sparta, Tyndarous, required all who came to ask for his daughter, Helen, in marriage to vow that they would assist with the utmost power to recover her if she were stolen. Thus, when she was taken by Paris, all Achaeans were drawn into that pledge.

It does not follow that the Greeks were more vicious than other peoples equally unhabituated to constant, vigorous, and well-regulated exertions of law and government. From the licentiousness were derived the manners, and even the virtues, of the times, and hence knight-errantry with its strange consequences. This was true all through the dark and into the middle ages among the more isolated tribes. [10]

Having retrieved for us proof beyond a reasonable doubt of the likely site of Troy by a rigorous comparison of like layers elsewhere during the Mycenaean age, we find Heinrich Schliemann also quotable as an historian. In our *Historians' History of the World* we find him quoted in the following summary:

"The Trojan war gives a great shock to Greece and hurls it for the first time against Asia. Herodotus saw very well in this war, still mixed with fables, but certain in its principal events and in its issues, the first act of this long struggle between Greece and Asia, which will have for [its] end the expedition of Alexander."

The Eastern armies are richer, their habits more slack, and their spirits less active and less enterprising. In Greece marriage is no longer a sale: Penelope is the companion of Ulysses; there is a nobleness in her sorrow; and her authority is a sign of the new destiny for women. Helen, herself, after her return to family life, will come and sit down, free and respected by the hearth of her spouse, as we related in Chapter 1. Women were far from equal, however, and could with no recourse be replaced in her husband's affections by a favorite slave. The Greeks, with their tribal insularity, were somewhat superstitious about the occasional wanderer. They were therefore exceedingly hospitable to guests, as it might be the gods who sent him. [11]

So the above information from Schliemann's writings here ends our saga, and we might hope he would reappear with his millions in personal fortune to rescue the repute of our hero, Sir Francis Drake. After all, what is more important than a man's legacy?

But there are heroes deserving of our actual gratitude. It is my hope that my book, inspired by the above research of Jensen, Viles, and Gitzen, as well as that of Samuel Bawlf of British Columbia, will inspire others to similar research, with additional attention to the geological development of the Nehalem Bay area during the past four hundred plus years.

Lest there be any doubt in my mind that that location was the one described by Francis Fletcher in *The World Encompassed by Francis Drake*, published in 1628, I have only to read what he wrote as they left Nehalem Bay, which I also included in the forefront:

"Not far without this harbor did lye certain Islands, we called them the islands of Saint James, having on them plentiful and great store of seals and birds with one of which we fell July 24, whereon we found such provision as might competently serve our turn for a while."

As Garry Gitzen says in citing this passage: "these nearby islands exhibit hard evidence that Drake stopped there to take on food supplies before sailing to the Moluccas from the Pacific Northwest Coast on July 25th 1579." The spectacular islands were declared the Three Arch Rocks National Wildlife Refuge by Theodore Roosevelt, the first of its kind, on October 14, 1907, in order to protect their wildlife.

I owe to Samuel Bawlf many thanks for my introduction to the neglected history of Sir Francis Drake in his 2003 *Secret Voyage* which first aroused my interest. To Gitzen, however, I offer my deepest gratitude for his book of 2008 which led me to discover the hidden, unheralded, unacknowledged, and principal labors of Sir Francis Drake in Nehalem Bay.

If it were possible, it is to Sir Francis Drake that I would offer my most profound homage for his dream, so expansive, so seemingly impossible, that he accomplished at such odds and for the grace with which he accepted his fate.

I would also add my own summary: "Heracles was restored by Hera to Mt. Olympus, and it is time we do the same for Sir Francis Drake."

NOTES

ABBREVIATIONS

HHW *The Historians' History of the World.* A Comprehensive
Narrative of the Rise and Development of Nations from the Earliest
Times. Edited with the Assistance of a Distinguished Board of Advisers
and Contributors, By Henry Smith Williams, LL.D. in Twenty-five Vol-
umes, Volumes XXIV — Index. New York: The Encyclopedia Britannica
Company, Copyright, 1904, 1907

Chapter 1
Drake's Legacy
A Labor Lost
1. Charles Knight. *A Popular History of England,*
        London,1856-1873, 8 vols. (III, 121-128), in HHW,
        vol. 19, p. 381
2. Ibid., p. 383
3. Samuel Rawson Gardiner. *A Student's History of*
        England, London, 1884, II, 458, in HHW, vol. 19, p. 382
Historians' Estimates
4. George Bancroft. *History of the United States*,
        Boston,1839-1874, 10 vols., I, 78-90, in HHW,
        vol. 22, p. 495
5. Ibid., p. 495

6. Charles Macfarlane and Thomas Thomson.
   Comprehensive History of England, London, 1861,
   4 vols., II, 241-248, in HHW, vol. 19, p. 459

Current Estimates

7. Harry Kelsey. *Sir Francis Drake: The Queen's Pirate,*
   New Haven: Yale University Press, 1998, p. 99
8. Garry D. Gitzen. (1) *Francis Drake in Nehalem*
   Bay 1579: Setting the Historical Record Straight.
   Wheeler, Oregon: Isnik, 2008, p. vii
9. Angus Konstam. *The Great Expedition: Sir Francis*
   Drake on the Spanish Main 1585-86, Oxford, England: The
   Osprey Press 2011

A Legacy Revealed

10. Gitzen. (1) op. cit., p. v
11. Gitzen (1) Ibid., p. 7
12. Garry D. Gitzen. (2) *"Edward Wright's World Chart of 1599",*
    in Terrae Incognitae, vol. 46.1, April 2014, **Journal of**
    the Society for the History of Discoveries
14. Gitzen. (1) op. cit., pp. 12, 14
15. Ibid., p. vi
16. Ibid., p. 80
17. Ibid., p. 21

Chapter 2
A Historical View

Black Holes of History

1. Henry Smith Williams, ed. *Historians' History of the*
   World, New York: Encyclopedia Britannica, 1904,
   vol. 1, pp. 1-4
2. Hubert Dreyfus and Sean Dorrance Kelly. *All Things*
   Shining, New York Simon and Schuster, 2011, p. 5
3. *"Herekles: Punished Again,"* review by Daniel Mendelssohn in New York Review of Books, May 23, 2013
4. Connop Thirlwall. *The History of Greece*, London, 1838-1845,
   8 vols., III, 77-199, in HHW vol. 3, p. 174
5. Williams. op. cit., p. 4
6. Ibid., p. 14
7. John L. Beaty and Oliver A. Johnson. *Heritage of Western*
   Civilization, vol. 1, pp. 45-47

8. George Grote. *History of Greece,* London, 1851-1856, 12 vols. in HHW, vol. 3, p. 646

The Roman Mind

9. Dr. Edward Meyer. *"The World Influence of Early Rome"*, writ ten especially for HHW, vol. 5, p. 2

10. Ibid., p. 4

11. Edward Gibbon. *History of the Decline and Fall of the Roman Empire*, London, 1853, 7 vols., in HHW Vol. 6, p. 664

12. Meyer. op. cit., pp. 105-6

The Rise of Christianity

13. Ibid., p. 108

Chapter 3
The Rise of Tudor England

The Plantagenets

1. Knight, *op. cit*. (II, 347-351) in HHW, vol. 18, p. 625

2. Ibid., p. 626

3. J. H. Ramsay. *Lancaster and York*, Oxford, 1882, 2 vols., (II, 551-552) in HHW, vol. 18, p. 630

4. Lord John Campbell. *Laws of the Lord Chancillors*, London, 1845-1848, 7 vols., (I, 407) in HHW, vol. 18, p. 632

5. Knight. op. cit., p. 635

6. G. M. Trevelyan. *A Shortened History of England,* New York: Penguin, 1942, p. 189

7. Ramsey. op. cit., p. 635

8. Richard Lingard. *History of England from the First Invasion by the Romans to the Accession of William and Mary in 1688*, London, 1859, 10 vols. (IV, 261-267) in HHW vol. 18, p. 623-625

9. G. J. Meyer. *The Tudors: Complete Story of England's Most Notorious Dynasty*, New York: Boston Books, 2011, pp. 45-47

10. Ibid., p. 48

The Spanish Connection

11. Ibid., p. 60

12. Ibid., p. 64

13. Ibid., p. 74

14. Ibid., pp. 82-3

15. Ibid., p. 84

16. Ibid., p. 80

16. Ibid., p. 90
17. Ibid., pp. 91-93

,

Chapter 4
Henry VIII, Character and Legacy

Early Years

1. Trevelyan. op. cit., pp. 212-213
2. Lingard. op. cit., vol. 19, p. 65
3. Ibid., p. 68
4. Williams, op. cit., vol. 19, pp. 148-9
5. Ibid., p. 150
6. Lingard. op. cit., p. 70

First Wives of Henry

7. Ibid., p. 160
8. Ibid., pp. 164-5
9. Ibid., p. 122
10. Knight. op. cit., pp. 187-188
11. Ibid., pp. 190-1
12. Ibid., p. 192
13. Lingard. op. cit., p. 193
14. Ibid., p. 194
15. Ibid., p. 195
16. Sir James Mackintosh. *The History of England,* London, 1853, 2 vols. (II, 89, 94) in HHW, vol.19, p. 198
17. Ibid., p. 201

Chapter 5
The Successors of Henry VIII

The Reigns of Edward and Mary

1. Thomas Knightley. *The History of England* , London, 1839, 3 vols. in HHW, vol. 19, pp. 197-201
2. David Hume. (1) *History of England from the Invasion of Julius Caesar to the Revolution in 1688,* London, 1754-1762, 6 vols. (IV, 266-280) in HHW vol. 19, pp. 202-204
3. Samuel Eliot Morison. *The European Discovery of America: The Northern Voyages*, New York: Oxford University Press, 1971, p. 228
4. Knight. op. cit., p. 219
5. Morison. op. cit., pp. 229, 231

Elizabeth's Court

6. Edward Augustan Freeman. *History of the Norman Conquest of England, Its Causes and Its Results*, 1871-1879, 6 vols. (VIII, 342-343) in HHW, vol 19, p. 267
7. C. F. Raumer. *Political History of England in the Sixteenth and Seventeenth Centuries*, London, 1837, 2 vols. (I, 141-149) in HHW, vol. 19, pp. 368-269
8. Tracy Borman. *Elizabeth's Women*, New York: Bantam Books, 2009, pp. 195, 196
9. Ibid., p. 202
10. Ibid., pp. 204, 225
11. Ibid., p. 215
12. Knight. op. cit., p. 291

Her Favorites

13. Motley. op. cit. p. 292
14. Ibid. p. 295
15. Ibid. p. 296

Chapter 6
Later Years of Elizabeth's Reign

Mary Queen of Scots

1. Borman. op. cit., p. 334
2. Ibid., p. 335
3. Ibid., p. 336
4. Ibid., p. 338
5. Ibid., p. 339
6. Ibid., p. 341
7. Lingard. op. cit. HHW, vol. 19, p. 341-342
8. Macfarlane and Thomson. op. cit., p. 342
9. Ibid., p. 343

Elizabeth's Privateers

10. Knight. op. cit., vol. 19, pp. 332, 385
11. Ibid., p. 384
12. Trevelyan. op. cit., p. 255

Drake's Voyage, as Edited

13. Macfarlane and Thomson. op. cit., vol. 19, p. 385

Chapter 7
Troubled Voyage

Naval Power of England
1. Trevelyan. *op. cit.*, pp. 248-249
The Plan
2. Morison. op. cit. , p. 581.
3. Ibid., p. 583
4. Ibid., p. 555
5. Ibid., p. 560
6. David Cressey. *"The Mystery of Francis Drake's California Voyage"* published in **History Today**, vol. 31, Issue i, 1981
7. Francis Fletcher. *The World Encompassed by Sir Francis Drake*, published by Bourne, 1628
Drake's Background
8. Samuel Bawlf. *The Secret Voyage of Sir Francis Drake 1577-1580*, Penguin Books, 2004, pp. 67-68
The Journey
9. Ibid., p. 73
10. Ibid., p. 80
11. Ibid., p. 88
12. Ibid., p. 90
The Trial
13. Ibid., pp. 100-101
14. Ibid., p. 102
15. Ibid., p. 104-5
16. Ibid. p. 110

Chapter 8
In Command

The Straits
1. Bawlf. op. cit., pp. 112-13
2. Ibid., p. 114
3. Ibid., pp. 115-16
4. Ibid., p. 118
5. Ibid., pp. 119-20
6. Ibid., p. 122
7. Ibid., p. 124-5
8 Ibid., pp. 127-8
9. Ibid., p. 129

10. Ibid., pp. 130-131
11. Ibid., p. 134
12. Ibid., p. 139
13. Ibid., p. 140
14. Ibid., p. 144
15. Ibid., p. 146
16. Ibid., pp. 148-150
17. Ibid., p. 158
18. Ibid., p. 161
19. Peter C. Mancall. *Hakluyt's Promise: An Elizabethan's Obsession for an English America.* New Haven: Yale University Press, 2007. p. 80

Chapter 9
The Lost Labors
Guatulco to Nehalem Bay

1. Bawlf. op. cit., p. 276
2. Ibid., p. 278
3. Ibid., pp. 279-80
4. Ibid. pp. 281-2, 285
5. Ibid., p. 286
6. Ibid., p. 291

Point of Position

7. Ibid., p. 308
8. Ibid., p. 315
9. Gitzen., (1) op. cit., p. 28
10. Ibid., p. 225
11. Ibld., p. 9-11
12. Ibid., p. 19
13. Bawlf. op. cit., p. 147
14. Gitzen. (1) op. cit., p. 24
15. Ibid., p. 139

Tillamook Indian Culture

16. Ibid., pp. 124-25
17. Ibid., p. 139
18. Ibid. p. 82
19. Ibid., p. 83

20. Ibid., pp. 140
21. Ibid., p.18

The Moluccas

22. Bawlf. op. cit., p. 196
23. Ibid., pp. 165-6
24. Ibid., p. 167
25. Ibid., p. 170
26. Ibid., p. 175
27. Ibid., p. 176
28. Ibid., p. 177
29. Ibid., p. 179
30. Gitzen. (1) op. cit., p. 11

Chapter 10
The Aftermath

Drake's Return

1. Trevelyan. op. cit. p. 256
2. Ibid., p. 257
3. Macfarlane and Thomson. op. cit., p. 386
4. William Camdon. *Annales,* London, 1586, 2 vols., (II, 256) in HHW, vol. 19, p. 386

The Siege of Antwerp

5. Thomas Colley Grattan. *History of the Netherlands*, London, 1850 (81-88) in HHW, vol. 13, pp. 506-507
6. Motley. *op. cit.,* p. 513

The Netherlands Fiasco

7. Grattan. *op. cit.,* in HHW, vol. 18, 372
8. Knightly, op. cit., vol. 13, p. 519
9. Ibid., p. 520
10. Lingard. op. cit., vol. 13, p. 521
11. Ibid., pp. 522-24

Hutton, Latest Favorite

12. Sir Julian S. Corbett. *Drake and the Tudor Navy,* London, 1898, 2 vols. in HHW, vol. 19, p. 409
13. Gardiner. op. cit., in HHW, vol. 19, p. 411
14. Motley. op. cit., in HHW, vol 13, p. 522
15. Knight., op. cit., (III- 197-198) in HHW, vol. 19, pp. 380-381

Chapter 11
Spain and the Inquisition
"Letters of Marque"
Expulsion of Jews
1. Paul Goodman. *History of the Jews*, 1904, revised 1930 and
      1953. Introduction by Abba Hillel Silver, p. 7
2. Ibid., Preface to the First Ed., 1904, p. 15
3. Ibid., p. 89
4. Ibid., p. 90
5. Ibid., p. 115
6. Ibid. p. 101
7. Ibid., p. 103
8 Ibid., p. 111
9. Ibid. , p. 112
10. Ibid., p. 114
Moslems in Spain
11. Theodor Noldeke. *The Scope and Influence of Arabic History,*
      written especially for HHW, vol. 8, pp. 2-4
12. Ibid., pp. 5-6
13. Ibid., p. 10
14. Ibid., pp. 13-16
15. Ibid., pp. 21-24
Persecution of Jews in Spain
16. Goodman, op. cit., p. 116
17. Ibid., pp. 116-117
18. Ibid., p. 119
19. Ibid., p. 120
The Rise and Fall of Spain
20. Macfarlane and Thomson, op. cit., vol. 19, p. 332
21. Williams, ed., HHW, op. cit., vol. 10, pp. 130-133
22. Ibid., p. 134
23. Hume. op. cit. in *The Spanish People: Their Origins,*
      Growth, and Influence, in HHW, vol. 10, p. 176
24. William H. Prescott. *History of the Reign of Ferdinand and*
      Isabella the Catholic, Boston, 1838, 4 vols. (I, 232-269) in
      HHW, vol. 10, p. 166

Chapter 12
The Invincible Armada

The Spanish Fleet

1. Lingard. op. cit., in *Maritime Exploits* (VI, 479-498) in
   HHW, vol. 19, pp. 383-389
2. Kelsey. op. cit., p. 321
3. Motley, op. cit., (II, 463-528) in HHW, vol. 19, pp 389-402

The Army of Palma

4. Ibid., p. 403
5. Macfarlane and Thomson. op. cit., vol. 19, p. 403
6. Motley. op. cit., pp. 389-404

Chapter 13
The Last Years of Elizabeth

Leicester's Demise

1. John Richard Green. *A Short History of the English People*,
   London, 1895, in HHW, vol. 19, p. 406
2. E. Lodge. *Illustrations of British History*, London, 1838 in HHW

Essex and the Invasion of Corunna

3. Lingard. op. cit., (VI, 515-544) in HHW Vol. 19, pp. 405-410
4. Knightley. op. cit., p. 411

Sir Walter Raleigh at Court

5. Gardiner. op. cit., (from an article about Raleigh in the **Ency
   clopedia Britannica**) in HHW, vol. 19, p. 413

The Capture of Cadiz

6. Lingard. op.. cit., vol. 19, p. 415

Summary of Elizabeth's Last Years

7. *Chronological Summary* (at end of Elizabeth's reign), in
   HHW, vol. 19, p. 641

End of the Tudor Reign

8. Ibid., pp. 641-2
9. Gardiner. op. cit., in HHW, vol. 19, p. 5

Chapter 14
A Legacy Denied

Upon Pain of Death
Fenton's Voyage

1. Mancall. *op. cit.*

2. Bawlf. op. cit. pp. 201-2
3. Ibid., pp. 198-9
The Making of Maps
4. Ibid., pp. 208-215
5. Ibid., p. 216
6. Ibid., p. 217
7. Ibid., p. 346 Nt. 16
8. Ibid., p. 218
9. Ibid., pp. 219-227
10. Gitzen. op. cit., (2) *"Edward Wrignt's. . ."*
Distorted Accounts
11. Bawlf. op. cit., p. 228
12. Ibid., p. 227
13. Ibid., p. 231
14. Ibid., p. 232-3
15. Ibid., p. 236
16. Ibid., p. 237
The Molyneux Globe
17. Ibid., pp. 238-242

Chapter 15
The Martyrs
The Final "No"
1. Bawlf. op. cit. , pp. 243-246
Spain's Secrecy
2. Daniel J. Boorstin. *The Discovery: A History of Man's Search To Know His World And Himself*, U. S.: First Vintage Books Edition, 1985, p. 263
The Passion for Discovery
3. Williams, LL. D., op. cit., in HHW, vol. 22, p. 411
The Martyrdom of Columbus
4. Ibid., p. 412
5. Ibid., p. 422
6. Ibid., p. 450
7. Ibid., p. 467
The Martyrdom of Sir Walter Raleigh
8. Gardiner, . op. cit., article on Raleigh in HHW, vol. 19, p. 413
9. James White. *History of England*, London 1890 in HHW vol. 19, p. 413

10. Gardiner. op. cit., vol. 22, p. 473
11. Knight. op. cit., vol. 22, pp. 563-4
12. Bancroft. op. cit., in HHW, vol. 22, p. 562

Chapter 16
Reprise

A Nod to Posterity
A Labor in Vain
Vested Interests
1. Garry Gitzen. (3) *"An Event That Never Happened"*, an article on
   http//www.fortnehalem.net/post/2012/11/
   november-27th-2012.html, p. 2
2. Ibid., p. 3
Beyond Reasonable Doubt
3. William Ridgeway. *The Early History of Greece*, Cambridge,
   1901, 2 vols. (op. cit., I, 1-2) in HHW vol. 3, p. 40
4. Ibid., pp. 44-5, 54
5. Chrestos Tsountas and J. Irving Manatt. *The Mycenaean Age*,
   Boston, 1897, 3 vols. (op. cit. I, 170-178) in HHW, vol. 3,
   pp. 52-65
6. Friedrich August Wolf. *Prolegomena ad Homerum,* in HHW,
   Halle, 1795, in HHW, vol. 3, p. 69
7. G. W. Bowersock. *"On the Road with Heracles,"* review in New
   York Review of Books, Feb. 20, 2014 of *The Discovery of
   Middle Earth: Mapping the Lost World of the Celts* by
   Graham Roth, Norton, 2013
8. Wolf. op. cit., p. 77
9. Ibid., p. 78
10. Ibid., p. 79
11. Henry Schliemann. *Troja*, London, 1884, in HHW,
    vol. 3, p. 97

BIBLIOGRAPHY

Bancroft, George. *History of the United States,* 10 vols. Boston,
    1839-1873, in HHW

Bawlf, Samuel. *The Secret Voyage of Sir Francis Drake
    1577-1580,* Penguin Books, 2004

Beaty, John L. and Oliver A. Johnson. *Heritage of Western
    Civilization,* vol. 1, Penguin Press, 2003

Boorstin, Daniel J. *The Discovery: A History of Man's Search To
    Know His World and Himself,* U. S.: Vintage, 1984

Borman, Tracy. *Elizabeth's Women*, New York: Bantam, 2009

Camdon, William. *Annales*, 3 vols. London, 1586, in HHW

Campbell, Lord John. *Laws of the Lord Chancillors,* 7 vols.
    London, 1845, in HHW

Chronological Summary at end of Elizabeth's reign, in HHW,
    vol. 19

Corbett, Sir Julian S. *Drake and the Tudor Navy*, 2 vols.
    London, 1898, in HHW

Cressery, David. *"The Mystery of Francis Drake's California
    Voyage"* published in History Today, vol. 31, Issue 1, 1981

Dreyfus, Hubert and Sean Dorrance Kelly. *All Things Shining*,
    New York: Simon and Schuster, 2011

Fletcher, Francis. *The World Encompassed by Sir Francis Drake,*
    published by Bourne, 1628

Freeman, Edward Augustan. *History of the Norman Conquest of
    England, Its Causes and Its Results,* 6 vols. London,
    1837, in HHW

Gardiner, Samuel Rawson. *A Student's History of England*,
        3 vols. London, 1900, in HHW
_____ article about Raleigh written for Encyclopedia Britannica,
        in HHW
Gibbon, Edward. *History of the Decline and Fall of the Roman
        Empire,* 7 vols. London: 1853, in HHW
Gitzen, Garry. (1) *Francis Drake in Nehalem Bay 1579: Setting the
        Historical Record Straight*, Wheeler, Oregon: Isnik, 2008
_____ (2) *"Edward Wright's World Chart of 1599"*, in Terrae Incognitae,
        vol. 46.1, April 2014, pp. 3-15, **Journal of the Society for the
        History of Discoveries**
_____(3) *"An Event That Never Happened"*, an article on *http//www.
        fortnehalem.net/post/2012/11/November-27th-2012. httm*l
Goodman, Paul. *History of the Jews*, New York: Dutton & Co.,
        1904, revised 1930 and 1953
Grattan, Thomas Colley. *History of the Netherlands*, London,
        1850, in HHW
Green, John Richard. *A Short History of the English People,*
        London, 1895, in HHW
Grote, George. *History of Greece*, 12 vols. London: 1851-1856,
        in HHW
Hume, David. *History of England from the Invasion of Julius
        Casear to the Revolution of 1688,* 6 vols. London,
        1754-1762, in HHW
Hume, Martin A. S. *The Spanish People: Their Origins, Growth,
        and Influence*, written especially for HHW, vol. 10
Kelsey, Harry. *Sir Francis Drake: The Queen's Pirate,*
        New Haven: Yale University Press 1998
Knight, Charles. *A Popular History of England*, 8 vols. London,
        1856-1873, in HHW
Knightley, Thomas. *The History of England*, 3 vols. London, 1839,
        in HHW
Konstam, Angus. *The Great Expedition: Sir Francis Drake on the
        Spanish Main 1585-86*, Oxford: The Osprey Press, 2011
Lingard, Richard. *History of England from the First Invasion by
        the Romans to the Accession of William and Mary in 1688,*
        10 vols London, 1859, in HHW
Lodge, E. *Illustrations of British History,* London, 1838 in HHW

Macfarlane, Charles and Thomas Thomson. *Comprehensive History of England*, 4 vols. London, 1861, in HHW

Macintosh, Sir James. *The History of England,* 2 vols. London 1853, in HHW

Mancall, Peter C. *Hakluyt's Promise: An Elizabethan's Obsession for an English America*. New Haven: Yale University Press, 2007

Mendelssohn, Daniel. *"Herekles: Punished Again,"* review, New York Review of Books, May 23, 2013

Meyer, Dr. Edward. *"The World Influence of Early Rome"*, written especially for HHW, vol. 5

Meyer, G. J. *Complete Story of England's Most Notorious Dynasty*, New York: Boston Books, 2011

Morison, Samuel Eliot. *The European Discovery of America: The Northern Voyages,* New York: Oxford University Press, 1971

Motley, John Lathrop. *History of the United Netherlands*, 4 vols. New York, 1860

Noldeke, Theodor. *The Scope and Influence of Arabic History*, written especially for HHW

Prescott, William H. *History of the Reign of Ferdinand and Isabella the Catholic,* 4 vols. Boston, 1838, in HHW

Ramsay, J. H. *Lancaster and York*, 2 vols. Oxford, 1882, in HHW

Raumer, C. F. *Political History of England in the Sixteenth and Seventeenth Centuries*, 2 vols. London, 1837, in HHW

Ridgeway, William. *The Early History of Greece*, 2 vols. Cambridge, 1901 in HHW

Schliemann, Henry. *Troja*, London, 1884, in HHW

Thirwell, Connop. *The History of Greece*, 8 vols. London, 1838-1845, in HHW

Trevelyan, G. M. *A Shortened History of England,* New York: Penguin, 1942

Tsountas, Chrestos and J. Irving Manatt. *The Mycenaean Age*, 3 vols. Boston, 1897, in HHW

White, James. *History of England*, London, 1890 in HHW

Williams, Henry Smith, LL. D. ed. *Historians' History of the World*, New York: Encyclopedia Britannica, 1904, 1907
_____essay on North American discoverers, in HHW, vol 22

Wolf, Friedrich August. *Prolegomena ad Homerum*, Halle, 1795, in HHW

ILLUSTRATIONS AND ACKNOWLEDGMENTS

The writer has made liberal use of historical maps and graphics from the 1904, 1907 *Historians' History of the World* (HHW), many with their captions, published by the Enclyclopedia Brittanica. Captions are provided for those not identified in the originals or in adjacent explanatory text. In addition, the writer has used many personally-taken photos and a few attributed area maps thought to be in public domain.

With much gratification the writer has received written permission and best wishes from Phillip A. Costaggini for use of his map of Nehalem Bay on page 104, his diagram of a relic on page 110, his map of relics found on Neahkahnie Mountain on page 112, and his survey and method of triangulation at "point of position"on page 113, all from his 1982 thesis at Oregon State University.

The Hondius Broadside Map on page 16—with its inset in the upper left corner of Portus Nove Albionis shown on the cover and pages 17 and 102— appears in numerous publications, the original residing in the Maritime Museum in Rotterdam, Netherlands and an engraved and hand-colored copy of which resides in the Library of Congress, Washington, D. C. The Edward Wright map on page 178 is to be found in the R. A. Skelton essay on Hakluyt's maps with a discussion of its merits in an appendix by Helen Wallis entitled 'Edward Wright and the 1599 World Maps' from the collections in the Hakluyt Society Handbook of 1974, and a copperplate engraved copy resides in the Newberry Library, Chicago, Illinois.

INDEX

    This index is thought to best serve the reader's interest by limiting its coverage to historical names, locations, events, and eras. Not included are general topics, categories, nor names in a general list. It is hoped that the index will guide the reader to a full treatment of each entry.

    The writer has occasionally included in the text the names of those historians whose work is being cited. The historians are again referenced for the most part in the footnotes at those points where their accounts are completed and are then available in the bibliography. Generous use is made of the work of Gitzen and Bawlf, contemporary historians whose work the writer is attempting to draw particular attention to, and their accounts and quotes are attributed in numerous footnotes.

N

O

P

Q

R

W

X

Y

Z

ABOUT THE AUTHOR

Erma Armstrong, pictured here at the Basket Slough Wildlife Refuge near Dallas, Oregon, is a retired musician and music educator. She holds Bachelor of Music and Music Education degrees with distinction from Colorado State University, A Master of Music and Piano Pedagogy from Lewis and Clark College, and a Doctor of Musical Arts Degree from the University of Oregon. She was an Assistant Professor at the University of Calgary, and has taught music at all levels in public and private schools in Colorado, Oregon and New York City. She has performed in numerous chamber music ensembles and has most recently retired as organist and choir director from various churches near her home outside Dallas.

www.ingramcontent.com/pod-product-compliance
Lightning Source LLC
Chambersburg PA
CBHW060045100426
42742CB00014B/2703

* 9 7 8 0 9 8 6 0 8 5 6 4 2 *